CREATIVE COMPROMISE

The MacBride Commission

A Firsthand Report and Reflection on the Workings of UNESCO's International Commission for the Study of Communication Problems

William G. Harley

UNIVERSITY
PRESS OF
AMERICA

Lanham • New York • London

Copyright © 1993 by
University Press of America®, Inc.
4720 Boston Way
Lanham, Maryland 20706

3 Henrietta Street
London WC2E 8LU England

Library of Congress Cataloging-in-Publication Data

Harley, William G., 1911–
Creative compromise : the Macbride Commission : a firsthand
report and reflection on the workings of UNESCO's International
Commission for the Study of Communication Problems /
William G. Harley.
p.   cm.
Includes index.
1. International Commission for the Study of Communication
Problems. 2. Communication—International cooperation.   I. Title.
P96.I5H38   1992   302.2—dc20   92–27092 CIP

ISBN 0–8191–8906–5 (cloth : alk. paper)

The paper used in this publication meets the minimum requirements of
American National Standard for Information Sciences—Permanence
of Paper for Printed Library Materials, ANSI Z39.48–1984.

TABLE OF CONTENTS

ACKNOWLEDGEMENTS

This is a page devoted to acknowledging with thanks those people without whom.... First in order must come Leonard Sussman, who first approached me with the idea of writing this book and who made valuable suggestions on its structure and general approach. Harriet Lundgaard did much of the editing of the early drafts and was always available to untangle my tortured syntax. Thanks go to Barbara Good and Christina Nobbe for French and Spanish translations of magazine articles and to Richard Nobbe for digging out foreign press reports in the archives at UNESCO head-quarters in Paris.

Without Elie Abel (the American on the Commission) who helped me prepare reports of the meetings, there would have been no basis for the book. He also looked over the manuscript to save me from egregious errors of fact and misinterpretations about the Commission and its work. Ray Wanner and John Fobes did the same for the sections on UNESCO and the UN. Dana Bullen of the World Press Freedom Committee, commented and let me rummage around in his meticulously kept files, Sandy Godfrey did the keyboarding, and Max and Bob Reed did the final editing and organizing to produce the camera-ready copy.

A final expression of gratitude must go to my good wife Jewell for tolerating many hours of solitude while I was holed up in my den, slaving away at the word processor.

FOREWORD

Leonard R. Sussman

The New World Information and Communication Order (NWICO)[1] is, for all effective purposes, dead. In its lifetime during the 1980s it was both hope and bogey: *hope* of the developing countries that Western governments and journalists could be persuaded or forced to provide Third World countries with better communication infrastructures and to report their news more favorably (if not objectively); *bogey* for Western journalists who inferred from even the valid criticism of their reporting that the Third World countries sought to censor the global news flows for being "unbalanced" and "imperialistic."

Raucous battles over NWICO ended with a whimper at the 1989 general conference of UNESCO under the guidance of its new Director-General, Federico Mayor. By then, the United States and the United Kingdom had withdrawn from the United Nations Education, Scientific and Cultural Organization (UNESCO) and the controversial communications programs of UNESCO were a major, if not the only, reason. The cap was placed on NWICO in 1990 when the United Nations General Assembly followed UNESCO's lead and removed NWICO as an agenda item. The United Nations in 1991 renewed that decision. For three years, then, NWICO was formally written into history, nothing more.

At the peak of the controversy, then Director-General Amadou Mahtar M'Bow sought to diffuse the stridency and, not incidentally, avoid the destruction of his organization. He created an international commission of sixteen Wise Men. (The unofficial name went out of use when one woman replaced a man. No reflection on her wisdom but Fifteen Wise Men and One Woman simply was not a catchy title.) That International Commission for the Study of Communication Problems was headed by Sean MacBride, the colorful Irish parliamentarian who had already earned both the Nobel and Lenin Prizes. He seemed like the perfect mediator for these intractable politico-communication issues.

---

[1]Sometimes referred to as the New World Information Order (NWIO) (see footnote 1, page 109).

The MacBride Commission reported its findings, book-length, in 1980. Those who favored NWICO found the Commission's report useful, but were somewhat disappointed. Those who had strongly opposed NWICO were somewhat relieved but, because of their great suspicions, not about to utter praise of anything that flowed from the long and bitter controversies. Why, then, resurrect the MacBride Commission now?

Precisely because the extensive argumentation inside the commission *now* provides us with factual bases with which to examine the real issues that were debated and, indeed, polemicized both inside the Commission and around the world. All participants--the Western news media, Western governments and, of course, Third World and Soviet polemicists--all based their arguments and their actions on premises and assumptions, not necessarily reality.

William G. Harley was present at all meetings of the MacBride Commission. He had already had a notable career in the field of domestic and international communication, in both the private and public sectors. He took copious notes and contributed ideas and drafts throughout the two years of the commission's existence. His recollections are important. They tell us how international agencies function, for better or worse, and how the vital communications sector of international diplomacy is influenced by the interplay of the private and public media of communication, and by their interactions with governments and intergovernmental agencies.

NWICO may be moribund, but the issues are very much alive. These issues will be high on the international communication agenda well into the twenty-first century. While never credited for having done so, the Commission put to rest the controversies over a politicized "new information order." But there is developing every day a new international communication system that will, indeed, change the lives of everyone on the planet. The Commission recognized the futility of imposing a single political communication order (press controls and the like) and modestly turned the focus where it will remain: on the vast potentials that new technologies provide for freely flowing information of many kinds.

This book records an important crossroad in the international politics of journalism and especially press freedom. The antagonists on all sides, West, East, North, and South, who argued without listening to one another, should read this book in these calmer, more helpful days for international communication. They should also applaud Bill Harley for conscientious reporting while the struggle raged, and an orderly analysis ten years later of that debate's flavor and substance.

PREFACE

When the idea was first proposed to me to write a book on UNESCO's[1] International Commission for Study of Communication Problems (better known as the MacBride Commission after its chairman), my first reaction was, "What's the point? The Commission's report generated a brief interest in certain limited circles when it came out back in 1980, but by now it's ancient history. And, besides, why me?"

Leonard Sussman, then Executive Director of Freedom House, the author of the proposal, explained it this way: I was uniquely placed to undertake such an assignment. I had attended every meeting of the Commission as it traveled around the world for two years and had a complete collection of reports I had sent back to the U.S. State Department, as well as all the UNESCO published materials on the subject. Furthermore, I had a file of relevant personal notes, memos, and letters, a comprehensive collection unique in all the world.

Sussman was of the opinion that publication of these reports on the Commission's work and its significance might constitute a useful contribution to the history of international communication and the role of UNESCO in the field.

This is not an attempt at an academic treatise. Rather, it is a personal account of the process that produced the Report and my firsthand, reflective observations about the personalities involved, and my opinion of what was accomplished. Preceding that is an account of how I came to be an eye and ear witness at what transpired.

I cannot pretend to have been completely objective in my reporting (but then, is anyone?). Having worked for the U.S. delegations, it is perhaps understandable that, despite a conscientious effort to include a wide range of views, my Western predisposition may have affected my writing here and there.

It should be noted also that these are unofficial writings and the views and opinions, unless attributed, are my own and not necessarily those of the U.S. government or any of its agencies.

---

[1]The United Nation's Educational, Scientific, and Cultural Organization.

Chapter 1

INTRODUCTION

Purpose and Outcome

This is a story about a study whose process was more important than its product. The MacBride Commission consisted of sixteen experts appointed in 1977 by the Director-General of UNESCO, Amadou Mahtar M'Bow. The announced purpose of the Commission was to "study the totality of communication problems in the modern world" and write a report that would remedy deeply entrenched problems. "Basic to the task," said M'Bow, "was the formulation of ways through which a freer and more balanced international flow of information and a more just and effective new world information order might be fostered." The unannounced purpose was to quench the firestorm of controversy over communication issues that had arisen in UNESCO during the 1970s, culminating in the 1976 UNESCO General Conference in Nairobi, an explosive situation that threatened to blow the conference apart and irreparably damage the beleaguered organization.

Yet, in the process of carrying out these objectives--selection of commissioners, bickering in the meetings, fighting between the staff and the chairman, concoction of a radical Interim Report, alarm-ringing by the Western press, along with producing a highly contentious Final Report--the result was an immediate fanning of the flames of discord in the international community.

Thus, the outcome did not produce the salutary effect hoped for- either in quieting Western concerns about how UNESCO was being manipulated in this area, in fostering Third World[1] hopes for a new world information order,[2] or in resolving other contentious international communication issues. Overall, however, it was a conscientious effort to reach a consensus in the study of controversial communications policy problems between and within nations and should afford the reader insights into the complexity of modern communications and their interrelationships with the economic, cultural, and social aspects of our interdependent world.

---

[1] A phrase used to describe the combination of developing countries.
[2] A collection of proposals to reduce global news flow in ways Western news media perceived as threatening to their independence. See footnote 1, chapter 2.

1

The reader will also find the reports of the meetings to be fascinating exercises in group dynamics, with proponents deeply grounded in philosophical differences vigorously promoting (sometimes to the verge of dangerous confrontation) their respective views, blocking political moves, or denouncing motivations, while still managing to seek a degree of commonality. Despite the multiple purposes and perspectives, the result is a careful balancing of frequently clashing views of the industrialized, the nonaligned, and the socialist countries.

At least the reader will not have cause here for the complaint of Gerald Long of *Reuters*, who grumbled that throughout the proceedings of the MacBride Commission we have never known who said what. The speakers are clearly identified here.

The meetings were not all peaceful by any means. Tempers flared, three commissioners at different times threatened to resign (one of them actually storming out of a meeting), and the chairman wanted to fire his chief-of-staff for his high-handed behavior and refusal to cooperate with two outside writers whom the chairman had brought in to improve the quality of the writing. In addition, there were cliques within the Commission, collaboration of the staff with certain commissioners, and undue pressure from the UNESCO Secretariat. On the other hand, it was not all serious and tense. This account recounts some lighthearted moments in the sessions, repeats many anecdotes, and provides observations on the personalities of the participants, including Director-General M'Bow.

Most important, there is a detailed account of the Commission's treatment of the proposed New World Information Order. This contentious concept, whose definition and adoption was ardently promoted by Third World participants as the sole purpose of the Commission, was thoroughly discussed and then dismissed. Despite enormous pressures, the Commission refused to define or adopt such a scheme. This decisive turndown, backed by the authority of this distinguished group, marked a turning point in the nonaligned countries' campaign to gain international sanction for establishing a New World Information Order. The decline of this value-laden issue, a decline that the Commission started, had widespread implications for all future communications debates in UNESCO and the United Nations. And this fact, as discussed late in this book, was the most important, although not the only, consequence of the Commission's work that had an impact on the world's communication development.

Origin of the Controversy

Through the 1980s and more, the Third World countries developed a set of assertions and demands that evolved from a series of "indignation meetings" about "disparities and anomalies, inequities, and injustices" reflected in the disequilibrium in the world's flow of news and information.[3] Their remedy was to propose establishment of a New World Information Order (NWIO), a concept (though ill-defined) that summarized their grievances and set forth an aggressive program for their relief. In their frustration at not being able to effect a rapid alteration of their situation, the Third World countries turned to international mechanisms, especially UNESCO, seeking the enactment of international regulations and efforts in this respect as a means of counteracting "Western imperialism" and for "throwing out the last vestiges of colonialism."

In addition, in 1972, the Soviet Union had introduced in the UNESCO General Conference two draft resolutions that were of a restrictive nature. The first of them was related to guiding principles on the use of the media.[4] The other, which was concerned with direct broadcasting by satellite, contained a stipulation requiring prior consent of a receiving country.

Such initiatives in UNESCO were bitterly opposed by the West as it struggled during the ensuing years to preserve free press values against Soviet and Third World attempts to replace diversity and freedom with restrictions and restraints.

Inevitable Outcome

It was in the light of this history that the MacBride Commission met to do its work, and the outcome was probably inevitable. Commission members themselves represented opposing ideological positions: the Third World's aspirations for restructuring the global communications system in order to redress the imbalance in news; the Soviets' preoccupation with maintaining control of news and information flow to preserve national sovereignty; and the West's concern with preserving the free flow of information internationally. Inevitably, therefore, there was conflict in the

---

[3]The Bandung Conference of 1954, attended by Nehru, Tito, Nasser, Chou En-lai and other leaders, was the beginning of the nonaligned group of nations. The First United Nations Conference on Trade and Development (UNCTAD) in Geneva (1964) marked the start of the group of 77. The two groups have operated as a kind of political tandem ever since, mutually supportive, yet preserving separate identities.

[4]*Declaration on Use of the Media*, Article 10, which urged that states be given the right to "correct" news deemed to be "erroneous," and Article 12, which called for each state to be made responsible for the international activities of media within its boundaries.

Commission's deliberations, and inevitably its Final Report, reflecting these differences, was a grand compromise. On the other hand, given the diverse political and ideological predisposition of the commissioners plus the short time they had in which to do their work, a surprising level of agreement was achieved; in certain areas, they found ground for practical action and could agree that there were legitimate concerns and communication disparities that require far-reaching changes.

With so many divergent pressures and counterpressures at work within the group, however, its Final Report clearly mirrored the strong difference in world opinion, which were not necessarily (but certainly were more clearly) delineated.

The Commission's Report

The disappointing aspect of the Commission's work was that, in attempting to be responsive to so many conflicting views, it failed to come up with some positive, concrete suggestions on what to do about the complexity of "communication problems in the modern world." Consequently it missed the opportunities to lay down a firm foundation on which international communication policy could have been built and to provide a vision for the future based on a broad perspective of all forms of information and their communication. "The amount of resources expended by capable people should have produced a major breakthrough in an understanding of the process of communication and to set an enlightened guideline for communication policies."[5] This disappointment was furthered by the manner in which the Commission's Report was handled.

In advance of its release, there was general expectation that the Commission would produce a definitive study that would become the bible for UNESCO guidance in this area.   And even when reading advance copies of the Report diminished this expectation, there was still the feeling that its presentation at the 1980 UNESCO General Conference in Belgrade would generate a lively debate over its recommendations and even produce some fruitful outcomes.

In this expectation, I presided over a U.S. government interdepart-mental committee that worked throughout the summer of 1980 to prepare U.S. positions on every one of the MacBride Report's eighty-two recom-mendations. However, there was never an opportunity to use these metic-

---

[5]"Many Voices, Many Worlds: Four Readings on the NWIO Debate in UNESCO," a paper by Elizabeth M. Tesser and W. Barnett Pearce of the University of Massachusetts, William Husson of the University of Connecticut, and Zulkarnaine Mohd of the University of Malaysia.

ulously prepared papers. UNESCO Director-General M'Bow announced at the start of the conference that the Report of the MacBride Commission had been prepared exclusively for his personal use and it was not, therefore, on the agenda. Rather, he said, it "was an excellent resource, deserving study and reflection, but not a reason for immediate decisions."

The reason for this surprising action is not difficult to discern. By the time the conference was due to start, tensions had become so high and apprehensions so inflamed that the Director-General realized that the conference might blow up if an attempt was made either to have UNESCO formally adopt the Report or if there was a move to adapt any of its recommendations. One also suspects that Mr. M'Bow was not unmindful of the effect on his chances for reelection if he were to become personally snared in this controversial situation.

The Report, though it did not in consequence represent UNESCO policy (it was not endorsed by the conference), did provide important insights into UNESCO concerns and it did delineate the issues, though somewhat murkily. Essentially a compromise (it acknowledged itself as "being more a negotiated document than an academic report"), it praised the Western concern of the need for access to information and the subservience of news media to "social, cultural, and economic and political goals" and displayed a strong bias against compromise. People found much to please as well as to displease in the MacBride Report; overall, the reaction was mostly critical.

This book emphasizes the process by which the Commission came into being, the trials and tribulations of working within the confines of the UNESCO framework, and the continuous give and take required to finally hammer out a document that, in Commissioner Abel's words, "was more than a first step toward understanding the contribution of international communication at a moment in history when mankind confronts glittering opportunities and all too stubborn problems in the field."[6]

This document, then, is an analysis, undertaken in an environment of still-unresolved communications problems within and among nations. It attempts to examine the work and appraise the significance of the MacBride Commission in addressing national and international policy concerns with a comprehensive global perspective. As Marshall Anderson's essay on the Commission's Report concluded, "No other single study or relatively short-term cooperative effort has had more potential for helping policy makers

---

[6]Quotation from Delegate Abel's intervention in the Communication Sector session at the UNESCO General Conference, Belgrade, 1980.

and the international community generally recognize the relationships between power and communication and the importance of information to the development of each individual, group, and nation."[7] Consequently, he believes, it deserves to be "seriously read and analyzed by policy makers, professional communicators, and scholars concerned about improving the quality and quantity of information around the world."

Four university professors supply the bottom line: "The MacBride Report...neither clarified nor resolved the issues which fueled the debate."[8]

---

[7]Michael E. Anderson. "A Primer on the MacBride Commission and Communication Policy for Tomorrow", a background paper prepared for the East-West Communication Institute for the Communication Policy Planning Project, April, 1980, Page 2.
[8]Ibid. p. 39, "Many Voices, Many Worlds: Four Reading on the NWIO in UNESCO," op. cit, p. 1.

Chapter 2

HISTORICAL PERSPECTIVE ON
INTERNATIONAL COMMUNICATION

In recent years, communication, information, and the role of the mass media have been moved swiftly toward center stage in the international arena; the flows of, access to, and interpretation of all forms of information have received increasing attention. And today there is a vast thicket of politically sensitive issues involved in the relations between the developed and developing countries and between the Western and Eastern blocs.

International information policy issues arise not only as the result of the flow of information across national boundaries, but also because of the growing awareness of the importance of the international exchange of information and information technology in their national affairs that motivates them toward increasing participation in the international debate on these issues.

These issues have come to the forefront and have been identified and analyzed primarily in two forums: those provided by the formal intergovernmental meetings of UNESCO and those of the nonaligned countries.

Just as a nation's overall foreign policy fundamentally tends to reflect its domestic perspectives, so too do a nation's international information policies reflect its domestic information policy perspectives.

The U.S. approach to information--its gathering, storing, clarification, transmission, and presentation--has stressed two themes: freedom from government interference domestically and free flow of information internationally. Beginning at the founding conference of UNESCO, the latter theme was promoted by the United States. It thus was incorporated as a fundamental tenet of the Universal Declaration of Human Rights, Article 19, which declares the rights of everyone "to seek, receive, and impart information and ideas through any media and regardless of frontiers." The concern for a free and unrestricted international flow of information has been a constant principle of U.S. foreign policy since the end of World War II. It has been vigorously opposed from two directions:

- From the USSR, which believed that the unrestricted flow of information across its borders might undermine its domestic authority and external influence and its policy mandating that the media must serve the purpose of the state.

- From the Third World countries, which have a conviction that their "dependence" upon Western media prevents their control over critical or embarrassing reporting and precludes adequate opportunity of expressing and defending their political and social systems in which the purpose of information and communication is to serve development plans.

At various meetings, some sponsored by UNESCO and some by the nonaligned countries themselves, Third World spokesmen have insistently presented a long list of complaints. In sum, they argue:

- There is great imbalance in the amount of news flowing between the advanced and developing countries.

- Most of the news coming into the Third World is controlled by Western news agencies that are owned by and directed from the industrialized countries.

- Western news reporting on the Third World countries focuses on the trivial or sensational to the neglect of "positive" developments.

- The dominance of ideas and information from the West constitutes a kind of cultural imperialism that is disruptive to indigenous cultures.

- The near total dependence of Third World nations on the developed countries' communication systems does not allow Less Developed Countries (LDCs) a significant role in origination of information.

- The free flow concept is just an excuse for unbridled commercial exploitation of the media internationally, free of responsibility or reprisal.

These concerns, along with many others, have been gathered up by the nonaligned countries into a package to justify their demands for a "New World Information Order (NWIO)." This is a derivative of the "New International Economic Order," essentially a claim by the "have-nots" upon the "haves" for what they perceive as greater distributive justice. The "New World Information Order" is a somewhat vague concept[1] but however it is defined, it reflects the East/West confrontation as well as the developing countries search for identity and growing nationalism.

The clearest elucidation of this concept appeared in a background paper prepared by a committee of the nonaligned countries for the MacBride Commission.[2] Its underlying theme was that the reason for information-flow imbalances is the fact that they are free (hence, uncontrollable) and they ought to be controlled by governments or by intergovernmental bodies like UNESCO. To developing countries, the NWIO was a scheme that would allow governments to regulate the flow of news and data across national boundaries and a means for reversing Western domination of news and information flow of communications technology. To the Soviets, it was a legitimation of their contention that the media are tools of the state and that control of the media is necessary for protection of national sovereignty. To the West, the NWIO was a "method to invest absolute power over all media and information, domestic and international, in the hands of government, stripping the private sector of its authority, independence, and freedom."[3]

Despite the explosion in communication technology in recent years, it was not until the political decolonization[4] was well along that the Third World countries became aware of the importance of information and communication at the national and international levels. The first governmental manifestation of this awareness came at the Nonaligned Summit meeting in Algiers in 1973. There decolonization of information flow was seen as a phase of the emancipation process. A similar meeting in Lima in 1975 recommended cooperative efforts to reorganize domestic mass media that is still dependent upon foreign countries or still a part of a colonial heritage. These themes were rearticulated that same year at symposia of media specialists meeting in Tunis in March and in Mexico City in May. Their recommendation for establishment of a pool of nonaligned nations' press agencies was ratified by a meeting of foreign ministers in Sri Lanka in August. Later that month a Nonaligned Summit in Colombia produced a resolution approving a "New Order of Information."

---

[1]I once defined it as "the constant reiteration of the forever unclear."

[2]Mustapha Masmoudi. "The New World Information Order" No. 31 in the Mauve Series of background papers prepared for the Commission (see Appendix I).

[3]Timothy Brown. *International Communications Glossary*, The Media Institute. Washington, 1984.

[4]becoming independent of the colonial powers that formerly exercised control of their media

The Soviets' continuing insistence that it is the duty of sovereign states to ensure against use of foreign media for "corrupting ends" and that in order to prevent undesirable material from being transmitted across national frontiers the state should control news flow, found ready acceptance among developing countries, particularly those with authoritarian regimes or those leaning that way. Almost all of them believe they must control news to some degree as a necessary step toward nation-building and think that only government is in a position to know what citizens should see and hear. Belatedly, they came to recognize that there is a linkage between communication and economic development, and sought through international political pressure to gain the technological resources they need and to impose restrictions on Western media as a way to counter Western "domination" of news flow. These efforts in UNESCO ranged from trying to gain international sanction for legalizing government censorship of foreign news and for licensing journalists to establishing universal codes of journalistic ethics and guarantees of the right of reply and rectification for alleged misinformation in foreign news.

The United States, along with its Western allies, has opposed all attempts to control mass media for such political or economic purposes. It has maintained that through a diversity of sources and through fostering greater growth of more open societies, mutual understanding among nations can be improved and the economic well-being of all nations can be benefited. Accordingly, "the United States has called for worldwide recognition of the principle of free flow with a minimum of government interference."[5] Not all nations, by any means, have agreed.

Communications in the United Nations' System

The United Nations (UN) is an intergovernmental organization created after World War II to preserve international peace and security and promote economic and social development. It came into being in 1945 at San Francisco at an international conference where its charter was drawn up. From the very start, the UN adopted the principle of Free Flow of News and Information by Word and Image and in 1948 enshrined it in article 19 of the Universal Declaration of Human Rights. After a false start, as we shall see, it floundered in this area and let others assume leadership.

Because its founders were of the opinion that many areas of economic and social cooperation requiring an intergovernmental approach

---

[5]Ambassador Diana L. Dougan, Luncheon Speech, Conference on "Mass Media and Telecommunications Assistance." Washington, D.C., 12/3/84.

could be more effectively served by relatively autonomous organizations, they created several specialized agencies, of which some have responsibilities in communications. These specialized agencies include The International Telecommunications Union (ITU), which administers agreements on international broadcasting and sets fees and standards;[6] the United Nations Educational, Scientific, and Cultural Organization (UNESCO), which carries out a wide range of projects that range from preserving cultural artifacts and fighting illiteracy to helping developing countries acquire scientific technology and train manpower for its use;[7] the United Nations Conference on Trade and Development (UNCTAD), which is mandated to promote trade (including telecommunications) between countries in various stages of development; and the United Nations Development Program, which funds projects for technical cooperation in the transfer, inter alia, of communications technology between developed and developing countries.

The United Nations' attention to communications has had an uneven history.

At a 1948 UN Conference on Freedom of Information in Geneva, in what was the first international effort to chart a course for information in the post World War II era, an informal agreement was reached concerning resolutions and draft conventions dealing broadly with the rights and responsibilities of the mass media and the respective roles of the UN and UNESCO. According to Julian Behrstock, the political aspects were to be the responsibility of the UN and UNESCO was to "concentrate on the more practical work involved in attempting to ease the flow of information across frontiers."[8]

Later, when the General Assembly got around to addressing itself to the draft resolutions adopted at Geneva, it established a Sub-commission on Freedom of Information and the UN Economic and Social Council began work on an International Code of Ethics for those engaged in disseminating news. Nothing ever came of these initiatives, however, and the only draft convention proposed at Geneva that was ever adopted--the Right of Reply and Rectification (for alleged misstatements)--was only ratified by six nations.

Even so, the General Assembly maintained Free Flow of Information as an item on its agenda and each year automatically deferred its discussion until the next year.

---

[6]ITU was established in 1865 and was made a part of the UN System in 1947.
[7]See the next chapter for more details on UNESCO's role and programs in communications.
[8]Julian Behrstock. *The Eighth Case: The Troubled Times of the United Nations*, p. 174.

Meanwhile, UNESCO had moved ahead with a variety of technical projects and was busy trying to help developing nations strengthen their communication capacities.[9]

In the 1960s, as it became obvious that the UN was floundering in the communications field, the nations turned to the only other agency with a mandate to deal with communication concerns, UNESCO, and it began to involve itself in the identical issues that the UN had shelved twenty-five years before. This move was accelerated by the impatience of two parties: the Soviets, who thought their ideological concerns were not being given sufficient attention, and the Third World, which wanted a more equitable global flow of news and information. And finally, the UN began to revive its interest.

It created a Committee on Publicity and Public Policy, concerned with overseeing the UN's public relations activities. In 1978, the General Assembly changed the name to the Committee on Information, expanded its membership from 41 to 61 (now 78), and added the responsibility for monitoring all communication matters in the UN system, including the establishment of "a new, more just, and more effective new world information and communication order." Beginning in 1980, this UN committee, as part of its responsibility for guiding the UN Department of Public Information (the publications branch), began holding annual meetings to formulate a set of recommendations on international communications policy. These forums inevitably involved the member states in the same controversies with which UNESCO had been struggling-- and with no better success. Each year, following two weeks of negotiations, the G77 (a massive voting block within the UN system) throws out the negotiated document and at the final session votes through its original set of proposals. Hence, unable or unwilling to achieve consensus, the Committee routinely forwards the G77's recommendations to the UN Political Committee, which routinely accepts the Committee's one-sided report.

Always, the sticking point in each meeting of the Committee on Information is the definition of a NWICO. This no longer seems to be a major issue in UNESCO, where a new Director-General is in charge; however, the debate on this issue in the UN, where this bone of contention had not been worried so long, seems destined to drag on.[10] Leonard Sussman,

---

[9]According to Hajnal (1983), UNESCO at that time served primarily a "technical role in promoting free exchange of books, newspapers, and audiovisual equipment."

[10]In 1990, however, the UN Committee on Information finally dropped its long-standing effort to promote the "establishment" of a NWICO.

quoted in *Press Time* sums up the situation this way: "The debate will go on in the UN probably indefinitely and bore the hell out of everyone. I think it is dead in UNESCO."

Historical Role of UNESCO in Communications

The United Nations Educational, Scientific, and Cultural Organization came into being in 1945 premised on the assumption that international conflicts result from peoples' ignorance of other peoples, and that if each could be better informed about the other, peace could be won in the minds of men. Consequently, the founders believed it was important that they work to break down blockages of free flow of information around the globe.

The Preamble to UNESCO's constitution says:

States believing in full and equal opportunity for education for all, in the unrestricted pursuit of objective truth, and in the free exchange of ideas and knowledge, are agreed and determined to develop and increase the means of communication between their peoples and to employ these means for the purposes of mutual understanding and a truer and more perfect knowledge of each others' lives.

And Article 1.2 states:

The organization will collaborate in the work of advancing the mutual knowledge and understanding of peoples through all means of mass communication and to that end will recommend such international agreements as may be necessary to promote the free flow of ides by word and image.[11]

As it turned out, as Tom Bethel has observed, "Information freely gathered and disseminated is as likely to cause conflict as it is harmony...especially in relation to the fortunes of national rulers who do not enjoy the consent of those they rule. It was the failure to even consider this possibility that was the principal error of UNESCO's founders and theoreticians."[12]

Research by Stevenson, Cole, and Shaw (1980) tends to support Bethel's contention. Increases in the amount and diversity of information, they found, do not seem to increase public understanding of a complicated world. "Certainly the American people, surrounded by information...are

---

[11]Article 1.2 (a). The United States was instrumental in getting this clause inserted.
[12]Tom Bethel. Introduction to *The Media Glossary*, Media Institute, 1984.

evidence that interest in the world does not increase as the quantity and diversity of information increase. And we have seen no evidence that other systems of mass media produce a more enlightened public." (Their explanation: poor use is made of the diversity of information available in all parts of the world.)[13]

The founders, though, had no reservation about the importance of free flow, and though in later years UNESCO turned away from unreserved commitment to this concept, it was certainly so committed at the start.

It is ironic, then, that UNESCO, which has always had a Division of Free Flow of Information and has a constitutional mandate for its promotion, has been the dominant forum for attacks on this principle. In the debate on communication issues, which has been going on for two decades, the doctrine of free flow has been under sustained attack. It is ironic, too, that through what Ian Christie Clark, former Canadian ambassador to UNESCO, calls "a reverse colonization," the institution that was conceived by the West to serve Western ideas and values has come "to serve not only the needs and anxieties of the Third World countries, but has become their spiritual home and forum in which they express their resentments.[14]

During the 1980s and longer, the Third World countries have turned to UNESCO for a wide program of assistance: training, conferences, seminars, research, and counseling, and as mandated by successive UNESCO general conferences (beginning in 1970), assistance in formulating national communication policies and plans. In attempting to fulfill this mandate, UNESCO came in for a great deal of criticism from the West.

A principal source of such criticism stemmed from a series of UNESCO-sponsored meetings held in Asia, Africa, and South America. The most notable example of UNESCO's problem in this respect was the 1976 conference in San Jose, Costa Rica, where UNESCO held the first series of regional intergovernmental meetings on communication policies. The conference aroused great controversy even before it began, because background papers submitted in preparation for the meeting suggested alternatives that seemed to favor government control of the press. UNESCO vehemently insisted that these were only the personal views of the consultants who had been hired to write working papers and did not represent UNESCO policy.

---

[13]Robert L. Stevenson. "Beyond Belgrade: Prospects for Balanced Flow of Information."

[14]Ian Christie Clark. From "Crisis to Renewal of UNESCO," article in the *Newsletter of Americans for the Universality of UNESCO*, September, 1988.

While all of the thirty-two resolutions adopted at San Jose called for greater government participation in every area of communications, some defended press freedom and some called for varying degrees of control over the media. A principal assertion was that "a free flow of information will really exist only when all countries have equal access to all the sources of information and take part on an equal footing in the control over the use of international channels of information."

Perhaps the most troublesome theme sounded at San Jose was the argument that the news media should be used to bring about social change. Communication was seen not as an end in itself but as a means to pre-conceived ends. Few would quarrel with the logic that communication (at least the information sources relating to health, agriculture, and education) should be integrated into overall national development planning, and that is what UNESCO urged. The problem, the West warned, was the danger that pursuit of such planning could easily lead to suppression of news the government considered harmful to national development and circulation of news limited to that considered nationally beneficial.

In any case, there were enough denunciations and enough resolutions of a restrictive nature drafted at San Jose to convince the West that UNESCO was set on an ominous course in sponsoring these regional conferences on communication policy.

A major source of difficulty in the North-South debate was the difference over the role of the media. Developing nations regard information as a social good and communication systems as an integral and necessary part of national development. Western media people regard such a concept as subversion of news and information by government for purposes of suppressing criticism, disseminating only favorable news, and perpetuating regimes of those in power.

The UNESCO Secretariat, officially neutral and ostensibly without any policy on governmental or nongovernmental control of the media, still managed to get into hot water in providing assistance to Less Developed Countries (LDCs) in the development of their communication planning. Presumably, UNESCO project teams were merely authorized to indicate to countries the options available and then assist them in drawing up policies within their national context. In practice, if the leaders of countries being helped had a socialistic predisposition, UNESCO teams lent themselves to helping governments do a more efficient job of controlling news and opinion.

A Third World country selection of a communication model and policy is governed by its first priority: national development, including creation of national unity, cultural cohesion, and social and economic improvement. Accordingly, in the view of many of them, the press must be mobilized behind government to "explain" national policy to the country and to promote national consensus.

British publisher Roy Thompson has said criticism in new nations may be subject to some degree of restriction because their journalists do not have enough experience and judgment to keep from printing "destructive or inflammatory criticism which exposed to populations which have not yet learned the art of political stability could lead to serious unrest and even revolutionary activity." I myself have sometimes startled audiences of foreign journalists by confiding that if I were the head of a new nation, I, too, would be inclined to keep control of the media until my country had a chance to get its roots down. Many Third World leaders would say "Amen." They assert that their fragile governments, lacking firmly established institutions and educated peoples, are not yet ready for freedom of speech and the press. (On the other hand, founders of the newly-created United States believed that free expression and a free press, undominated by the state, were so important that they guaranteed those freedoms in the Constitution of the new nation.)

As a Third World representative reminded me at the 1979 Stockholm Conference on World News Agencies, the Western traditions of free expression were slow in developing. "Even though press freedom is a desirable goal the world over, it is a concept of rather recent vintage," he said. "It took England, the bastion of democratic freedoms, 300 years to arrive at this point. You must not be impatient with us; it will take time."

Nevertheless, Western leaders and journalists have frequently expressed impatience. Elliot Abrams, while U.S. Assistant Secretary of State for International Organization Affairs, once wrote, "There is no country that is too poor to be free or to have a free press." And I, on the other hand have often argued with U.S. journalists who cannot understand why Third World countries cannot set up media that are owned and operated by the private sector. My answer: In many cases there is insufficient capital for media enterprises and not enough economic base to make advertising revenue a means of financial support.

UNESCO's Director of Free Flow of information Handy Kandil, in a speech to the UK National Commission for UNESCO (3/30/83) asked, "What could have been the alternative to government, especially in the early days of independence? Where could a market have been found for national commercial interests? Did the possibility of national private interests exist at the time?" My answer: In many cases in the early days of independence, private media enterprises were begun and were operational, and were then shut down by the new governments precisely because they were private. David Lamb, in his book *The Africans*, reports that an estimated fifty percent of the African press was closed by governments, not by economic necessity.[15]

What it comes down to, concluded the U.S. Deputy Assistant Secretary George Dalley, "is the need to recognize the fact that in many emerging countries the choice is between government-sponsored media and no media. And with the increasing recognition of the application of the mass media to national development, we can understand why they are unwilling to wait until all factors are in place to support a private communications system and the fact that some countries find it necessary to control the media during a period of national development."[16]

The belief that Western-style journalism is not appropriate for Third World countries is widely held among nonaligned communication theorists. As Rosemary Righter of the *London Times* has pointed out, governments in the past have argued that their developing societies are too vulnerable to withstand the Western probing style of reporting; at that time, however, they were attacking the Western model as undesirable in itself. Even if they could afford it, they said, its importation would sow dissent instead of promoting the unity and cohesion needed for nation building. She concluded that an organized campaign has been undertaken to give this view international respectability through sanctions of UNESCO and the United Nations, and to help governments develop the techniques and ideological framework for a comprehensive revision of communication along these lines.

UNESCO has been the chief vehicle for forwarding this campaign. Not only has it provided forums for debate, resolutions, and declarations, but also, through its Secretariat beginning in 1970, it has attempted to establish global criteria for proper content of information and the responsibilities of journalists.

At its 1970 General Conference, UNESCO took up for the first time the theme of imbalance in the flow of information and its presumed effect on cultural identity. This theme was subsequently raised in the 1972 Helsinki Conference on Cultural Policies, in the conference for ASEAN Ministers in Jakarta in 1973, in the meeting of African Ministers in Accra in 1975, and in the ministerial cultural conference for Latin America in Bogota in 1978.

---

[15]Reported in *The Media Crisis* published by the World Press Freedom Committee, 1982, p. 86.
[16]Testimony before the Senate Foreign Relations Committee (6/19/79).

Balance and Free Flow

On the basis of these regional meetings, UNESCO reinterpreted its constitutional mandate so that it called not just for promotion of a free flow of ideas but for the free and *balanced* flow of ideas two concepts that were invariably linked under the presumption that there was an indivisible connection between "free" and "balanced" as the desideratum in international information flow.

Director-General M'Bow asserted that "the concentration of media in the hands of a few developed countries affects the direction of the flow of information and its content. This is what justifies the demand for a better balance in the production, dissemination and circulation of information."

Western managers of international communications insisted that they were using them impartially and expressed fear that attempts to achieve balance would restrict free flow. "These arguments were denounced as specious justification for self-serving practices which perpetuated international patterns of colonial domination."[17] In any case, spokesmen for the "receivers" insisted that there could never be true free flow unless the developing countries were freed from their state of perceived information dependency.

News and information media in the United States and in other information-rich countries export a vast amount of news and information via word and image, but import very little. A similar imbalance persists in the distribution of technical resources, with the Third World almost totally dependent on the industrialized world for communication equipment. And the rapid development of this technology each year consistently widens the gap.

The uneven distribution of communication facilities also increases the Third World's dependence for media software (content), with the consequence that programs imported from the United States and other producing countries inevitably impact on the culture and media of the receiving countries. It is estimated that 80 percent of the world news flow emanates from the four global news agencies in the United States, Great Britain, and France (Associated Press, United Press International, Reuters, Agence France Presse). In 1977, UPI alone was delivering news, news pictures, news films, and audio services to 6,000 subscribers in 116 countries and territories. An estimated 4,500,00 words of copy were transmitted by UPI every day.[18]

---

[17]"Many Voices, Many Worlds: Four Readings of the NWIO Debate in UNESCO" op. cit. p. 10.
[18]Report of the Committee on Foreign Relations, U.S. Senate. June, 1977, pp. 9-10.

"The effects of this one-way news flow are considered disastrous by the receiving countries, which complain that intellectual and cultural subjugation is as pernicious as economic and political dependence."[19] Socialist spokesmen see in this process an interference in domestic affairs and a violation of national sovereignty.

The Soviets claim that the term "free flow of information" appeared after Winston Churchill's Iron Curtain speech in 1946 and that it became a part of the Cold War strategy as well as a means of helping the United States maintain a worldwide hegemony.

Other countries say the free flow doctrine is used to propagate a Western model of social, economic, and cultural development at the expense of indigenous (what UNESCO insists on calling "endogenous") national systems. Still others see the doctrine as providing a protective umbrella over the activities of transnational corporations that distribute media products.

Elie Abel suggests that these differences cannot be resolved by compromise. "Few decisions made in the name of any nation are more intrinsically political than those basic decisions about how media institutions are to be owned, operated, and regulated...We do not ask of others that they do as we have done. The Bill of Rights, starting with the First Amendment, is peculiarly American. It was not designed for export."[20]

A study of the four Western global news agencies (Associated Press, United Press International, Reuters, and Agence France Presse) by Stevenson and Cole puts the worldwide flow of news in a different perspective. Some of the complaints about the Big Four agencies they say are legitimate, but others are outright contrary to the evidence.

To begin, while the four Western agencies do supply a large amount of news, they are not alone. There are 104 government agencies, representing 68 percent of all nations. These agencies participate in the international news flow by exchanging copy with each other or distributing their files to other agencies. "The services of AP, UPI, and Reuters are sold to the government agency rather than straight to the media. This arrangement empowers the national news agency to control the picture of the world that is painted for the nation's readers, viewers, and listeners. If the Western (and other foreign) agencies provide an off-color or alien view

---

[19] C. Anthony Gifford. "The New International Information Order," Edward R. Murrow Symposium, Washington State University, Pullman, Washington, 1979.
[20] Seminar on "New World Information & Communication Order," Geneva, 8/12-15, 1981, Working Paper No. 19, p. 9.

of the world, the national agency has the power to correct that distortion...the fact is that very little Western wire copy contains labeling of any kind. Most of it is added at the national news agency."

In response to some of the charges, the researchers offer four generalizations:

1. The amount of information available to the Third World, on the whole, is less a problem than the kind of information available.
2. The assertion that the Western agencies ignore the Third World in regional service in those parts of the world is simply not true.
3. The argument that the Third World is singled out for special treatment is also not supported by data.
4. The information revolution increases the amount and diversity of information but does not seem to increase the quality of it or the public's knowledge and understanding of a complicated world.

"The real task of journalism," conclude Stevenson and Cole, "is to find ways to transform the flood of information into a coherent view of the world that enlightens as well as informs."[21]

Another cause of misunderstanding is the difference around the world in what constitutes "news." What the Third World people would like to have reported about themselves is not necessarily what Western editors consider newsworthy for their readership. The events that occur, usual or unusual, are news, as opposed to propaganda or information about economic or social development. In blunt terms, the housewife in Oskaloosa, Iowa or the farmer in Bedford, Indiana is not much interested in the new highway construction in Uwagadougou. Put another way, it is not news when airplanes take off and land routinely every day, but when one crashes it is news.

This action orientation, of course, tends to emphasize disasters and violence wherever it occurs, and this is why people in the Third World assert that the global news agencies report largely negative news about their countries and neglect the positive developments.

This accounts, in part, for the deplored underreporting of the Third World in Western papers, but it also true of news everywhere that what interests people the most is what happens close to home--to friends and

[21]From a paper presented at the International Communication Association in Mexico in May, 1980, reproduced in *Editor and Publisher* (7/5/80). Robert Stevenson is associate professor of journalism and Richard Cole is dean of the School of Journalism at the University of North Carolina. Cole and Stevenson were participants in a cooperative study of foreign news in 25 to 30 countries, undertaken by the International Association for Mass Communication Research, requested by UNESCO, following the 1976 General Conference in Nairobi.

neighbors and people in their own community, region, or country. And that universal truth dictates what editors choose to publish in the Third World as well as elsewhere.

It should also be noted that another reason for inadequate Western reporting of news in the developing world is the cost and primitive communications facilities. It costs a Western agency more than $100,000 per year to keep a reporter in the field. Covering a continent the size of Africa is not only enormously expensive but also very difficult because of the problems in communication and transportation. Contrary to some claims, the global news agencies do not make a profit on their services to Third World subscribers, but maintain them at a loss in order to be a full world service.

Soviet Initiatives in UNESCO

In the past, the Soviets, who regarded UNESCO as a handy mechanism to be manipulated in their national interest, were quick to exploit Third World discontent with Western media domination by initiating several major resolutions in that body.

In 1972 they introduced a resolution on direct satellite broadcasting, which carried a provision for prior consent by the receiving country. The United States denounced this provision as contravening Article 19 of the Universal Declaration on Human Rights, and it registered the only dissent in a 100-1 vote by which it was adopted.

Also in 1972, the Soviets introduced a resolution calling for a declaration on the use of the media, which sought to impose a variety of regulations. The West objected to this declaration as an attempt to gain international sanction for government control of the media. Third World spokesmen supported the Soviet resolution because it challenged the basic Western tenet on free flow of information. After long and bitter debate in three successive UNESCO general conferences, a greatly modified version of the Soviet-sponsored Declaration on the Media was adopted in 1978.

Western strategy made this outcome possible. While the head of the U.S. Delegation, Ambassador John Reinhardt, and publisher William Attwood were engaged in off-stage negotiations with Director-General M'Bow, Western delegates carried on a week-long mock negotiating session with the Soviet and Third World representatives. On the final morning, the Soviets were called into M'Bow's office and were confronted with a *fait accompli* that had been worked out behind the scenes.

This version was acceptable to the West because, as Assistant Secretary George Dalley explained, "Gone were all mentions of government control, replaced by affirmation of freedom and diversity in the flow and exchange of information and encouragement of action toward increasing the abilities of all peoples to participate in and benefit from the new communication technologies."[22]

Herbert Schiller, a professor of communications at the University of California in San Diego had a different view. "The U.S. prevented the approval of a resolution aimed at establishing criteria for the content of international information flows--a recommendation viewed by U.S. media and government officials as an international move to censorship, and, more menacing still, as a direct and dangerous thrust against the system of private ownership of the media."[23]

The Global Ball Game

Another consequence of the communications revolution was the fact that information became linked to global issues. Not only did it become an aspect of North-South dialogue, but it became a major factor in the competition between East and West for influence in the developing world.

In the first place, this change dramatized the new ball game in the world arena--the dramatic shift in power resulting from the influx of 100 new decolonized nations into the UN system. The alliance of nonaligned countries called The Group of 77 (G77) was formed in the late 1950s, as a massive voting bloc within the UN system. The realization by the Less Developed Countries (LDCs) that they now held the balance of power in international forums led to all sorts of cleavages and realignments-- cleavages between former allies and unexpected alliances of former enemies. What happened on the Draft Declaration on the Media is a case in point.

In 1975, at the intergovernmental meeting of experts in Paris convened by UNESCO to develop a new Draft, the Soviets put together a strong coalition with the Arabs and the Africans. The come-on for the Arabs was the inclusion of a reference in the preamble to UN Resolution 3379 equating Zionism with racism. Since the Declaration forbade the promotion of racism through the mass media, the implications were obvious and highly damaging to Israel. The Africans, possibly sensitive to the Arabs new-found oil muscle, joined with them. Despite strong protests from the West, this coalition was able to vote inclusion of this reference; consequently, twelve Western nations withdrew from the conference. The

---

[22]George Dalley. Statement on "UNESCO and Freedom of Information" op. cit., p. 10.
[23]Herbert Schiller. *"Cultural Domination Adjusts to Growing Demand for NWIO,"* paper for seminar on international communications, Amsterdam. 10/6-8, 1987, p. 4.

result was to leave the Third World and the Soviets in possession of the field, free to prepare a Draft with far more stringent limitations than would have otherwise have been possible.

But one year later, in Nairobi, the Soviets lost their coalition. By then, many people realized that things were on a collision course. The Africans, following the lead of the first African to ever head a UN agency (M'Bow), refused to side with the Soviets and instead, joined with the West and its allies in postponing the Draft Declaration. This time the General Conference had the good sense not to steam-roll through, by brute force of the bloc vote, a one-sided Media Declaration that would have produced a great pyrrhic victory.

Another factor in securing a large measure of Third World support for the West in preventing adoption of the Declaration was the expressed willingness of the United States and its allies to help developing countries improve their communication capabilities. Ambassador Reinhardt, head of the U.S. delegation, promised such support in his plenary address; and the United States backed a Tunisian resolution that provided UNESCO funds for communications research, training, and consultation projects for developing countries.

Some labeled this a patent trade-off; others considered it a turning point in the international communication controversy. At Nairobi, realizing that there could be no progress without gaining cooperation from the Third World power bloc, and finally beginning to appreciate the possible consequences stemming from inattention and unresponsiveness to the underlying causes of their discontent, the West started to respond in an understanding and positive way.[24] During the debate, the Western representatives listened sympathetically to the problems outlined by emerging countries, acknowledging that the Western press agencies were not without fault and that, indeed, there was a gross imbalance in the world's news and information flow. They argued, however, that the way to improve the world media situation was neither by restricting the media capacities of the industrialized countries nor by embracing self-defeating controls for developing countries that would strangle their own communications and cut them off from the free international exchange of information. A better way was for the LDCs to improve their own communication capacities so they could make a larger contribution to the world's free flow of news and ideas--in

---

[24]Clayton Kirkpatrick, then editor of the Chicago Tribune and a member of the U.S. delegation, electrified the delegates with this statement: "The world's best hope for a wider extension of freedom and a freer flow of information lies in the universal and instinctive desire for self-determination. Our best course is to assist in every way the development of information services in the Third World countries."

other words, not limit the capacities of *some* but increase the capacities of *all*. This, the West argued, was the way to help redress the admittedly enormous imbalance in international media. And to help bring this about, the West offered technical assistance to improve the quality and quantity of media production and provide professional assistance to increase the competence of media management and performance. This initiative was the precursor of the U.S. proposal that led to the establishment of UNESCO's International Program for Development of Communication, whereby contributions from industrialized countries are matched with communication priority needs of developing countries.

While some Third World representatives remained skeptical, more moderate elements (especially among the Africans) were willing to cooperate with the West by accepting this pragmatic approach as more productive than continued denunciation. The leaders of the nonaligned countries recognized that it would require more than fervent rhetoric and moral indignation to bring about significant changes in the information order. It would have to be, they reluctantly conceded, an evolutionary process that would require the cooperation not only of both the First and Second Worlds, but also of the Third World as well. Not only would normative actions unsupported by consensus be ignored by the developing countries, but presumed LDC gains would be meaningless without the cooperation and involvement of the countries with advanced technological capacitance. They were going to be heavily dependent upon the West for help, and for a while this mutual recognition seemed to bring about some amelioration in the controversy.

The West was slow, however, to make good on the promises made at Nairobi. The United States, experiencing a slow-down in its economy, did not back up its Ambassador, and aside from offering free transponder time on its INTELSAT Satellite System for experimental use in four areas of the developing world, it provided no new assistance initiatives along this line until much later. There was some increase in the training programs provided by England, West Germany, and Scandinavian countries. And in the United States, spokesmen for the private sector, speaking through the World Press Freedom Committee (WPFC), pledged that they would make a substantial effort to raise funds to upgrade professional journalism training and provide other assistance. (To date, the WPFC has completed 120 projects that aid journalists and news media in need of help.)

Communications scholar Michael Anderson suggests that the Nairobi UNESCO conference marked the high point in the level of emotion and fervor in the East-West confrontational debate on communication issues.   At various international meetings shortly after Nairobi, there seemed to be a growing disposition by various parties to seek clarification. Even so, experienced observers believed it would be naive to expect too much.

To begin, there was still an enormous gap in the perception of the role of the media. Developed countries thought of communication in terms of news and journalism; Third World countries, striving for survival, considered information an essential aspect of national development in all its forms and channels. The Soviets and some others considered media as instruments of revolutionary and political change. Traditional societies felt threatened by the new technology and its impact. These varied perceptions inevitably created conflicts and distorted the dialogue.

Perhaps the greatest obstacle to reasoned discussion of the international media issues was the insistence by media nonprofessionals on exploiting legitimate grievances of the developing countries for external political purposes, including Third World communication theorists and politicians intent on advancing authoritarian principles and perpetuating their power and officials from Bloc countries bent on fostering government control of communications as a standard for the world. Another possible obstacle was the suspicion that the UNESCO staff had a vested interest in perpetuating the controversy. If, as Western news media spokesmen like Leonard Sussman (Freedom House), George Galliner (IPI), and George Beebe (WPFC) insisted, the controversy were left to the journalists themselves, real progress could be made in improving the global communication system. But in any conference of UNESCO, whose membership consists of sovereign states, the involvement and dominance of government officials is unavoidable.

In Summary

The foregoing provides a rough outline of the communications controversy as it developed in the UN and UNESCO up to the time the MacBride Commission came into being. It was essentially a conflict between those who believe the media must be independent of government, led by the United States, and those who believe the media must be instruments of the state, led by the USSR. In between are the Third World countries who hold the balance of power. Some of these countries are oriented toward authoritarian forms of government, some toward democracy, and some are in transition or undecided. The ability of the United States and its allies to convince the LDCs that they will respond sympathetically to their media priorities and give practical help in their achievement, will likely determine the extent of participation by the developing countries in exploring cooperative remedies for readjusting the world's information system in the interest of all peoples.

With the best of good will on all sides, the international media issues remained difficult to confront. They would remain so as Chairman MacBride and his fellow commissioners began their study of International Communication Problems.

Chapter 3

ESTABLISHMENT OF THE MacBRIDE COMMISSION

My Involvement and How It All Began

The communication debate at the UNESCO General Conference in Nairobi in 1976 was so volatile that it had threatened to blow the conference apart. This would have been a catastrophe for the Paris-based United Nations Education, Scientific and Cultural Organization (UNESCO), because this conference was its first ever to be held on the African continent. Furthermore, it was being led by an African Director-General, the first African to head a UN agency, Amadou Mahtar M'Bow, of Senegal. The Secretariat, then, was anxious to quench the fire and an initiative from the U.S. delegation helped. In the final intervention by the United States in the Communications Sector at the Nairobi conference, after reiterating our objections to the Soviet sponsored Declaration on Use of the Media and endorsing a Scandinavian proposal to send technical assistance to Third World countries, I concluded with a suggestion that aroused widespread interest.

The night before, along with Richard Nobbe (another member of the U.S. Delegation), I had dinner with Gunnar Naesselund of Sweden, UNESCO deputy Director-General for Culture and Communication. Our conversation centered on our mutual frustration and discouragement about the fruitless two-week debate in the Communications Sector of the Conference concerning the policy and program of UNESCO in this field. It had been nothing more than a rehash of stale arguments that had been going on for years in UNESCO. Charges and countercharges had gone back and forth--assertions without substance and claims without proof were made with no supporting data to back them up; in short, delegates didn't know for sure what they were talking about. As a result, we weren't getting anywhere and the possibility of ever resolving the issues seemed increasingly remote.

Naesselund recalled that there had been similar lack of progress in the Education Sector until UNESCO commissioned a committee, chaired by Edgar Faure of France, to study the problems in this field from a global perspective. The resulting report, *Learning to Be*, had a positive impact on education worldwide. Nobbe and I both jumped at the idea. "Why not do the same for international communication," Naesselund said, "Why not?" We decided that I should add such a proposal to the end of my presentation the next morning at the final session of the Communications Sector.

In my statement (an "intervention" in UNESCO parlance), I reviewed the debate on the Media Declaration, pointing up the myriad concerns it had raised and the enormous complexity of the problems involved. We had debated these matters for two weeks in Nairobi and for several years before that, and we seemed no further along in resolving our differences or finding solutions. I then recalled the success of the Faure Commission in confronting a similar situation in the field of education. I suggested that "the Director-General consider establishing a high-level committee of outstanding communication scholars, practitioners, experts, and representatives of professional media organizations to advise UNESCO on drawing up a long-term comprehensive plan and program. Such a plan is necessary to a rationalized determination of objectives and priorities. U.S. Secretary of State Henry Kissinger recently stated that world development has "lacked a coherent strategy by which the benefits of technology...can be made available in a disciplined, and farsighted and cooperative manner." The approach we have suggested for UNESCO, I concluded, might well prove just such a strategy for sharing the benefits of communication technology.

To my surprise, the speech provoked considerable excitement, with delegates crowding around to get copies. I was especially impressed by a note on beautifully engraved stationery that complimented me on the presentation and was signed "the Holy See." (The Vatican holds official observer status in UNESCO.)

Nobbe was so concerned that this effort not be in vain that he rushed up to the Rapporteur (or Secretary) to make certain that the U.S. Delegation's proposal was duly "noted" in the Report of the Communications Commission and thus brought to the attention of the Conference plenary--and of the Director-General.[1]

That's the inside story of how the MacBride Commission came into being.

---

[1] Guidance notes of the Medium Term Plan adopted by the 19th UNESCO General Conference.

Amadou Mahtar M'Bow

Because the Commission was appointed by M'Bow and (as he insisted) its Final Report was prepared exclusively for his personal use, it seems appropriate to accord him special attention in this book. Furthermore, supporters and critics alike consider that most of UNESCO's recent troubles originated during his regime.

Although I had a professional acquaintance with the Director-General for more than a decade, my personal observations here are supplemented by what I have been told by colleagues, particularly, by observations of Julian Behrstock, a long-time member of UNESCO's Free Flow of Information Division.

Mr. M'Bow became Director-General in 1974. Earlier he had headed Senegalese delegations to UNESCO General Conferences in 1966 and 1968 and had become chairman of The Group of Seventy-seven (G77) of nonaligned countries. In 1970, he was appointed Assistant Director-General for Education in UNESCO. In 1974, at the age of fifty-three, he was elected Director-General.

He is a contradictory personality. Although he was a stern disciplinarian at work, he was all affability and charm in social situations. With a broad smile on his round face, he would stand for an hour in a reception line, warmly greeting guests. Even though I might not have seen him for two years or more, it was always, "Ah, Mr. Harley; so glad you're here," despite the fact that he might be well aware that I had that very morning made a strong intervention against some aspect of his program. According to Behrstock, he had "the politician's gift for never forgetting a name or a face, an amiability which was to baffle those who encountered his doctrinaire, stubborn postures in official contacts." Behrstock offers the further observation: "Although lacking in any notable intellectual depth or erudition, he had a sharp intelligence and a gift for behind-the-scenes maneuvering in conference situations...with a capacity for adroit manipulation and reconciliation of opposing views to avoid votes and achieve consensus--usually on positions in accord with his own views."[2]

My one protracted personal negotiation with him occurred in 1982. As one of the architects of the International Program for Communications Development (IPDC), I had hoped that the IPDC might be established as a free-standing entity outside of UNESCO, but the Third World majority would have none of that (see Appendices). Failing there, I next tried to

---

[2]Julian Behrstock.. *The Eighth Case: Troubled Times at the United Nations*, University Press of America, New York, London, p. 120.

ensure that, even though the IPDC was to be located in UNESCO, its program director would have the independence of reporting directly to the IPDC Administrative Council rather than to some UNESCO bureaucrat. To this end, I sought an audience with the Director-General.

I ascended to the top floor of the UNESCO headquarters building in Paris via the Director-General's private elevator and was shown in to the luxurious duplex apartment specially built for his residency (and on which, I was told, he refused to pay rent).

Mr. M'Bow listened politely to my plea, expressed apparent sympathy with my view, and then lowered the boom. He brought out a copy of the UNESCO constitution and pointed out the section that made him ultimately responsible for *all* activities of UNESCO. Consequently, this precluded him from ever surrendering under any circumstances his answerability for whatever went on in the organization, including activities of the IPDC. I left his headquarters feeling rather like a schoolboy who had been properly chastised for failing to do his homework.

I should explain that Mr. M'Bow's "lecture" to me was done via an interpreter for, although he had a rudimentary knowledge of English, he was not able to carry on any real conversation in the language. He was, however, fluent in French; I was not.

My overwhelming impression of M'Bow was of a man of great ambition and great pride--and he had much to be proud of. Beginning life in 1921 in modest circumstances in Senegal, he rose through various posts in the Senegalese government and in UNESCO to become the first African to head a UN agency. And during his career he was awarded forty-five honorary doctorates, three gold medals, forty-one decorations, and four honorary professorships.

Along with his pride, M'Bow had a strong self-righteous streak. This was reflected in his tendency to indulge in lengthy monologues, largely devoted to defensive rhetoric and self-justification. I heard him speak at several so-called press conferences going on without interruption for an hour or more, leaving no time (or very little) for questioning. He was known to address the UNESCO Executive Board for hours at a stretch, and one observer at many of these sessions told me that he was always disappointed in M'Bow's presentation. His passion for particularization never allowed him to disentangle himself from the mass of details so he could organize them into a coherent vision for the organization.

Because of M'Bow's righteous self-image, he had difficulty in handling criticism and accepting suggestions or challenges. He was incensed by the drum beat of criticism and constant scrutiny by the Western press. He never understood the Western media's watchdog role and the practice of investigative reporting. Instead, he was convinced that Western journalists were personally "out to get him."

The particular irritants were Ron Koven, former *Washington Post* foreign editor, who camps on UNESCO's doorstep in order to provide daily detailed reports for the World Press Freedom Committee in Washington and cooperating organizations; Paul Chutkow, who covered the UNESCO beat for the Associated Press; and Rosemary Righter, a constant critic of UNESCO, writing for *The London Sunday Times*. Ms. Righter was an especially difficult proposition for the Director-General.

Due to his cultural background, M'Bow was never comfortable in one-on-one confrontations with professional women, especially when they were as aggressive as Ms. Righter. A case in point occurred at the First Talloires conference, an assemblage of free-world journalists organized in 1981 by the World Press Freedom Committee. At the beginning of the question period following M'Bow's address, Rosemary marched up the center aisle, planted herself six feet in front of the Director-General and announced that because he had not returned her telephone calls for weeks, she was pleased to have this face-to-face opportunity to ask him some questions. She then ticked off a series of public promises she said he had made and demanded to know why he had not fulfilled them. M'Bow, obviously flustered, hemmed and hawed a bit and then, losing his cool, launched into an angry accusation of misrepresentation. It was not one of his best performances, and an appearance that had been intended as an attempt at reassuring the Western journalists about UNESCO's intentions, ended by reaffirming their suspicions about the intentions of both Mr. M'Bow and UNESCO.

That he was ambitious was manifested by his rapid rise within UNESCO, culminating at a comparatively young age with his election to the top post of Director-General. Near the end of his second term it was common knowledge that, though he would settle for a third term, he harbored even higher ambitions: to become secretary general of the UN or to win the Nobel Peace Prize, "an ambition not unrelated to gratuitous pronouncements he had been making on crises in the Middle East and Central America far outside UNESCO's purview."[3]

As it turned out, none of these ambitions was realized. When the Soviets let it be known that they thought two terms were enough, and four countries--West Germany, Switzerland, the Netherlands, and Japan--

---

[3]Ibid., p. 121.

indicated they were ready to resign if M'Bow were given a third term, his candidacy was doomed. A Spanish scientist, Federico Mayor, was elected.

In the end, Mr. M'Bow's power base in the Soviet Union and in the developing countries failed him. It was this base that he used during his two terms to decisively shape UNESCO's work. His predilections are not surprising when one considers his background. During his three years at the Sorbonne he became head of African Students Federation of France, an experience that undoubtedly was the inception of his reputation as a militant for the African heritage. After college, he was active in the G77 and became thoroughly attuned to that group's grievances and plans for their redress. And, of course, as a native of Senegal, he was a Third Worlder himself. Perhaps based on his background in education, he saw UNESCO as a "bully pulpit" to educate the world.

It must be said that Mr. M'Bow was sincere in seeing himself as a champion of the poor and oppressed, particularly of his native Africa, but also of all the developing world, as an advocate of the new international economic order that would provide for a more equitable distribution of the world's goods and services, and as an ardent promoter of a new world information order that would help the newly independent countries develop their own cultural identity and project it to the rest of the world.

During M'Bow's regime, UNESCO undoubtedly made commendable advances in many aspects of science, education and culture. And even in the communication sector there were positive contributions through workshops, seminars, training programs and research. On balance, however, the politicization of the communications issues that his leadership engendered far outweighed UNESCO's minor accomplishments in this field.

Finally, it should be said that anyone who could hold the post of Director-General for thirteen years had great abilities as a politician and statesman. It is unfortunate that, as Director-General, M'Bow saw fit to employ those skills to tilt the balance in UNESCO rather than play the proper role of an even-handed international public servant.

Selecting the Commission Members

Director-General Amadou Mahtar M'Bow, bought the commission idea, all right, but he took his time about implementing it. He was conscientious about finding appropriate representation of geographical and ideological areas as well as people with relevant experience and expertise. UNESCO, in a press release, put the process on a higher level of prolixity: "...the Director-General stressed himself that his choice had been guided by a concern to reconcile the demands of pluralism and the need for unity and homogeneity...also by the need to ensure currents of thought, intellectual trends, and cultural traditions which reflect the large number of professional circles concerned and the diversity of economic and social systems and situations in the major regions of the world."

Another reason for delay was dissention within the staff as to the scope and mission description, as well as several lists of possible members. M'Bow was cautious in resolving the disagreements, but wanted it clear that the final design was his. His first job was to pick a chairman--and here he made a superb choice: Sean MacBride, an Irish politician, lawyer, and journalist. As winner of both the Lenin and Nobel Peace Prizes, he possessed credentials that were about as balanced as one could wish. He was well-known on the international scene for holding many important posts including founder and chairman of Amnesty International, president of the International Peace Bureau, president of the Special NGO Committee on Human Rights, secretary general of the International Council of Jurists, president of the Council of Ministers of the Council of Europe, and vice president, of the Council of Organization for European Cooperation. Elected to the Irish Parliament for four terms, he also held the post of Minister for External Affairs from 1948 to 1951.

MacBride came literally from fighting Irish stock. His father, Major John MacBride, organized an Irish Brigade, which fought on the side of the Boers in the Transvaal Wars. Major MacBride was one of the leaders in the 1916 Rising in Ireland and was subsequently executed by the British Military. Sean's mother, Maud Gonne MacBride, was one of the leaders of the movement for emancipation of the peasants and Irish national independence and was often imprisoned.

Sean himself was active in the movement for Irish national independence and was imprisoned on a number of occasions. While engaged as a journalist in his younger years, he also acted on occasion as secretary to Eamon de Valera.

According to a *Herald Tribune* article October 12, 1980, MacBride as a boy spent time in the home of William Butler Yeats, who tutored him in English and Irish and considered himself a foster father. Another family friend was Ezra Pound, from whom he learned Latin. Despite these associations, MacBride confessed, he was never good at poetry.

In speaking of MacBride, the same article added that, "His international activities began in the 1920s, when he attended anti-imperialist congresses and became acquainted with such figures as Ho Chi Minh and Jawaharal Nehru and renewed many of those contacts as foreign minister."

A prominent international barrister, MacBride argued many leading cases in Ireland and Africa and before international courts, especially in litigation on human rights.

At the time MacBride accepted the chairmanship of the International Commission for Study of Communication Problems, he was 74 years old, somewhat frail in body, but still possessed of fighting spirit and resolve as well as impressive intellectual power.

Mr. M'Bow said he chose Mr. MacBride because "he possesses rare qualities of integrity and courage which he has shown during a lifetime devoted to the struggle for freedom, justice, and mutual respect." I have not always agreed with Mr. M'Bow's judgement, but in this matter he was right-on.

With the chairman chosen, the Director-General turned to selecting the remainder of the Commission. Unannounced were M'Bow's concerns with the public relations aspects of his selection process; he wanted to stud the Commission with celebrities and people of worldwide reputation. This was well illustrated by his North American search. He insisted on appointing Marshall McLuhan, the Canadian communication guru, despite warnings from Canadian officials that McLuhan had a personal problem. It was not until McLuhan himself rejected the appointment that M'Bow gave up. McLuhan's reason: "I never go to meetings."

From the United States, Mr. M'Bow wanted the prominent *New York Times* columnist James Reston. The Director-General even sent a representative, the London journalist Byron Jones, to try to persuade Reston to accept the appointment. He was not interested. When Jones conferred with the State Department, he was given a list of possibilities that I had made up after consulting with various media people. Time went by and nothing happened.

Months later, when I was in Paris checking on UNESCO activities, I got an early-morning phone call from Gunnar Naesselund, who needed to know immediately whom the United States wanted to nominate for the Commission. The Director-General was about to leave on an extended trip and he wanted the names of three American nominees.

My first move was to talk to staff of the U.S. Permanent Delegation to UNESCO, recommending Elie Abel, distinguished in both broadcasting and journalism as an NBC commentator, foreign correspondent for the *New York Times*, and then dean of the Graduate School of Journalism at Columbia University. They agreed. Next, I got on the transatlantic phone (I couldn't use government communications because Vice President Mondale was in Paris and all the lines were tied up) and talked with the chairman of the U.S. National Commission for UNESCO, Sarah Power, and her publisher husband; they agreed. I also talked to Russell Heater at the State Department and asked him to contact the heads of the associations for newspaper publishers and editors, as well as the president of the National Association of Broadcasters (whom he finally reached in Hawaii). When he called back, Elie Abel was the unanimous first choice. I immediately gave this information to Naesselund, who gave it to M'Bow before his departure.

Again, nothing happened.

Meanwhile, the State Department, in its fashion, decided to thoroughly "vet out" the matter. It put together a list of thirty-two names of possible candidates, then narrowed the list to eleven, and finally to three. And again the name of Elie Abel was first on all the lists--both alphabetically and deservedly.

An unconscionable amount of time went by (ten months after Nairobi) before M'Bow announced the appointments, partly because of his futile time-consuming efforts to sign up Reston and McLuhan, and partly because it was just plain difficult to contact all the nominees, scattered as they were around the world.

Announcement of the appointments was made September 21, 1977. In making the announcement, the Director-General emphasized that members were on the Commission as individuals, not as representatives of their countries.

Membership of the Commission

MacBride, Sean (born 1904) Ireland. Barrister, politician, former journalist. Founder and Chairman of Amnesty International. Winner of both the Lenin and Nobel Peace Prizes.

Abel, Elie (born 1920) USA. Journalist, Broadcaster, Educator. Professor of Communications, Stanford university. Previously Dean of the Graduate School of Journalism at Columbia University. Former foreign correspondent for NBC and the *New York Times*.

Beuve-Mery, Hubert (born 1902) France. Journalist, Founder of *Le Monde*, President of the Center for Training and Professional Upgrading of Journalists.

Elebe Ma Ekonzo (born 1933) Zaire. Journalist, Director General of the Zaire Press Agency, former Ambassador to Belgium.

Garcia Marquez, Gabriel (born 1928) Colombia.   Writer, Novelist, Journalist.   Author of *One Hundred Years of Solitude*.   Nobel Laureate.

Losev, Sergei[4] (born 1922) USSR.   Director General of TASS, the official Soviet news agency.

Lubis, Mochtar (born 1922) Indonesia.   Journalist, President of the Press Foundation of Asia, Previously Editor of the daily *Indonesia Taya*.

Masmoudi, Mustapha (born 1937), Tunisia.   Permanent Delegate of Tunisia to UNESCO.   Former Secretary of State for Information.   President of the Inter-Governmental Coordinating Council for Nonaligned Countries.   Former Director-General of the Tunis *Afrique Press*.

Nagai, Michio (born 1935) Japan.   Journalist and Sociologist.   Editorial Writer, *Asahi Shimbun*.   Former Minister of Education.   Former Director of the East-West Communication Institute.

Omu, Fred Isaac Akporuaro (born 1935) Nigeria.   Research Professor at the Center for Social, Cultural and Environmental Research, University of Benin.   Former Commissioner for Trade, Industry, and Cooperatives.   Previously Head of the Department of Communications, University of Lagos.

Osolnik, Bogdan (born 1920) Yugoslavia.   Journalist, Politician.   Vice President of the Federal Council of the National Assembly.   Previously Editor of the newspaper *Komunist*.

Oteifi, Gamal (born 1925) Egypt.   Lawyer and Legal Adviser.   Honorary Professor at Cairo University.   Former Minister of Information and Culture.   Deputy Speaker of Parliament.

Pronk, Johannes Pieter (born 1940) Netherlands.   Economist and Politician, Member of Parliament, and Member of the Brandt Commission.   Minister for Development Cooperation.

Somavia, Juan (born 1941) Chile.[5] Executive Director of the Instituto de Estudios Transnacionales, Mexico City.   Previously Chairman of the Board of the Andean Development Corporation.

Verghese, Boobli George (born 1927) India.   Journalist and Gandhi Peace Foundation Fellow.   Head of the committee on Autonomy for Broadcasting in India.   Previously Editor of *Hindustan Times*.

---

[4]Replaced Zamiatin after the third meeting of the Commission.

[5]A Chilean national now serving as Chilean ambassador to the United Nations. He was in exile in Mexico during the period of the Commission; he had been an official in the government of Salvador Allende.

Zamiatin, Mitrofanovich Leonid, USSR.   Ambassador and Journalist. Director-General of TASS. Member of the Supreme Soviet.

Zimmerman, Betty[6] Canada.   Director of Radio Canada International. Previously Director of International Relations, Canadian Broadcasting Corporation. The only woman on the Commission.

The Commission membership clearly was carefully apportioned regionally, although a majority of the members were "slanted" (as is UNESCO itself) toward the developing countries. As the biographical notes indicate, half of them were active or had been active in government and most had had journalistic experience.

As Power and Abel pointed out in an article, "The Commission membership reflected the political arithmetic of the contemporary UN system: four members from African countries, three Asians, two Latin Americans, two North Americans, five Europeans (three from Western Europe), and one each from the Soviet Union and Yugoslavia. The weight of members lay with those who favored one degree or another of state control."[7]

In any case, it was a distinguished assembly of international talent representing an impressive body of experience in media and diplomacy. Individual biographies will be fleshed out with anecdotes and personal observations about their personalities as they are revealed in meetings of the Commission.

Earlier Association with Elie Abel

I had come to know and respect the commissioner from the United States from earlier contacts. I, of course, remember hearing him on the radio as a foreign correspondent for NBC, broadcasting during the 1960s from London, Cairo, and Moscow. And I was aware that he had left broadcasting to become Dean of the Graduate School of Journalism at Columbia University. So Abel had quickly come to mind two years earlier when, in my capacity as the communication specialist on the U.S. National Commission for UNESCO, I set out to form an informal advisory group to the Commission.

----

[6]A late appointment, Zimmerman replaced McLuhan when he refused to serve.
[7]Philip Power and Elie Abel. "Third World vs the Media Power," *New York Times Sunday Magazine*, 2/9/60, p. 122.

With this in mind, I went to see him at his office at Columbia University. Our meeting was warm and cordial, and I was even more impressed by the man in person. An imposing figure--tall, mustachioed, dark-haired--in his belted, military style trench coat (as I was to see him so many times later), he looked the perfect personification of the celebrated foreign correspondent.

At this initial meeting, we spent a half hour or so discovering mutual acquaintances in broadcasting and journalism and discussing international communication matters as they had developed within UNESCO, especially the Declaration on the Media, at that time still an unresolved issue.

It was not until our second meeting, however, that Abel signed on as a member of the National Commission's informal advisory group. The occasion was a Santo Domingo meeting of the Inter American Press Association. Abel agreed to join a group consisting of Leonard Sussman, Executive Director of Freedom House; George Beebe, Chairman of the World Press Freedom Committee; Hugh Donaghue, Vice President of the Control Data Corporation; Jonathan Gunter, COMSAT; George Kroloff, President of Ruder & Finn; and Will Sparks, Vice President for Public Relations, Citibank. This group (or at least some of the the people involved) met several times in Washington to react to new communication developments in UNESCO, especially various versions of the Mass Media Declaration.

This group was subsequently modified and augmented to bring in media specialists with whom Abel could consult about issues likely to come before the MacBride Commission. The new members were Philip Power, President of the Suburban Communications Corporation; Richard Schmidt, General Counsel for the Society of Newspaper Editors; Sue Wonderman, CBS; Clayton Kirkpatrick, Editor of the *Chicago Tribune*; Arch Madsen, President of Bonneville International; Professor Ithiel de Sola Pool, MIT; and Barry Zorthian, Vice President, Time, Inc.

The group met in New York (June 29, 1978) shortly before Abel's departure for the first meeting of the MacBride Commission. I had over-conscientiously prepared a six-page outline for the discussion, which I passed around to each participant. Abel, as the chairman, wisely ignored this "agenda" entirely, proceeding to set forth his concerns and then throwing open the meeting for general discussion--a far better approach than the pedantic scenario I had prepared for such an informal gathering.

I had a good association with Elie Abel, both before and after his appointment to the MacBride Commission, and I was confident that the United States would be well served by his participation in that body.

Serving as Aide de Camp to Abel

On the eve of the initial convening of the MacBride Commission in Paris, December 14, 1977, the Chairman of the U.S. National Commission for UNESCO, Sarah Power, and the State Department's Assistant Secretary for International Organization Affairs, William Maynes, decided that, in light of the potential importance to the United States of this new enterprise, I should accompany Elie Abel to all of the Commission meetings in order to provide first-hand reports promptly. This may appear to have been a rather extravagant procedure, but it reflected the hyperanxiety that had been growing in both the private and government sectors about what UNESCO was up to in the communications field. Also, since this Commission was a U.S. idea, it was natural that our government should take a special interest in how its proposal was carried out. And I, as the proposer, I suppose, seemed the appropriate choice for observer. Another reason was that I, as part-time consultant, could be more easily spared for such an assignment. In any case, I was delighted at the prospect of being associated with Elie Abel in his responsibility as U.S. member of the Commission.

In the beginning, although I could attend public sessions of the Commission, I was not allowed to be present at its executive sessions, which were limited to members of the Commission and its staff. Consequently, after each session, Elie would sit down with me while I tape-recorded his report of what had transpired, together with his views and observations--always insightful and frequently hilarious. With this tape as a guide, I would write a detailed report of each meeting and mail it to the State Department for typing and distribution to selected officers.[8] Modified copies of these unclassified reports constitute the principal basis for this book. I only wish that I still had the unexpurgated tapes to review, because they contained many pithy comments on the personalities involved and candid speculations on motives, which I was precluded from incorporating in my reports to the Department of State.

Understandably, I very much wanted to sit in on the meetings themselves rather than experiencing them secondhand. I did get acquainted with all of the commissioners by mingling with them at coffee breaks and at social affairs. At the third meeting in the historic walled city of Dubrovnik, I at least was able to listen in on the discussion. Appropriating one of the headsets providing instantaneous translation of proceedings, I stationed myself in a corridor that ran behind the meeting room; in this way I was

---

[8]Greatly modified and condensed versions of these reports were mailed to a select list of leaders in the U.S. media industry to help them keep abreast of the Commission's work.

able to hear most of what went on. Unfortunately, on the second day the UNESCO staff member who headed the Commission staff, Asher Deleon, caught me in the act and I had to quit my eavesdropping. He subsequently complained to the chairman and accused me of being from the CIA! MacBride dismissed this charge as nonsense.

I was not easily discouraged, however, and at each session I kept edging further and further into the proceedings. At the fourth meeting, I was allowed to sit at the back of the room and at the fifth meeting, I sat immediately behind Abel and did so at all subsequent sessions. This breakthrough came about because of an Abel intervention. He observed at this meeting that Soviet Commissioner Zamiatin had brought an aide (an East German woman) to sit with him at the table, and Abel demanded the same privilege. At subsequent meetings, Commissioner Somavia was accompanied by Fernando Reyes Matta, a member of his staff.

Being able to sit right in the meeting was, of course, a vast improvement, although Elie and I continued the routine of conferring immediately after each session in order to tape a report. Now, however, I could share my firsthand perceptions with him and we could argue or agree on our interpretations of what we had both observed and heard.

Chapter 4

WORK OF THE COMMISSION

In advance of the initial meeting of the Commission, the UNESCO Secretariat prepared an elaborate pamphlet setting forth in great detail the duties and responsibilities of all those who would be involved in the Commission's work. That pamphlet is quoted in the passages that follow.

ASSIGNMENT OF DUTIES

1. Role of the President

"The President is responsible for the Commission's work as a whole, on behalf of the Director-General and of the organizations and people that collaborate with it. He presides at each session and directs the discussion in accordance with generally accepted rules. In cooperation with the Executive Secretary, the President ensures continuity of the work carried on between meetings, keeps in touch with members, convenes sessions, and decides which institutions and specialists will take part in all or part of each session or to assist in specific tasks. He is to spend ten days a month in Paris to guide the Secretariat."

2. Role of the Secretariat

The Commission Secretariat is provided by a group of UNESCO staff members headed by Asher Deleon, who had served as executive secretary of an earlier UNESCO commission on adult education. He is assisted by four professionals and a small staff responsible for secretarial, documentation, and translation services.

To facilitate the Commission's work, the Director-General directed that various support services provide assistance and backup. These include all divisions of the Culture and Communication Sector, the Bureau of Studies and Programming, the Division of the General Information and Program, the office of Public Information, and the Office of Statistics.

3. Role of Advisers

Because of the complexity of communication problems, it was believed necessary to enlarge the members' knowledge and experience by providing for the assistance of outside consultants "so as to enable the Commission to reflect the plurality and wealth of opinions, trends and lines of research which coexist in the field of communication and in allied disciplines." These specialists would constitute a group of permanent advisers providing advice to better reflect diversity of views. (The idea, I gathered, was to avoid having the Commission work in an ivory tower.)

4. Role of Commissioners

Members of the Commission are expected to participate actively in each meeting, study the documents submitted to them, draft reports, and contribute according to their experience and aptitudes. They are invited to contribute to work being done between meetings by writing comments, preparing drafts of Report sections, and submitting suggestions to solve problems. Each member can make proposals for the inclusion of specific agenda items for discussion during subsequent meetings.

MEETINGS

The dates and duration of the meetings are fixed by the president, with the duration usually three to five days and the location normally at UNESCO headquarters in Paris.

Usually the sessions are limited to members of the Commission and its Secretariat. In some sessions, however, members of the general Secretariat or of other specialized agencies will be invited. Some sessions may be open to representatives of intergovernment organizations, leaders of professional associations, communications specialists, university teachers, and researchers. It is up to the president to draw up a list of such organizations and individuals to be invited to take part in certain sessions. The president also has the right to decide if certain sessions may be opened to the press.

Working languages of the Commission are English and French; documentation is in the two working languages, and simultaneous interpretation in English and French is provided at each meeting.

Meeting I	Paris	December 14-19, 1977
Meeting II	Stockholm	April 28-29, 1978
Meeting III	Paris	July 10-14, 1978
Meeting IV	Dubrovnik	January 8-12, 1979
Meeting V	New Delhi	March 28-30, 1979
Meeting VI	Acapulco	June 4-8, 1979
Meeting VII	Paris	September 9-14, 1979
Meeting VIII	Paris	November 19-30, 1979

MANDATE AND METHODS OF WORK

The Commission's mandate, as defined by the Director-General, outlined four main lines of inquiry:

1. to study the current situation in the fields of communication and information and identify problems that call for fresh action at the national level and an overall approach at the international level.

2. to pay attention to problems relating to the free and balanced flow of information in the world, as well as specific needs of developing countries.

3. to analyze communication problems within the perspective of a new international economic order and of measures to foster a new world information order.

4. to define the role the Commission might play in making public opinion aware of the major problems besetting the world and how to solve them by concerted action at the national and international levels.

DOCUMENTATION

It was agreed at the start that no primary research should be undertaken at the Commission's instigation because of the impossibility of completing original scientific work within the prescribed time limits. It was decided that the documentation to be compiled should essentially identify priority problems and crucial aspects for analysis and clarification. In this connection, two major documentary sources were envisioned: a) factual and descriptive documentation, providing as objective an overview as is possible on the state of communication and information systems of the world, and b) a collection of opinions and ideas concerning current problems and suggested solutions representing widely different trains of thought from all parts of the world. The documents will include:

1. documents of a descriptive nature relating to both quantitative and qualitative aspects of communication and information in different parts of the world.

2. comparative documents describing communication systems, national and international infrastructures, networks, broadcasting, production centers for books and files, etc.

3. analytical documents treating such problems as obstacles to free flow of information, imbalances in news circulation, and participation of individuals and groups in this area.

4. documents synthesizing results of past studies and research as well as present trends in research in this field.

5. documents pertaining to the work and direction of research of international, intergovernmental, and nongovernmental organizations.

6. collections of selected texts of pertinent extracts from specialized works, speeches, declarations, research reports, and articles.

7. bibliographical documents including lists of research centers, selective bibliographies, and descriptions of principal research activities currently underway.

The first series of documentation of "facts and findings" are to be prepared largely by the Commission staff and members of the UNESCO Secretariat. A second series (ultimately called The Mauve Series because of the covers) is to be prepared by members of the Commission or by selected individuals from different regions who were invited to write on general themes of a philosophical nature (freedom, cultural identity, etc.) or specific themes such as one-way flow or juridical aspects of communication.

These documents are to be translated into English and French. The Commission staff, taking account of the view expressed by the Commission during their meetings and an analysis of the documentation, will prepare an

Interim Report "consisting of a synthetic study of communication problems in the modern world." This draft will be sent to members of the Commission and to selected organizations, institutions, and specialists for comment. Its publication, the Secretariat observed, "should be the occasion in the following months to start a worldwide debate."[1]

And indeed it did, as we shall see--a debate carried over into the 20th General Conference of UNESCO in 1978 in Paris. The Final Report of the Commission's work was presented at the 21st General Conference, held in Belgrade in 1980. It, too, provoked a storm of controversy, not because of its content, which was not at issue by decree of the Director-General, but because of the way its presentation was linked to a set of accompanying resolutions forced on the West by the Third World majority.

---

[1]*Methods of Work*, Number 3 in the Mauve Series of UNESCO documents prepared for the Commission (see Appendix I).

Chapter 5

THE MEETINGS

UNESCO HEADQUARTERS

Before getting into the meetings, we should describe the UNESCO headquarters in Paris, where the majority of the meetings were held. Located at 7 Place de Fontenoy, the impressive, modern, curving, Y-shaped structure covers almost the entire block facing the rear of the Ecole Militaire and not far from the Eiffel Tower. It was designed by the Italian architect Pier Lugi Nervi, who pioneered the use of concrete rib structures.

It has been called one of the most imaginative pieces of contemporary architecture in France, unsurpassed in Paris as regards both design and the caliber of its works of art; inside, murals by Miro and Picasso, and outside, sculpture by Henry Moore and a mobile by Calder. Also on the outside are an impressive Japanese garden by Noguchi and a colorful row of flags of the member states on the Rue Lowendal side. The main complex is composed of four units linked together: a seven-story building housing offices of the Secretariat, the Conference annex with one large assembly hall, a small separate office building in the Japanese garden, and a two-story underground structure with offices and three conference rooms or salles. These latter are lighted from a series of innovative sunken gardens designed by Nervi.

The first floor is dominated by two large auditoriums that face one another; these are the sites for plenary meetings of the general and other conferences. They are adjacent to a large delegate lounge from which a stair leads to a somewhat smaller auditorium on the second floor. Other floors are mostly offices, with the top floor devoted to a restaurant with windows on three sides that afford magnificent views of Paris and the Seine. It is here that the Director-General regularly holds receptions.

Whenever the Commission met in Paris, it was in Salle B in the basement of the headquarters building. It was reachable from either end of the building but only through a series of winding stairs and a confusing maze of intersecting corridors. (I got completely lost the first two times I had to contend with that labyrinthian underground.)

The meeting room itself was a rather stark, high-ceilinged rectangle with a row of glassed-in translators' cubicles (like a stadium press box) set high in the wall at one end and a row of tall windows across the other. Commissioners sat at long tables arranged in an open rectangle with the chairman and his chief of staff beside him. Other members of the staff and observers sat in the rows of chairs behind the commissioners.

At each commissioner's place was a microphone, not because they needed amplification to hear one another across the room, but for the benefit of the interpreters who provided instantaneous translation of their comments into French, English, and Russian.

Since there were no decorations or pictures on the walls, about the only relief from momentary boredom with the proceedings was to gaze out the windows, though that was not especially edifying since the only "view" was of an unrelieved grassy bank that rose steeply away from the basement wall. Once, however, we had the welcome distraction of watching a workman systematically mow that grassy bank. Absorbed in his work, he was totally oblivious to the fact that just a few feet away from him, prestigious diplomats were earnestly engaged in discussing, what to them, were matters of world-shattering importance. He couldn't have cared less.

The sessions began at 10:00 A.M. and went until about 11:30 when there would be a coffee break, Two huge carts were wheeled down the corridor just outside the meeting room. We would line up to get a beverage and cookie and then move to an adjacent parlor to mingle and converse. I was always struck by the fact that these were cordial conversations that betrayed no sign whatsoever of the fact that moments before the commissioners may have been engaged in a very heated argument.

I especially enjoyed these breaks each morning and afternoon, because they gave me an opportunity to get better acquainted with the commissioners and the staff and to ask questions and exchange views. As is always the case in structured meetings, some of one's best insights are likely to come from corridor conversations.

The morning sessions continued until about 1:00 P.M., resumed at 3:00 and ran until about 6:00, unless the interpreters could be persuaded to work late (for overtime pay).

Whenever the Commission met at headquarters, there were, of course, many other activities going on in other parts of the building--a constant stream of seminars, conferences, and meetings in support of UNESCO's projects in such areas as illiteracy, cultural preservation, communications development, and some eight hundred scientific programs.

And almost every evening there was a concert, a play, or some other cultural presentation with an international flavor.

MINUTES OF THE MEETINGS

These are informal minutes of the eight meetings of the Commission that were held over a period of two years, December 1977 to the end of November 1979. Because the commissioners believed they could gain valuable insights from on-site discussions of communication problems, meetings were held in five different countries and in each place local specialists were invited to present their views.

Although all sessions other than the opening one were closed, Elie Abel, as previously indicated, gave me daily briefings that were augmented by talks with members of the Commission and its staff, and by the fourth meeting I was allowed to sit in on the sessions.

These accounts are essentially a recast of unclassified reports sent back to the U.S. State Department.

MEETING I, PARIS, DECEMBER 14-19, 1977

This was the public launching of the International Commission for Study of Communication Problems (ICSCP), with speeches by the Director-General and Chairman MacBride. In addition to the usual ritualistic noises, obligatory at such occasions, the two speakers focused on world communication problems from the Third World perspective. M'Bow asked that the commissioners work with terms of reference related to UNESCO`s concerns for establishing a "new world information order." MacBride, after stressing the importance of communications and their impact upon every aspect of society, concluded by asserting that four key questions must be answered:

What is meant by "free and balanced flow of information"?

What does the "new information order" mean?

How may the "right to communicate" be achieved?

How can objectivity and independence of the media be preserved and protected against irresponsible use of the media?

First Session (December 14)

Abel (U.S.) raised the question of opening the sessions to the press and the public, pointing out the irony of a commission devoted to studying free flow of information closing itself off from outside scrutiny. Zamiatin (USSR) objected on the grounds that the Commission was still engaged in housekeeping details that were not of general interest. He was supported by Ekonzo (Zaire). There was agreement that the Friday morning session would be "open," but the policy for future meetings was left undecided.

Chairman MacBride (Ireland) announced that he had personally received an invitation from the Swedish Government to hold the second meeting of the ICSCP in April in Stockholm, to be preceded by a two-day meeting of the "Big Five" global news services, together with news agencies and representatives of the Third World.

Deleon (ICSCP Executive Secretary) gave a report on existing research being collected and on additional research that the Staff has commissioned. Abel asked for a list of commissioned research projects being considered for commissioning. He also took the occasion to express the view that disproportionate attention was being given to print media and not enough to the electronic, particularly radio, which is the major medium of communication in the Third World. He was strongly supported by Somavia, the exiled Chilean living in Mexico.

The afternoon session began with Zamiatin (USSR) demanding to know by what authority the Secretariat had used the phrase "obstacles to communication" in its ICSCP report #2 (*Origin and Mandates*): "In Socialist countries there are no obstacles to communication," etc. Deleon replied that this phrase was well established in UN and UNESCO documents and resolutions and that there are, indeed, political, financial, and cultural factors that constitute obstacles to communication. He stressed, however, that the Commission was not bound by any previous documents or resolutions. Lubis (Indonesia) supported Deleon, saying that in his and other Third World countries there were a great many obstacles to communication. Oteifi (Egypt) observed that, as an example of such obstacles, the press of one country (USSR) never mentioned Sadat's historic visit to Israel, a journalistic lapse that hardly served the cause of free flow of information.

Zamiatin blustered that he personally had mentioned Sadat's "four points" on a TV program, though he said nothing about TASS. He then launched into a half hour set speech following the usual Soviet line about the responsibility of the press to combat war propaganda, racism, and apartheid; he insisted that the sole function of the press was to be trustworthy and report the news "with respect to topicality" with accuracy. In that connection, he remarked dryly, he would refrain from mentioning Radio Liberty.[1] He concluded his speech by warning the Third World that the establishment of news services to compete with the Big Five would take

---

[1] An America broadcasting station with transmitters in West Germany and Spain.

an enormous amount of investment capital. TASS, of course, was trying to help Third World news agencies and now had agreements with seventy Third World countries.

Abel then asked for recognition. He remarked that as his Soviet colleague had refrained from mentioning Radio Liberty, he wouldn't either (laughter). Abel stressed that he was speaking as a private citizen, not as a representative of the U.S. government. Whereupon Zamiatin broke in to say, "You soon will be!"

Abel, picking up on Zamiatin's earlier remarks, observed that topicality certainly was an important consideration in defining what was newsworthy and that Mr. Sadat's visit to Israel unquestionably met such a test. He thanked Zamiatin for mentioning the high cost of news services and observed that this was an example of the kind of obstacle to communication that Deleon had been talking about. When Abel attempted to expand his discussion of news topicality with additional illustrations, Chairman MacBride cut him off by asserting that recent historical events were not relevant to the Commission's work.

There were a number of minor interventions by other commissioners. Vorghese (India) said he wanted to talk about communication issues from a national rather than an international perspective. In his country there was a tendency to assume that they could replace people with hardware, overlooking the need for developing adequate trained personnel necessary for its management. For example, they were now considering installing color television in India and would probably discover in twenty years that what they needed all along was radio.

Omu (Nigeria) made the standard speech about how Africa was constantly being misrepresented in the Western press and suggested that there should be a World Press Council that would impose sanctions on press services that behaved irresponsibly. He conceded that balanced news flow did not mean numerical equality. Research, he asserted, should be done in four African areas: Socialist-oriented states, federated states, authoritarian states, and Rhodesia-South Africa.

Somavia (Chile) made a Marxist-oriented philosophical disquisition including his usual mouthing of the views of Herbert Schiller, Professor of Communications at the University of California at San Diego.

Second Session (December 15)

Opening minutes of the session were devoted to a discussion of semantics. Nagai (Japan) complained that Japan was neither a developed nor a developing country. He suggested that the distinctions be "early" and "late" developing countries, e.g., Japan is highly industrialized today but was late in developing. Somavia (Chile) suggested that to avoid pejorative implications it would be preferable to use "industrialized" and "Third World" as designations.

Nagai also picked up on Verghese's comments of the day before, saying Japan shared India's problems and those of Third World countries, that is, because the flow of information is chiefly from the West, the only link they have with neighbors is communicating in English. It's only the Asians, who are already influenced by the West, who can communicate with one another.

Two points came up regarding the Secretariat's proposed advisory council of fifty to sixty members: (1) Abel suggested that this was far too large a number, so big as to wag the Commission. (2) MacBride observed that since no women had been included on the Commission, women must be included in the advisory council. He suggested that the selection of these women be turned over to the Women's International Democratic Federation (East Berlin). Abel objected on the grounds that each of the commissioners was capable of proposing a suitable woman communications specialist from his own country.

Although no decision was made as to the size of the advisory council, Zamiatin strongly supported Abel's view that it was too large, and there was general agreement that the commissioners themselves might nominate women as candidates for inclusion in the group.

The balance of the session was devoted to planning the next meeting of the Commission, tentatively scheduled for April in Stockholm. The Chairman confessed he was a bit fuzzy about what this second meeting should address. Abel, supported by Osolnik (Yugoslavia) and Elebe (Zaire), said that in view of the plan to have the news agencies meet in advance of the Commission's meeting, the transnational news agency issue ought to be the sole agenda. Egypt also agreed. There appeared to be consensus.

MacBride then suggested a working plan for the Stockholm meeting involving four panels on various aspects of news services:

1. *Technical* - What are the promises and possibilities of using technology in LDCs for news agency pooling?
2. *Content* - What are the relationships of news content to economic, cultural, political, and regional interests?
3. *Accuracy and Balance* - What are the problems in importing and exporting news? (MacBride originally suggested "Objectivity," but Abel protested that this was a "slippery word" that defied precise definition.)

4. *Relations Between the State and Media* - What are the problems in relations of the State to news agencies, electronic media, and reporters? What can be done to protect journalists?

Zamiatin (USSR), who was only present for the morning session, reported on having been given a demonstration of a new machine the Germans were trying to sell to TASS. He said it would print out twelve hundred words a minute and his reaction was that this was too fast. Even TASS would not be able to handle such a rapid flood of words. Too many employees would be needed to make use of such high-speed production.

Third Session (December 16)

Osolnik proposed that, in addition to the meeting in Stockholm devoted to news services, the third meeting should concern the "new information order." Zamiatin immediately attacked the proposal on the basis that no such thing existed. "What are you talking about? There is no such Order! Paragraph 8 in page No. 2 is nothing but a Utopian study. We are living in a real world of sovereign states which have their own legal systems. TASS may differ from Western news services, but we can't change them. You can't just announce that there is a new world order and then put it into effect. Remember what happened in Europe when a certain person tried to impose a new order!"

Abel agreed, saying he had just recently heard this term and didn't know what it meant. Neither did many others. He saw no point in calling a meeting on a topic when nobody knew its meaning. It appeared to be nothing but an empty phrase, and if it was not, why was it so hard for Third World countries to explain it?[2]

MacBride raised some questions about organization of the Stockholm meeting and suggested that the main topics related to the news services should be:

1.   Technological Positions
2.   Structural Organization
3.   Geopolitical Problems
4.   Ownership and Control
5.   Defects in the Present System

---

[2]Nordenstrong, president of the International Organization of Journalists (Prague), deplored the absence "of a solid theoretical basis to determine the conceptualization of a NWIO and today, especially in the UN and UNESCO, the formulations are virtually hanging in the air or...floating in the ether of diplomatic-political tactics." *Handbook of World Communications*, p. 35.

Abel opened the afternoon session by suggesting that a study be made of the Latin American trend toward licensing journalists. He was concerned that such procedures might constitute an obstacle to journalistic freedom. Since Dr. Mary Gardner, Michigan State University, had already begun such research he suggested that she be commissioned to undertake a study for the Commission. Somavia supported the proposal. Oteifi (Egypt) said that, of course, they did things differently in his country. Egypt does not have licensing and does not permit expression of views that differ from those of the government. However, when he was Minister of Information, he tried the experiment of inviting leaders of other political parties to appear on Egyptian television and these programs drew the largest audiences in history.

Omu (Nigeria) said that his country does not license journalists but does require them to register; this procedure, he believed, adds to their professional status and places them in the same company of such recognized professionals as doctors and lawyers. However, he added, in Nigeria "openness" is not encouraged.

Abel pointed out that the study he proposed was to be made of licensing practices in Latin America only, and that he hoped his colleagues would recognize the possibilities of such a practice for subverting journalistic freedom. At this point Beuve-Mery (France) spoke for the first and only time in the three days. He reminded his colleagues that in all their deliberations they must keep in mind considerations of human liberty and the rights of man.

The remainder of the third session was devoted to a presentation by Frank Goodship (UNESCO Secretariat) concerning new developments in communications technologies. He was interrupted repeatedly by Zamiatin, who kept challenging his statements or reporting technical information that TASS had acquired.

MEETING II, STOCKHOLM, APRIL 28-29, 1978
Swedish News Seminar

This second meeting was something of a two-ring circus, with Commission members active in both rings. It was in conjunction with a three-day seminar hosted by the Swedish government on the subject of "Infrastructures of News Collection and Dissemination in the World," which preceded their own Commission meeting by a day-and-a-half and involved them as participants and group discussion leaders.

Because this was the first time that they could perform independently in a public forum, some of them seized the opportunity to exploit the occasion and use it as a platform for promoting their personal views and ideological persuasions. Consequently, some of the commissioners did a bit of grand-standing and became involved in heated arguments and exhortations, which carried over into the Commission sessions that followed.

In addition to the Commission members, some 100 editors and directors of news-agency radio and television organizations attended this seminar.

The debates, expressing dissenting and divergent views on many basic information issues, reflected the sociopolitical realities in many parts of the world, but they also suggested that some areas of agreement and understanding were increasing. There was a consensus that access to the means of communication is unevenly distributed and that there is an imbalance in both information flow and stages of development. Disagreement, as always, came in debate on what to do about it.

Western speakers were uniformly moderate, offering cooperation, and (somewhat surprisingly, in view of prior pronouncements) representatives of the three U.S. global news agencies insisted they were not opposed to national news agencies so long as they were not monopolistic.

Third World spokesmen dwelt on the following: the need for more national news agencies and pools, the importance of news quality over quantity, the inseparability of journalistic rights, the necessity of media refraining from interference with the affairs of other countries, and the significance of the New World Information Order.

Also, surprisingly, Bloc-country spokesmen (especially from the USSR) attacked the NWIO, expressing concern over establishing possible rights or standards that might jeopardize the sovereignty of nations. Some participants wanted the seminar to adopt a USSR-proposed UNESCO Declaration on Use of the Media, due for debate at the next General Conference.

The inclusion of a number of government officials raised the level of confrontational rhetoric, though, and on occasion there was blunt language and demagogic tirade. On the other hand, the debates were not so bitter as those at the Nairobi General Conference, and many were spiced with wit and even moments of rare eloquence.

Highlights of the Plenary

Western representatives led off in a markedly positive and forthcoming fashion. Max Snijder (International Press Institute) agreed that there was a need to reduce certain news flow imbalances. Richard O'Regan

(Associated Press) insisted that the role of international news agencies was not competitive but complementary to that of national and regional news agencies. Frank Tremaine (United Press International) said that his agency did not oppose national and regional news agencies, because it is in the best interest of everyone that the worldwide flow of information be increased and improved. George Beebe (American Newspaper Publishers Association) echoed Tremaine and said ANPA was not opposed to the Third World Press Pool, provided it was not a monopoly.

The general mood of moderation was shattered late in the first day by Saad Majber of Libya's Jana News Agency. An impassioned orator, he denounced press freedom as a device that let the big powers do as they pleased. If news agencies in developing countries were state-controlled, it was no business of the industrialized countries.

On other occasions, Majber took the floor to deliver heated polemics, often ending with threats of military retaliation if the big powers didn't stop meddling in the internal affairs of Arab countries.

Other speakers, including Nigeria's Commissioner Omu and Indonesia's Commissioner Lubis, were generally more moderate, and dwelt on familiar Third World complaints: that Western news agencies distort accounts of events in developing countries and emphasize disasters; that dependence on foreign news agencies is a colonial holdover; and that there is need to place news within the proper cultural and economic contexts.

Western speakers insisted that there must be freer access of correspondents to and within countries if the development story is to be effectively covered. Foreign correspondents were frequently harassed, denied visas, and expelled.

The reaction of Third World and Bloc speakers (including Tunisia's Masmoudi, Chile's Somavia, and the Soviet's Zamiatin) was that yes, there must be freedom, but it must remain the prerogative of the state to decide who should be granted visas and whether journalists should be required to behave in accordance with the laws of each country.

The most heated seminar discussion concerned journalistic accreditation and who was to determine it. Western speakers (including Elie Abel) were firm in insisting it was sufficient for a publisher or owner to make the certification or, at least, a national professional society of journalists. Others were equally firm in insisting that accreditation must be the prerogative of the states, both for resident journalists and visitors.

An offshoot of this debate concerned an international code of journalistic ethics. While there was general Third World support for such a development, including Yugoslavia's Osolnik; Abel and Zamiatin were opposed. The former objected to establishment of such a code except by professional organizations, and then only on a national basis; the Soviet concern was that such a code might interfere with the jurisdiction of state sovereignty.

The most interesting interventions in the entire seminar were made by Commissioner Zamiatin, who as a member of the USSR Central Committee and immediate past Director General of TASS, was probably the most prestigious of the participants. His initial presentation took forty-seven minutes and covered a wide range of topics.

I report his views at some length here because, as he confided to Abel, he had just been elevated to a specially created position in which he was to deliver the Party line to all Soviet media. In effect, he was to be the communications "czar" of the Soviet Union. He left the meeting early to take charge of Brezhnev's up-coming visit to Bonn. Obviously, Zamiatin's comments can be taken as reflecting Soviet communication policy--as of that time.

1. The NWIO, he said, was ill-defined, vague, and incapable of understanding. The idea of imposing some sort of international order on top of sovereign states is unthinkable. NWIO is nothing more than a mere slogan. "It may be all right to bandy this slogan around in the corridors of the UN, but to me it means nothing. Remember the last time somebody tried to impose a new order on the world."

2. Zamiatin opposed all suggestions to form any sort of international media tribunal or council to which journalists' complaints could be referred--a favorite Masmoudi proposal. Such mechanisms could only make recommendations and enforcement could only be through the jurisdiction of national courts according to each country's laws. "We already have sufficient documents in the UN."

3. Regarding the problem of protecting journalists, Zamiatin said there could be no question of developing immunity for journalists. "We can not go beyond provisions of laws of each state. Foreign and visiting journalists have the right to work only within the framework of national laws."

4. Rather than try to invent new international agreements on the rights of journalists, it would be better to pay attention to the Helsinki agreements. "Let's leave fantasy and do what is possible in relation to already existing agreements."

5. We are in a period of ideological struggle. We must not get into another psychological war as in 1941. Mass media are tools that must be used carefully, and journalists must not lead us in that direction. Responsibility for war propaganda must be on journalists and their papers. "We kept the peace for thirty years; let us not have a psychological war!"

Western observers felt that the Soviets lost ground with the Third World countries at this seminar, due largely to Zamiatin's intemperate scoffing at the NWIO, his generally patronizing and rude attitude toward developing countries, and his raw attempt at censorship. This latter business produced the most bizarre incident in the seminar.

The chairman of Working Group II on Accuracy and Balance was Elie Abel (USA) and the *rapporteur* was Anatoly Krasikov (TASS).[1] The draft of the latter's report, in French, which Abel had approved the previous evening stated that the group had agreed that foreign journalists ought to have free access to the public *including access to opposition sources within a country*. When Abel saw the English version the next morning, he found that these words (presumably at Zamiatin's order) had been excised. Accordingly, following the rapporteur's presentation of the report for Group II, Abel was recognized for the purpose of correcting the record "so it would truly reflect what had been said in the group." He described frankly what had happened, including how the text that he had approved had been altered.

Zamiatin immediately objected. He said it was ridiculous to speak of opposition in the Soviet Union since everyone knows that "Opposition in the Soviet Union ended in 1922!" (Laughter.) He charged that Abel was attempting to use his remarks just to oppose the USSR and the Socialist Bloc. Abel replied mildly that he had not named any specific country, "but if the shoe fits, that's your concern, not mine." (More laughter.)

In addition to Zamiatin and Abel, the other commissioner who played a prominent role in the seminar was Masmoudi, the Tunisian Minister of Information. He came to the seminar fresh from a meeting in Havana where he had surrendered his chairmanship of the Intergovernmental Council of the Nonaligned Countries and he constantly defended the NWIO, a concept of which he is generally regarded as the principal author. He proposed that the International Right of Reply and Rectification, promoted by the French in 1948, be reestablished, especially in the Third World countries where they were unable, he claimed, to

---

[1]One of the 75 Soviets later asked by the French to leave Paris because of alleged espionage.

exercise their right of reply. "In those days, the LDCs were not in the majority; now they can give this right its proper place," he explained.

Masmoudi (Tunisia) also played a prominent role in promoting an open letter that attacked the UNESCO Secretariat for stacking the composition of the seminar in order to give preference to members of the International Press Institute (IPI, based in London) and rigging discussions that perpetuated the communication dominance of the industrialized countries. This letter, initially unsigned, was first circulated in the seminar by a Mr. Kaarle Nordenstreng, a Finnish Marxist, and president of the International Organization of Journalists (based in Prague) and his fellow professor at Helsinki University, Tapio Varis. Later, Saad Mujer of the Libyan News Agency, presented the gist of the letter orally in the seminar's final plenary session. Still later, Masmoudi brought this letter into the Commission meeting.

First Session (April 28)

It was expected that the Commission would begin its meeting with a critical examination of the just-concluded seminar, and indeed, its staff had prepared a summary of its conclusions for this purpose. In fact, no critique occurred and virtually no mention was ever made of the seminar. This is not to say, however, that the seminar had no impact, because it did have the effect of politicizing the Commission meeting. Zamiatin and Masmoudi carried over the polemicizing from the seminar into Commission sessions by repeating their speeches in that forum. Other reverberations from the seminar included the introduction of the Masmoudi-endorsed open letter, and attempts to have the Commission consider the UNESCO Draft Declaration on Use of the Media.

The commissioners began by agreeing on a meeting schedule and then turned their attention to preparation of an Interim Report, which it was required to submit to the 20th UNESCO General Conference. Should it be detailed or brief? Should it be analytical? Should it anticipate proposals for action that might emerge at the end of this long study?

Abel began the discussion by saying he had difficulty envisioning such a report if it were to go into great detail. He pointed out that the Commission's initial meeting was a get-acquainted session devoted to a general exchange of views, and the only aspect of the Commission's charge examined at the second meeting was scheduled to be limited to news agencies; yet here they were considering writing an Interim Report when they had not even worked on motion pictures, radio, television, literature, and other forms that are important parts of the communication process. He appealed, therefore, for a modest approach, "because we haven't come to grips with these questions."

Lubis (Indonesia), as he often did, supported Abel's position, while Osolnik (Yugoslavia) held out for the need to be analytical. Somavia (Chile) sided with him, saying, "Let us be analytical and forward-looking."

Verghese (India) agreed that the Commission's work had been rather limited until now. It had considered only the print media, whereas in Asia and Africa communication was traditionally *oral* rather than written. This made radio news important because it jumps the literacy barrier. "We need to go into all aspects of communication."

At this point Zamiatin (USSR) made his major intervention, explaining that he would not be present for the session next day. He began by observing that there was no dearth of discussion about communication issues. These topics had been covered in recent meetings in Jakarta, Tripoli, and Havana, all of which had called for more news of the Third World. The USSR, he added, was trying to find ways of helping LDCs enter the world's information stream through news pools and world agencies.

He warned that national news networks, because they demand extensive infrastructures, will take a long time to build and we should, therefore, see what help we can give via UNESCO and other means for the short term.

Beyond the matter of the technology, he continued, there was a need for equitable criteria for the flow of information and we should not be disseminating war propaganda and the like.

Zamiatin then teed off on the working paper prepared by the Secretariat for development of an Interim Report. He said it contained too many studies, and would take far too long to go into all these matters. We need to guard, he said, against one-sidedness on the part of our consultants.

In the section of the working paper on the Interim Report dealing with "Communication and Power," he professed not to understand what that was. Power is the prerogative of states, he said, and as to standards, people had raised questions about human rights. Because this subject had occupied four months in Belgrade, he didn't want to get into that again, though of course it was perfectly all right to bar racism, war propaganda, and apartheid. He couldn't understand another item on the agenda, the one about rights of individuals--private rights. He was not interested in getting into private rights of individuals. Western newspapers get into private lives of this and that millionaire, but he believed that "we shouldn't put our finger in this pie."

Masmoudi (Tunisia), who was obviously representing the nonaligned group, said he wanted to discuss the results of the seminar immediately. Zamiatin opposed that, and MacBride said it would be difficult to do because the notes were "rather scrappy," the minutes weren't much good, and he believed that this consideration was best postponed until the Secretariat had a chance to complete its report.

At this point, Somavia (Chile) brought the discussion back to the Interim Report and suggested that the elements of this report ought to include:

1. *The present structure of information in the world and the existing pattern of news flow.* It's important to distinguish between public information transmitted through the media to the people and data flows across state borders. In addition, we should look at certain trade flows and transnational enterprises.

2. *Analysis of the social impacts of the existing system.* It is important to assess the educational role of the communication structure, especially with regard to the Third World, because it has problems in transferring information to a largely illiterate population. Moreover, one must consider the economic implications of the industry.

3. *Identification of the problems of the existing system and areas in which it doesn't work as well as it might.*

4. *Methods of dealing with the problems and determining the level at which they should be handled.*

Pronk (Netherlands), who was absent from the first meeting, then made his maiden intervention. He said that the Secretariat had offered an excellent outline, but one should avoid becoming too analytical at this early state. He thought it would be better to concentrate the analysis and recommendations in the Final Report. The Interim Report was not in itself very important; Somavia's plan was more appropriate to the Final Report, which, he added, ought to indicate what the world will look like in the year 2000.

Masmoudi (Tunisia) said he thought the seminar was a sign of big progress. He then distributed an open letter to Chairman MacBride (similar to the one previously distributed at the Seminar) about alleged overrepresentation of members of IPI, which thus undermined the Third World "progressive journalists." At the same time he asked the Director-General to distribute the December draft of the Declaration on Use of the Media and to bring the matter to vote at the 20th General Conference.

Masmoudi further attacked the balance of representation at the seminar, saying that in the future one ought to measure representatives, not just in terms of the number of countries involved, but in terms of the aggregate population they represent. He also indicated that the Arabs were unhappy because there was no Arabic translation, although it is an official language used at other UNESCO meetings.

Masmoudi then introduced a matter he had brought up during the seminar, namely, the 1948 French proposal for the International Right of Rectification. It's in the archives of the United Nations but nothing has ever been done about it. It should be brought out and put into effect. The Commission, he believed, should study what he termed "intellectual imperialism."

Finally, he proposed two undertakings for the Commission: inviting fifteen to twenty experts to hold a UNESCO seminar on the proposed New World Information Order, thus informing the Commission members about this concept a day or two before the July meeting, and consideration of the Draft Declaration on Use of the Media so the commissioners will not be "out of step" with whatever emerges in connection with this development. "We should be informed," he concluded, "let us see the text."

Zamiatin then asserted that the Draft Declaration was a matter for government not for the Commission. "It is within the general purview of UNESCO but not in ours. Keep it out!" MacBride agreed that the Commission had no function in regard to this Declaration.

Oteifi (Egypt) said he supported Masmoudi on the importance of the New World Information Order and that a definition of it was needed by July. He then picked up on the point of India's Verghese about the importance of traditional (aural) information sources as opposed to modern ones. It will take a long time to get telecommunications spread around Africa, he continued, and therefore the Interim Report should address itself to the nature of traditional forms of communication in countries that could not afford large expenditures.

At this point Abel (U.S.) said he associated himself with Pronk and Oteifi, because he believed that the time had not yet come to delve too deeply into philosophical questions or to try and come up with solutions, as Somavia had proposed, when they had barely started work. Somavia's outline was best discussed with regard to the Final Report. Omu (Nigeria), echoing Verghese's point, stressed the importance of interpersonal communication in his society. He cited Nigerian studies that show that propaganda for family planning, for example, is much more effectively communicated in meetings between individuals than through mass media.

Verghese pointed out the problem of the allocation of radio frequencies at the World Administrative Radio Conference (WARC) in 1979. The Commission ought to study the matter and possibly put some views before the WARC.

Nagai (Japan) said his country was not a member of the Third World, but it had suffered greatly from news imbalance in relations with the United States for 100 years, even in the postwar years when relations with America were considered to be very close. As a former minister of education, he had noted that the Japanese schools teach a great deal more about America than Americans do about Japan. However, he admitted that even though Japan was on the short end of the relationship vis-à-vis the United States, it is just as one-sided with regard to the Asian countries. "Just as Americans by and large ignore us, so we ignore Asian countries." As Minister of Education, he had made a special study to determine how Japanese children could be better informed about the rest of Asia. He found it took six years to get books written and published and six years to train the teachers. His own paper (*Asahi Shimbun*), he added, has established news bureaus in every Asian country and prints news of these countries daily, but preliminary studies indicate that people don't read it. In Japan, the average family spends three hours a day watching TV and thirty minutes reading newspapers.

Beuve-Mery (France), who rarely intervened, talked briefly about the problem of newsprint; the Soviets would be happy to publish more but they have a terrible shortage. "It is not for nothing that *Pravda* publishes only four pages most days," he said.

He agreed that people watch more TV and listen more to radio nowadays, but newspapers are here to stay and are more important because one can go back and look at them a second time, "whereas TV and radio are in one ear and out the other," he concluded.

Zamiatin then repeated a story he had told at the first Commission meeting as a warning to the Third World about the problems of getting into sophisticated telecommunications technology. He had seen a demonstration of the Siemans printer, which produces 1200 words a minute, but both AP and TASS had found the speed to be faster than they could work. They both required additional help, and the printer became uneconomical. The implied warning to the Third World was not to go for everything that salesmen presented.

He then praised the Japanese for being "first in the world in educational television," but asked if we ought to plunge these new nations "into the depths in which we now flounder" with our fancy new equipment?

"Let's stay out of the realm of science fiction," he said. (Abel told me later he thought this was an appeal to the Secretariat not to get too "airy-fairy" in its view of technical possibilities for the future.)

Masmoudi talked about the need to strengthen Third World communication. He stressed the puzzling disparities in postal rates that added to the difficulties of the LDCs.

Lubis (Indonesia) referred back to the newsprint problem and recalled that years ago the Food and Agriculture Organization (FAO) had studied the possibility of using Asian forests for paper and reported nothing could be done. The Philippines, however, went ahead and now produce 80,000 tons of newsprint per year. There are other problems of dependence. The Third World depends on the developed world not only for paper but also for printing machinery. Sometimes they bought things they shouldn't; maybe small, simple equipment was more suitable than the large and sophisticated.

Pronk (Netherlands) suggested that the Commission ought to warn the Third World of four dangers:

1. too much concentration of power in hands of producing countries.
2. purchase of sophisticated communications equipment that may have the perverse effect of widening the gap between the developed and developing countries.
3. conflict with national sovereignty from news and information flowing across national boundaries.
4. conflict of data constituting an unwarranted intrusion into private lives of citizens.

At this point, Chairman MacBride defended the idea of a working paper for the Interim Report. He suggested that such a report would at least show UNESCO that the Commission is still alive. It would also show the member states what had been done so far, so the Commission would benefit from their reactions.

Masmoudi then repeated his call for a special seminar on the New World Information Order in advance of the next Commission meeting. MacBride was firmly opposed, saying "Let UNESCO and the United Nations meet first and we can deal with this matter later." Oteifi, however, suggested that Zamiatin's attitude on this matter might be right, because the New International Economic Order was more than four years old and nothing had been done about it yet. He contended that it was just sloganizing.

Osolnik suggested that a definition of the New World Information Order might well emerge at the end of the Commission's work.

Zamiatin agreed with Oteifi about the slogans. He said that he personally had no understanding of the concept of the New World Information Order and believed it was just a slogan and nothing more.

Somavia asserted that this was not an issue that can be avoided, because it's in the mandate given the Commission by the Director-General, and the Commission will eventually have to take a position on it.

Abel then suggested that if Masmoudi was so eager to talk about the NWIO, he would invite him to an Aspen Conference at which such topics would be studied.

Masmoudi responded angrily that it was too late to eliminate the words of the New World Information Order from the dictionary. "Let us accept it or reject it. Forgive my passion, but I feel very strongly about this," he said.

MacBride responded in kind, saying he saw no value whatsoever in discussing slogans in a void. "We don't need experts; I don't acknowledge that there are any experts in this field. We are as good experts as there are, and we can't agree on a definition."

Zamiatin then suggested that everyone was tired and they should ask MacBride to review the matter and then have the Secretariat let the commissioners know how they perceive it.

Masmoudi kept demanding that they vote him up or down, but the Chairman was firm and refused to bring the issue to a showdown. The Secretary would prepare a paper. The whole purpose of this Commission was to study the existing system, to find its shortcomings, and to try to recommend elements of a new communications system. MacBride therefore refused to treat the NWIO as a separate assignment.

Second Session (April 29)

Abel led off with several points.

The New World Information Order seems to be the skeleton of an idea, but it has no flesh on it. If there are people who know what it means and how it would operate, maybe the Commission would benefit from getting their views. However, rather than compiling (as UNESCO so often does) a listing or reports of earlier UNESCO meetings, it would help to have several papers, including some done by people who have been seriously thinking about this concept.

Abel reviewed what he thought was the tone and feeling of the seminar. He was not one of those who were pessimistic. It seemed to him that there was a fairly marked change in atmosphere--less confrontational than previously. In addition, the global news agencies had showed a considerable "forthcomingness" with respect to Third World news agencies and pools.

He then read a portion of a speech by Keith Fuller, president of the Associated Press, showing the parallel between the AP's history in breaking away from a cartel with Reuters and Hesse some fifty years ago. He also made the point that Claude Roussel, Director General of Agence France Presse, had talked in a very welcoming way about the Third World news agencies and maybe the time had come to stop flogging a dead horse. Abel also talked a little bit about the *actual* as against the *imagined* activities in the nonaligned world, drawing on research of Tom Finch, a USIA official. He cited figures on the number of governments that subscribe to news agencies as against private or direct-line distribution. This is the kind of data we need more of, he maintained. There's far too much "bunk" in UNESCO files, much of it is rhetorical and lacks a solid data base. "It's time we get away from sweeping generalizations and get down to cases," he announced.

This view was supported by Nagai, who repeated some of what he had said the day before about Japan; while not a Third World country, it was on the short end of the exchange with the United States. However, the Japanese had made a virtue of the imbalance, which is something that other countries ought to think about. It's true that the Japanese are behind in certain areas, but the fact that they had been behind in communications is what fueled the enormous growth of Japan's electronics industry; thus, he concluded, there's more than one way of looking at imbalance.

Nigeria's Omu said he was astonished to hear Abel say that things were improving (with respect to news imbalance), and that he would like to discuss this matter with him in detail. It was not the quantity but the quality of news that counted, he said.

Abel replied that his comment was not intended to be comprehensive. He was talking mainly about the services the big news agencies supply to the developing countries, he said, rather than what comes out of those countries and is printed about them. Omu, not satisfied with this response, said he wanted to answer Abel when there was an opportunity.

The balance of the session was devoted to the research plan, notably, the papers that had been and would be commissioned. Some had been received already, some were in preparation, and some remained to be assigned.

MacBride began the discussion by saying there was far too much paper already and suggested that they go through the list and eliminate the ones that were not needed. They ended, instead, by adding twenty, an inevitable outcome once the matter was opened for discussion.

Masmoudi pointed out that in this or that field there was a Western paper and an Eastern paper but no Third World paper--and there should be.

The only item in the list dealing with ownership and control of the news media has been assigned to a Mrs. O'Brien, who worked at the University of Leicester in England. Abel made the point that it was important to consider not just the monopoly resulting from concentration of ownership in the private media, but also public monopoly: states in which there is only one source of news and that one is rigidly controlled by the government. If this lady will not include this point in her paper, he added, a special study should be commissioned for the purpose.

Somavia proposed ten individual research topics and said he would suggest names of people to do them later. Verghese and Lubis also had some suggestions for research papers.

The Commission concluded its activities by attending a luncheon hosted by the Swedish Minister of Education.

Notes on Commissioners and Staff

The most colorful actor at the Commission's Stockholm meeting was Zamiatin. An imposing figure of a man with a commanding presence, he spoke up often and with authority to assert traditional Soviet views, especially concerning any threat to national sovereignty.

He repeatedly ridiculed the NWIO and was obviously disdainful and patronizing toward Third World members of the Commission. I was reminded of a picture I once saw of a great stag striding along shaking off little puppy dogs nipping at his heels.

A notable aspect of Zamiatin's behavior was his marked preference for the company of US delegate Elie Abel. Ideologically they were miles apart, but the constant yapping by Masmoudi and others about the need to make concessions to the Third World inevitably put the United States and the Soviet Union into a "have" relationship with the "have-nots." This was especially evident when Masmoudi kept demanding that LDC's be given a greater share of the electronic spectrum, an area of communications in which the United States and the Soviet Union enjoy the greatest number of assignments. It was obvious that Zamiatin had no patience with proponents of a scheme that would rip up the existing international communications structure; hence, his contemptuous dismissal of the NWIO.

Abel and Zamiatin quite frequently found themselves together in common unhappiness over the Secretariat's predilection for overpretentious plans, prolixity in its prose, and a deplorable tendency to lapse into UNESCOese. They also shared with MacBride a resistance to having the Commission make a study of the universe or to have it used as a convenient dumping ground for every problem others had failed to solve.

Zamiatin would sometimes link his arm through Abel's and stroll off with him as if to say, "Let us, as representatives of the two most powerful nations in the world, leave these people behind." This behavior was a bit surprising to me, because in all previous international meetings I had attended, I discerned a marked disinclination of Soviet representatives to show any evidence of Westward leaning.

I expect Zamiatin's independence reflected his confidence that as a deputy of the Supreme Soviet he could behave pretty much as he pleased.[2] For Abel, it was a bit discomfiting to be placed, as it were, in bed with the Soviets, but he accepted the situation with wry amusement. This "unholy partnership," I hasten to add, in no way diminished the vigor of the adversarial debates in which these two frequently engaged.

Chairman MacBride, who despite his age and frail physique, could be firm, stopped Masmoudi in his tracks when the self-appointed spokesman for the nonaligned countries attempted to introduce the Declaration on Use of the Media. He said it was not a proper topic for the Commission. He also refused to permit a showdown demanded by Masmoudi on his proposal to hold a seminar on defining the NWIO.

On the other hand, MacBride did not wield a firm hand in directing the discussion; consequently, it rambled back and forth over a variety of topics, and the Commission, as at its first meeting, failed to come to grips with any of the issues.

The relationship between the Secretariat staff and the commissioners and, in particular, the relationship with the Secretary (Deleon) were strained. The commissioners were again highly critical of the Working Paper prepared by staff, and MacBride was most annoyed at Deleon for allowing the circulation of that open letter and for allowing a signer of the letter to sit in on the Commission's executive sessions. The individual in question, Fernando Reyes Matta, a member of Somavia's staff, was allowed to attend the closed meeting because, the secretary lamely explained, he had previously been a consultant to the Secretariat.

Masmoudi, the immediate past chairman of the nonaligned countries' information group, behaved as though he refused to accept the fact that he

---

[2]Zamiatin is currently Soviet ambassador to the Court of St. James.

was out of office, or perhaps he was running hard for reelection. He made several long interventions at this meeting and hosted a big cocktail party on the last night of the seminar. He clearly thought of his role on the Commission as the defender of the NWIO and the designated hitter for the Third World. In consequence, he spoke as a politician, which in fact he is, representing a particular constituency; thus, every issue that came up was subject to North-South confrontation.

He reiterated the same points so often and dwelt at such length on his favorite themes that even his nonaligned cohorts stopped attending to his words. As soon as he started to play the old record, commissioners automatically tuned out.

Asher Deleon and John Masse (a former US newspaper man on the Commission staff) were very defensive about suggestions that they were acting in anything other than a completely even-handed manner in the conduct of the Secretariat's work. They took Abel and me to dinner to find out what was bugging us about their work. We told them that we were concerned about the imbalance in research assignments. Of the fifty or so papers already commissioned, only five had been given to Americans, and two of these could hardly be considered researchers; moreover, many of those chosen from other countries were less than distinguished in the communications field. Deleon defended them on the basis of not having received any recommendations from the United States. I protested that I had handed MacBride three names in Ottawa on February 8, which Deleon claimed he had never received.

I gave him seven more names, and Abel promised to send him a list as soon as he got back to his office. Masse confided to me later that because 90 percent of the people who had done research in communications lived in the United States, they had begun by concentrating their efforts in finding people elsewhere.

As he did at the first meeting, Zamiatin warned the Third World members about the enormous costs of establishing news agencies and cautioned them about acquiring expensive, sophisticated communications equipment. Since the Soviet Union had so far been long on offers of training and exchange and short on supplying funds or equipment, I figured this was a means of signaling LDCs that they must not count on the Soviets for help in strengthening their infrastructures.

MacBride told me that he thought Zamiatin's attack on the NWIO stemmed from dislike of Deleon for his insistence that the Commission's study must be undertaken within that conceptual framework. At the end of the Commission's work, when Zamiatin had been replaced by another director of TASS (Losev), the Soviets had done a 180-degree turn and were staunchly backing their Third World colleagues in support of the NWIO. The reason may simply have been that the removal of Zamiatin's opposition allowed Soviet diplomacy to revert to its traditional pose of supporting Third World proposals. Verghese was soft-spoken and thoughtful; he clearly shared (along with Nagai) Western views on the free flow of information. At the time, he was chairman of a commission studying the reorganization of Indian broadcasting. Pronk, a Dutch economist and political radical, spoke infrequently, but when he did, he took a leftist approach, particularly on economic matters. He later wrote one of the background pieces for the Commission (called "Mauve Papers" because of the color of their covers) on the linkage of the New International Economic Order with the New World Information Order.[3]

Omu (Nigeria) and Ekonzo (Zaire) generally sided with Masmoudi on Third World issues, though their interventions were infrequent. Lubis (Indonesia), while a Third Worlder, spoke from a background of having been imprisoned by Sukarno and was understandably a strong advocate of press freedom. Oteifi (Egypt), while sharing Third World concerns about communications inequities, was careful and moderate in his comments and often sided with Abel. Somavia, an exiled Chilean radical, was very bright and displayed a philosophical bent. He also displayed an anti-American bias and an inclination to blame transnational media agencies for all of the world's communication problems.

Betty Zimmerman, who was chosen instead of Marshall McLuhan upon his refusal of the opportunity, was the Director of International Relations for the Canadian Broadcasting Corporation (CBC). She came to Stockholm with four days' notice of her appointment and, perforce, sat and listened in early sessions. She had a rich background in radio, television, and film and was expected to make a significant contribution from that perspective and also from a concern about the role of women in media.

Mustapha Masmoudi was the putative author of the first written formulation of the concept of a New World Information Order. Whether he was the principal author or not, he was certainly the instigator and organizer of the *ad hoc* committee of a handful of nonaligned members who met in Tunisia in 1978 to hammer out the details of a concept that had been evolving in a series of nonaligned meetings beginning in 1973. This *ad hoc* meeting, financed by Director-General M'Bow and prepared in advance of

---

[3]In Mauve document (No. 34), Cees Hamelink claimed that unless the concepts and principles of the NIEO are used to determine the shape of the NWIO, it may become "yet another mechanism to subtly integrate the dependent in an international order which perpetuates their dependence."

the third meeting of the Commission, was a forceful articulation of what had previously been bits and pieces of resolutions and bitter rhetoric. Now the concept had form and substance. It became the *locus classicus* of Third World complaints and demands.[4]

Masmoudi, at the time the Tunisian Ambassador to UNESCO and President of the Coordinating Council of the Nonaligned Countries, tried from the very start to make the NWIO the sole subject of the Commission's work. He never succeeded in that objective, but that did not stop him from interjecting the concept or parts of it into every session of the Commission to such a degree that commissioners became quite bored with his "Johnny-one-note" routine. At the same time, and even after the Commission ended, Masmoudi traveled the world preaching the NWIO gospel. In the end, it appears he rode this horse into the ground, for the Tunisian government shortly thereafter relieved him of his neglected Paris post.

Aside from his NWIO mania, Ambassador Masmoudi was an engaging conversationalist with a suave and charming manner. In an article in the *New York Times Magazine* of September 12, 1980 by Phillip Power and Elie Abel, Masmoudi was described as "a product of French education grafted on to French colonial stock. With an MA in law and economics from the University of Paris, Masmoudi served as Minister of Information, thereby becoming familiar with the ways government can shape and control the news media in a developing country before he assumed his post as Ambassador."[5]

Elie Abel (by reason of his training and experience, and as a scholar, teacher, editor, reporter, and broadcaster) was especially well qualified to serve on the Commission. Canadian born, he was a reporter and editor for Canadian newspapers before beginning a distinguished journalism career abroad, a career that included serving as foreign correspondent of the *New York Times* and London bureau chief for the National Broadcasting Company (NBC).

For several years, Abel served as Dean of the Columbia University Graduate School of Journalism in New York. Currently he is the Harry and Norman Chandler Professor of Communication at Stanford University in California.

Abel had a difficult time on the Commission because of the way the cards were stacked, but he held his own in the give and take, and was determinedly even-tempered despite frequent provocations to behave

---

[4]Chie-Woon Kim. "The Struggle Over the New Information Order," *World Media Report*. Vol. 1, No 2/3, p. 67.

[5]"Third World vs the Media," op. cit., p. 121.

otherwise. He staunchly defended free-press values and was especially vigilant in refuting charges against the Western press and in exploding various "myths" about the operation of global news agencies.

In settling for what he believed were, under the circumstances, justified compromises, he was accused of betrayal by some Western critics, who seemed to think that Abel single-handedly should have been able to keep out of the Report all items unacceptable to the West.

As one who sat in the meetings and watched his valiant efforts to promote libertarian concepts and thwart efforts to insert items promoting press control, I insist that such accusations are unfair and unjustified. Abel was an able representative of American principles in both name and performance.

Gabriel Garcia Marquez, journalist, novelist, and Nobel Laureate, was arguably the most celebrated personality among the commissioners. Author of the best-selling *One Hundred Years of Solitude*, he had a worldwide reputation and following, especially in Latin America. Whenever he emerged from a plane in whatever country, there was invariably a group of fans on hand to greet him.

Marquez did not attend many of the meetings and usually remained silent when he did. The notable exception was the sixth meeting in Acapulco. Stimulated by Commissioner Ekonzo's description of restrictions on journalists in Zaire, the Nobel Laureate launched into an impassioned denunciation of the conditions in Colombia in which journalists worked. If they told the truth, they risked going to jail; it was a matter of complying or starving. Consequently many were moving out of the field in his country (and in much of Latin America) and taking menial but safer jobs.

Asher Deleon, a Yugoslav adult education specialist, was the former secretary of the UNESCO Faure Commission on Education. Because of this experience, M'Bow brought him back from India in the summer of 1977 to head the staff of the MacBride Commission. Before his UNESCO experience he had worked in the trade union movement in Yugoslavia. Because he was a Third Worlder himself, he was biased in that direction and tended to associate himself with Masmoudi, Osolnik, and Somavia.

Abel and Zamiatin continued to poke fun at the staff's penchant for technical jargon and gobbledygook--and with good reason! This kind of writing, commonly called UNESCOese, was amply illustrated by the following excerpt from the Commission's Final Report, page 38:

It is argued that a world built on mutual understanding, acceptance of diversity, promotion of detente and coexistence, encouragement of trends toward real independence, not only needs but makes room for new, different patterns of international communication. If the conception of development as a linear, quantitative, and exponential process, based on transfers of imported and frequently alienating technology, is beginning to be replaced by that of an endogenous qualitative process focused on man and his vital needs, aimed at eradicating inequalities and based on appropriate technologies which respect the cultural context and generate and foster the active participation of the populations concerned, then there can be no doubt that communication between people and nations will become different.

MEETING III, PARIS, JULY 10-14, 1978

The third meeting had two principal agenda items: the Interim Report, which the Commission was obligated to submit to the 20th General Conference of UNESCO, and a paper on the New World Information Order prepared by Commissioner Masmoudi, the Tunisian Secretary of State for Information. The first item was the previously announced topic; the second was introduced without prior notice and preempted discussion of the Interim Report draft for the entire second day.

The introduction of these two topics considerably enlivened the level of discussion compared to that of the previous two meetings. For the first time, the lines of political-ideological differences, earlier obscured by polite interchange, began to emerge. The confrontation was less intense in the East-West dialogue than in the North-South debate. This was due primarily to the insertion into the agenda of the paper on the New World Information Order into the agenda, a highly controversial formulation.[6]

First Session (July 10):
New World Information Order Paper

This document had its origin in the April 1978 meeting in Havana of the Intergovernmental Coordinating Council for Information of the Nonaligned Countries, of which Masmoudi was the president. He was

---

[6]"The New World Information Order," presented by Mustapha Masmoudi, Tunisian Secretary of State for Information. This is number 31 in the Mauve Series prepared for the Commission, which was established in application of Resolution 100, 1978 UNESCO General Conference (see Appendix I).

asked by the Council to develop a synthesis of the Council's views for presentation at the UNESCO 20th General Conference and for the UN General Assembly. Accordingly, he brought to Tunis at UNESCO expense (personally authorized by M'Bow) a group of media specialists from various regions of the world, including Cuba, Vietnam, and East Germany. The document was the product of their combined effort, though Masmoudi is generally considered the principal author. Because it was formulated at the request of the Council under the direction of its president and reflected the work of representatives from the major areas of the Third World, the document can be considered an "authorized" statement of the nonaligned movement's demands for what it considered distributive justice.

The document ends by listing measures to be undertaken by both the developed and developing countries and the international community about what it regards as the causes of the inequities in the world's media system and analyzes them from a political, legal, cultural, technological, and economic standpoint. The main points concerned:

1. dominance of transnational corporations.

2. demand for independence and equity in access to global information sources.

3. demand for assistance to speed communication development.

4. promotion of the nonaligned news agency pool.

5. imposition of duties, encumbrances, and responsibilities upon the media.

6. mandated right of reply.

7. legitimizing limitation of access to sources.

8. right to censor or restrict flow of information across national borders.

9. establishment of a supranational mechanism to monitor media and serve as a recourse for complaints about false or biased advertising.

10. establishment of an international deontology (theory of moral obligation) governing information and communications.

The Masmoudi paper found ready acceptance among the Third World commissioners, who hailed it as an answer to the mandate given the

Commission by Director-General M'Bow to "Analyze communication problems within the perspective of the establishment of a new economic order and initiatives to be undertaken to form the installation of a new world information order."

Abel and Zimmerman were the only commissioners to speak out strongly against it, although reservations were expressed about various sections by Lubis, Zamiatin, Verghese, and Nagai.

Osolnik (Yugoslavia), who had also prepared a paper on the NWIO, said there were no basic differences between his paper[7] and Masmoudi's; accordingly, no further mention was made of the former and the debate was confined to the Masmoudi document.

Zamiatin led off the debate, observing the importance of developing new information systems that would make it possible to do away with many imbalances and colonization of information and would allow developing countries to compete more efficiently and report the views of their own countries. However, this must be viewed as a long-time endeavor, recognized that some of these matters are being discussed in other forums, for example, the World Administrative Radio Conference (WARC). Nations simply cannot be compelled to redistribute their radio frequencies, he said.

The struggle of developing countries to achieve equality of information has the full support of the USSR; however, this does not mean that the present be negated and that the terminology of the NWIO is not satisfactory. It does not suggest that all that has been done be scrapped.

Mr. Masmoudi's proposal holds the answer to many of the problems of imbalance and should be pursued, he said. Those who already have control will gain even greater power to flood small countries with unwanted materials. The USSR introduced the resolution requiring prior approval by the receiving country of programs transmitted by direct satellite broadcasting. But it is a fact of life that those who have the power and the ability broadcast to Latin America, and must pay London to transmit to India. It was simplistic to say that states who own satellites should lower their rates. Masmoudi was not opposed to attempts to lower rates, he said, but wishing will not alter realities.

Summarizing his intervention, Zamiatin said that developing countries cannot erect barriers to the free flow of information because nowadays any country can transmit to other countries; however, the media should take responsibility for what is transmitted. (In other words, Zamiatin was say-

---

[7]"Aims and Approaches to a New World Information Order," a document prepared by Bogdan Osolnik. Number 32 in the Mauve Series (see Appendix I).

ing, the USSR is fully supportive of efforts of developing countries to achieve equality of information providing such efforts do not conflict with its own dominant position.)

Zamiatin concluded his peroration by denouncing *The London Sunday Times* for carrying what he considered a distorted story about his intervention at Stockholm. The media should report the true situation, which has to do with ethics.

Oteifi (Egypt) observed that the right of rectification could be a part of such a code of ethics, but the question is how could such a code of conduct be enforced.

Lubis (Indonesia) pointed out that ownership of media systems by banks and corporations and use of data to manipulate the market gave them special advantages. Media supported by advertising provided several examples of cultural impact on Indonesia, whereby the rich countries were dominating all aspects of Indonesian art via the media. It is important that developing countries have a clear vision of their goals; otherwise they will fall into the same dehumanizing trap. Little was being said in these papers, he maintained, about the responsibility of states to guarantee the rights of citizens. The Commission would be remiss if it did not show the problems and benefits of both rich and poor societies.

Pronk (Netherlands) then launched into a long lecture on economics and the relation of the NWIO to the new economic order, ending with the assertion that there should be control over data that afford multinational agencies special advantage.

Abel then made his initial response to the two papers. He began by saluting both authors for ambitious undertakings and especially for their cautionary words that this concept can't merely be presented, it must be developed organically. It would take a long time and a lot of good will and hard work. The Marshall plan to restore war-torn countries in the 1940s involved only a ten percent investment by the United States; the rest came from the rebuilding countries themselves. Similarly, this sort of undertaking must depend upon the developing countries as well as the rich.

The text of Mr. Masmoudi's report contains many stereotypes, he said. For example, competition was treated as a dirty word. Competition is not necessarily a bad thing. Competition between the *New York Times* and *The Washington Post* in the area of investigative reporting was a good thing that led to the Watergate exposé. Word monopoly is used throughout the report as applied only to commercial news systems, with no mention of government monopoly, which is a danger. Many governments do not trust their own people and do not grant them human rights. The desire of most governments to control the media may be motivated by other reasons other than protecting their citizens from cultural invasion, he said.

Mr. Masmoudi makes some assumptions that need to be questioned, he said--for example, the undue emphasis by Western press upon violence and *coup d'etats*. Research does not support these opinions. A more appropriate question might be, "Why was there no story before the coup, or the next week?"

"There are some items I can support, such as opposition to discriminatory rates" said Abel. "The redistribution of spectrum allocations is a highly technical matter that will be attended to at the WARC."

The means of obtaining more space for coverage of the Third World will have to be a matter of consciousness-raising, and that's not unthinkable. "Consider what has happened in the past few years about women's rights! I am not so pessimistic as to regard news editors as unregenerate!" he said.

The U.S. government can't tell the press what to do. There is a constitutional amendment that prohibits such action, so any measure calling upon the press to do certain things is doomed to failure in countries with similar traditions.

Some nations take the position that their national news agencies should have exclusive control over gathering and disseminating news about their country, he noted. It's not reasonable, therefore, in those situations to expect the world news agencies to subscribe (as Masmoudi's paper urges) to Third World news agencies.

There are serious questions about the feasibility of codes of ethics, Abel continued. It's hard to see such a code on which Soviet and U.S. journalists could agree. Codes have had some success at the state level in the U.S., but attempts to broaden them nationally have not been effective. The National News Council failed because national news agencies refused to join.

There was also an overuse of the word "control" in the documents, according to Abel. It should not be used to sanction narrowing and restricting the press in countries where a free press exists.

Abel concluded his comments by observing that when a correspondents and reporters attempt to interpret a foreign country they must communicate with their audience and write with that audience in mind. There is a tendency to blame a foreign correspondent from writing in ways that the subject country perceives as wrong but the approach may be right in terms of the audience.

Omu (Nigeria) responded that it was sad indeed to say that the responsibility of journalists begins and ends with giving people what they want. Monkeys and leopards jumping into hotels is what U.S. audiences want to hear about Africa, so U.S. journalists will write such stories. "I am called a tribesman, but I am a member of a nationality, not a tribe. Journalists should be sensitive to cultural differences so that they can report about a foreign country with sympathy and understanding. Removal of the dependence pattern in communication will enhance the LDC's cultural and political identity; removal of dependence in one area strengthens independence in all areas," he said.

Somavia (Chile) praised the documents and chose to reemphasize some items. Information, he said, has become a resource as important as any other resource and should be treated as a resource for development. Communication is a process, information is a product. It should be dealt with in this context.

Somavia went on to lecture the Commission on the need to establish the principle of communication as a social need and the way it should be organized as a social process. Preferential treatment, he said, should be used in examining communication issues. Protection of infant industries in the Third World is necessary to allow them to compete with powerful outside forces.

Replying to Abel, he agreed that journalists write for their audiences and if the AP and UPI wrote for Americans only there would be no problem. But they in fact write for the whole world, and thus shape the news in certain ways. This question of news values is linked to news as a commercial product. Writing for the audience is writing for the market and therefore producing what that market wants. This commercial model is a constraint, he said.

Zimmerman (Canada) stressed the importance of continuing research on low-cost technology that could be used by the Third World, and Lubis (Indonesia) said there was a need to get a clear picture of the various systems of the world and to relate the Commission's work to that of other international bodies.

Verghese (India) emphasized that there are many variables regarding developed and developing countries. Balance must be studied internally as well as internationally. "There is no truth," he said, "just many perceptions."

The constant development of new technology, Verghese said, coupled with rapid obsolescence, makes it difficult for developing countries. Attention needs to be given to production of technology appropriate to the developing world, for example, slow-scan television. The scarcity of paper is still a concern of developing nations.   The development of journalistic codes is a long-time process, but press councils might be advanced as an idea.

Masmoudi then took over. He asserted that there appeared to be a broad consensus emerging. In some areas it may be possible to reach some consensus--certain imbalances and discriminatory rates, for example--but other areas are not subject to agreement. At least we *seem* willing to be able to move in this direction. But when one is urging the set-up of a new order, minor changes will not suffice; major moves must be made. The NWIO has not automatically come into being. It has, however, stirred the consciousness of the world, he maintained.

"On the basis of our discussions, none of us would challenge the need to bring about change for the benefit of the developing world, so our report should reflect that situation. It will be useful to get the reaction of the General Conference to it. If it can be broadly discussed, we can then proceed to the determination of action to be taken."

He gave his view that in some countries there was no choice but to have a state monopoly of the media. It is often the only body that is capable of owning a TV or radio station and private individuals may not wish to run the risk of starting a paper.

Masmoudi wound up his presentation by asserting that journalists cannot be a law unto themselves, and Watergate, when viewed from the historical perception, may turn out to be judged as having been "a wrong challenge to central authority."

Osolnik (Yugoslavia) announced that we must abandon old ways of thinking. To be against private monopoly was taken to mean one is in favor of state control and vice versa; if one is for state control, one must be for censorship, etc. New ways of thinking about these matters are emerging, he stated. There is presently more active participation of the public in the communication process than previously, and there is not only monopoly by private enterprise and by the state but also by professional media manipulators.

Second Session (July 13):
Reviewing the Interim Report

The other two-and-a-half days of the meeting were devoted to a discussion of a draft of the Interim Report (IR), prepared by the Secretariat with the assistance of five specialists brought to Paris for a month: James Halloran, Leicester University; Fernando Reyes Matta, Mexico; Louis Echeveria, former president of Mexico; John Lee, an American academic, and Francis Balle, a French media researcher. Chief of Staff Deleon emphasized that the Interim Report had not been finalized, nor was it in the form it would take when properly edited. It was to be circulated to member states of UNESCO in September and submitted to the 20th General Conference in October (1978).

As a consequence of its multiple authorship, Deleon said, the document was filled with broad generalizations, unsupported assumptions, gratuitous expressions of opinion, and false data. It made assertions about matters the commissioners never discussed and foreshadowed conclusions the authors obviously wished would be included in the Final Report, due in 1980.

Part I, which concerned the origin, mandate, and roster of the Commission, was readily accepted; part II, however, which contained such sections as "Socio-economic, Socio-political, and Socio-cultural Effects of Communication," "Today's Communication Problems," and "Communication Tomorrow: Trends, Prospects and Utopia," provoked considerable controversy.

Masmoudi, Somavia, and Zamiatin spoke the most frequently and at the greatest length. Masmoudi gave repeated performances of his original outline of the NWIO and at every opportunity championed the cause of the developing countries. He began by observing that the Interim Report failed to dwell sufficiently upon the gaps between developed and developing countries, nor did it give proper attention to the role of the state in many LDCs in planning and financing communication systems, and to the right of the state to intervene. "We should not underestimate the role of the state in communication."

Developed states are still attempting to dominate developing states via neocolonialism and hegemony, he stated. Examples within the document included the comment that in the distribution of radio wavelengths, the developed countries have 90 percent of these natural resources and former colonies are using equipment that can only receive, not transmit. "Colonization is not over!" he said.

Masmoudi went on to list a number of other points he thought had been omitted or not sufficiently elaborated. Among these were rights to communicate, financing problems, international regulations, ethical consideration, and discriminatory rates.

Somavia (Chile), whose colleague Fernando Reyes Matta was one of the principal authors of the draft, spent part of his time objecting to proposed deletions and the rest of the time in supporting and reinforcing aspects of the report that, not surprisingly, happened to accord with his own views. Several times he listed points he believed needed elaboration. For example, he said there should be a statement on the functions of communication which might:

1. help in understanding events and processes.
2. serve as an instrument of socialization.
3. recognize cultural diversity and protect cultural integrity.
4. serve to promote peace and understanding.

Zamiatin (USSR), as usual, made a number of rather long interventions. He began by observing that the Interim Report did not give sufficient emphasis to the role of communication in decolonization, the domination of developed countries over LDCs, or the "slant" of industrialized countries that prevents developing countries from reporting their own news. Greater attention should be given to the struggle of the LDCs in eliminating discriminations of the past, he proposed, but mention should be made also of the increasing role of media in fostering international understanding.

The reference to the Stockholm discussions has been watered down and distorted, he said. The problem was not on freedom of information; rather the focus was on the imbalance of information, on the need for decolonizing the information process, and for a NWIO.

Zamiatin criticized the writing in Part A as having been "drafted most unfelicitously" and cited a number of scientific and philosophical terms that could not be understood, for example, "epistemological." "For the love of God," he asked, "what does that mean? There will have to be explanatory notes that will be longer than the report."

Zamiatin continued to play the role of friendly supporter of Third World aims and sympathizer with complaints about the West. He was unhappy with a tendency to include TASS (along with Western news agencies) as one of the "dominating influences." And wherever there were demands for redistributing the electronic spectrum or demanding that the LDC share satellite or other sophisticated technology, he scoffed at these parts of the text as having been written by people out of touch with the real world.

Verghese (India) volunteered that there should be greater emphasis upon national and regional situations because international information flows from national situations. Advertising should be given attention, because it is the basis of much of the financing. Also, the relationship of news as events as an aspect of national development should be addressed, he said. News agencies handle things as a reflection of cultural differences; distortions are not deliberate but are the consequences of differing cultural perceptions.

Abel reminded his colleagues that they had agreed in Stockholm to produce a short, simple report, and now they were setting a trap for themselves by not leaving more time to deal with these complex issues. He suggested that the Commission should not claim to have achieved so much. "Section C goes in for too many half-baked ideas not yet discussed, and there is much language of communication theorists that I don't understand. Freedom is not a 'mirage'; I won't stand for that!"

MacBride commented that this is a provisional report and should eliminate conclusions and remedies. Masmoudi protested that if the Commission submitted too brief a report, the General Conference "would not be able to take advantage of our work and provide responses to our concerns."

Pronk (Netherlands) then listed a number of ways in which he found the draft deficient. Among them were: the definition of communication was not sufficiently precise; questions were asked that were not preceded by enough discussion; there was inadequate attention to access and economics; and no mention was made of the growing importance of the transfer of secret information.

Zamiatin asked for an example of the last item. Pronk said he was talking about the transfer to affiliates by multinational corporations of market data of which governments are unaware, or exchange by governments of information of which the public is unaware. This secret information, not publicly controlled, may be decisive in making important decisions.

Zamiatin replied that he still didn't know what Pronk was talking about. He had been in the press field for twenty years and had never encountered secret information. Secret information is a concern of commercial corporations of which there are none in the Soviet Union. This commercial espionage is the business of these corporations themselves and is not a concern here, he said.

At that point Abel and Omu (Nigeria) got into a debate on access to information, which Abel thought should be emphasized. Omu said that there was too much misuse of access--an excess of access. Abel acknowledged that there have been abuses, but that journalists who have been granted access have performed valuable functions. Omu responded that nobody was challenging the principle of access; the question was about indiscriminate access.

Zamiatin then chimed in to stress that they weren't talking about uncontrolled access, because access must be subject to laws of each country.

Various commissioners made other comments about the text, including this by-play:

Abel: "I am a bit uncomfortable about being called, in paragraph 16, 'a distinguished figure'."

Zamiatin: Why not? I have no doubt of *your* distinction; I only have doubts about my *own*.

Third Session (July 14)

The third and final day of the meeting was devoted to group editing of Part II of the draft, which, in turn, provoked more discussion and debate.

Zamiatin observed that there are areas on which they could agree despite ideological differences; there are other areas where the views are irreconcilable. But, he added, it may be possible for consensus on a number of measures that might be taken in the context of this pluralistic world.

MacBride then raised the question of whether more attention should be given in the draft to educational uses of communication. Zimmerman described the excellent work in instructional television that has been done in Canada, the United States, and Japan, and Zamiatin responded with a detailed description of the variety of instructional TV services in the Soviet Union.

The Chairman indicated that the draft also lacked a reporting of scientific developments and asked whether the Commission might not recommend reexamining the situation regarding discriminatory cable rates. Abel was willing, provided the Commission made a very general comment on this highly technical and complex area. A memorandum on the legal and technical aspect of rate imbalances could be appended to the report. Zamiatin cautioned that the Commission should not say that the rates be changed because that is not within its province. There are government-owned and privately owned channels and they set their own rates over which users have no control.

"This is not a simple matter," Zamiatin said, "In the USSR we set our own rates, but TASS can't get a reduction for photo telegraph transmission even though we have no private competition in the USSR! Masmoudi has a rather utopian idea. I agree with his intention, but reality suggests this is something outside our control."

MacBride said he understood that the growth of broadcasting was reducing the number of newspapers. Zamiatin, asserting that this was the first time he had disagreed with the Chairman, said it did not work that way in the Soviet Union. Since the retention of radio-TV content is fleeting, people need the backup of newspaper and magazines to ponder on what has been broadcast. "We can't print enough books to keep up with the demand!" he asserted.

Lubis (Indonesia) suggested that greater emphasis be given to the obstacles to communication within countries, because all the attempts to improve communication internationally would be to no avail if there are no changes made in domestic communications. In some countries, there are political structures and oppressive regulations; communication is only from the top down and the economics of these societies are under the control of the elite, who believe they have the right to manipulate communication for their own purposes.

At this point, Beuve-Mery (France), who had scarcely spoken a dozen words in two previous meetings, chose to intervene. He stated that the Commission was not a political tribunal; nevertheless, it had given credence to pluralism but some of the statements in the draft did not jibe with this concept. Thus it would not be appropriate to delete (as Zamiatin had suggested) the paragraph urging avoidance of bureaucratic or oligopolistic controls. Pluralism means abhorrence of monopolistic controls by government, commercial interest, or professional journalists.

Zamiatin replied that he had come here to participate in this distinguished Commission to explore the means for helping developing countries in communications. "And here we are getting into a consideration of trivial matters proposed by Commission members!"

MacBride raised the question of whether the Commission should submit a paper to WARC '79. Abel opposed this on grounds that the Commission is not competent to advise the WARC and the fact that all countries, including those at the table, would be represented there.

There followed an editing session on Part II. Abel objected to foggy and arty language, overuse of jargon, and the pretentious and pompous style. Oteifi wanted to eliminate all footnotes, and Osolnik proposed reducing Section A from ten to three pages. Zamiatin took offense at the "pseudo-scientific--in fact, stupid--language."

Turning to Section B, Oteifi said it was too long and poorly organized. Abel and Zimmerman pointed out a number of inaccuracies relating to assertions about broadcasting, and Zamiatin objected to a sentence lumping TASS with AP, UPI, Reuters, and AFP as dominating agencies. "That is a word that has political meaning. The sentence should be redrafted so as to have no political overtones."

Zimmerman (Canada) then made one of her major interventions. She deplored the failure of the Interim Report to deal with injustices, the role of women in communication, and the role of entertainment as a social need.   She went on to point out that broadcasting systems are not necessarily either state-owned or private, and Abel made the point that there is no conspiracy to force U.S. programs on other countries. They buy what they want. *Caveat emptor*!

Verghese added that in India there is public advertising (for promoting family planning) and such advertising contains development messages that have no commercial purpose; this distinction should be made.   Also there is a difference between the funding of commercial entertainment films and the public funding of documentaries.

Pronk expressed concern about the definition of communications as being too broad to distinguish it from other concepts. Lubis agreed with Osolnik's belief that emphasis should be accorded the importance of sharing information. Abel reminded his colleagues that an important function of communications is to *inform*, to let people know what is going on. Zamiatin thanked Abel for reminding them of a function they seemed to have lost sight of. He then went on to raise objections to portions of Section C, including the statement that we live in a world of information chaos. "This is not true; the present order is not topsy-turvy. There are systems and they work."

Abel ended the morning session by objecting to the many sweeping generalizations. "Let's agree that we cannot accept sophomoric writing that puts expressions of biases in our mouths."

In the afternoon, the Commission concentrated on the new text of Part I, revised by the Secretariat on the basis of the discussion at the first session of this meeting.

Verghese led off by saying the text was still dull. It failed to point up the consequences of the speed of technological development--the problems of the integration of communications into the social, political, and economic systems. Unless national inequalities in communications systems can be improved, the objective of obtaining improvement in the global system cannot be realized.

In Omu's view, however, the text overstressed the imbalance of communications at the national level, while a much more important matter was the inequities at the international level.

Zamiatin said that these inequities are caused by the concept of free flow, because it comes up against obstacles laid down by the states. If countries deplore the flow of information on a moral basis, they cannot permit unrestricted flow of information. In the Soviet Union, he declared, the media would never carry a story on homosexuality--not because of official censorship but because of the self-censorship journalists would impose on themselves. Freedom of information means that the media should be the property of the people; where that is not the arrangement, there can be no true freedom of information. Marx wrote that there can be no freedom of information where information is a commodity. "This is the concept upon which freedom of information rests in the Socialist countries," he said.

"We are in favor of freedom of information, but not of free flow of information. If you desire to retain that concept it must be in keeping with national legislation. We need to talk about the accountability of journalists; if journalists are not accountable, it opens the doors wide for distortions of events and defaces images of foreign countries to their audiences.

"The concept of free flow leads to cultural domination," he continued. "No country's system is based on the principle of dominating any one except for domination as regards technology. But this is not a sin, because it is necessary for development. This (the sentence linking TASS with other 'dominating' new agencies) should be deleted. The clients of TASS, UPI, and other news services voluntarily accept information by contractual agreement, so how can you talk domination? If one doesn't like *Reuters*, he can turn to AFP, and so on. Freedom of information stands in the forefront of human rights, along with the right to work, to one's country, and to one's nation. These are part and parcel of all other freedoms.

"What is the meaning of 'information rich and information poor'? Information-rich countries are not super powers. You can divide the world into 'haves' and 'have nots' but now we have 'developed' and 'developing' countries," he concluded.

Osolnik observed that the right to communicate should be put on the same level as concern for inequalities. "Our whole purpose is to see how to put communication into the service of mankind." Lubis seconded him. Communication should foster the enhancement of the environment for all living things he said, but it should be directed at promoting international understanding and peace.

Masmoudi then launched into another of his lectures. He recalled the role of *laissez faire* in justifying unfair economic behavior and said the same attempt was being made now in the information field. "Everyone recognizes that there should be redress of injustices in the economic world; I would like to have the same approach used in communications." He continued with a recital of many other points in his NWIO paper, ending with the observation that domination may not always be deliberate but that itis the natural outcome of the system; therefore, the system must be changed.

Zimmerman complained that the text asserts that the Commission is going to do this or that, whereas such statements are premature "We do not yet agree. All we have agreed to is to ask questions."

Abel said he had listened to the discussion with some sadness. "We've met to consider means for redressing imbalance in the media process. Now we hear complaints that there is *too much* balance! Around the table diverse views are represented. UNESCO is a worldwide organization of nation states representing the world in all its diversity, so any efforts to diminish the representation of an idea not shared by others is something I would regard very gravely. I have no quarrel with what the Soviet press prints or doesn't print. Homosexuality is a social problem, and in a free press it is currently the fashion to discuss this problem."

"Mr. Zamiatin and I are agreed on the overuse of the word 'domination.' I endorse his view that no country is obliged to subscribe to news services and if it does, it is because it wishes to increase the variety of its information services. Many countries subscribe to a foreign service but don't use the copy unless it fits the needs of that country. There is also the 'split level distribution' of the news in which the national agency subscribes to various services, but a large part is distributed to the elite and is not passed on to the public.

"I was saddened also by the discussion of freedom of information and of free flow," he continued, "This could have been avoided if the authors had been less polemical and less concerned with setting up straw men to knock down. It would have been useful to present the historical evolution of these concepts, which are enshrined in UN documents. The tone of the document is polemical and foreshadows conclusions, for example, phrases like 'such is not our view.' Who is 'our'?"

Abel then responded to Omu's concern about giving audiences what they want to read, pointing out that papers like *Le Monde* and *The Los Angeles Times*, neither sensational papers, have been gaining audiences, so it's not necessary to publish trash in order to increase readership. Omu misunderstood what he had said. The point was that a journalist must write with sufficient skill and make the story so appealing that people would want to read it.

"Talking about distortions!" he continued, "this is a distorted document. Journalists are human and do make errors. But these are not the result of dishonesty, but the result of the tendency to compress stories in the time frame. Perceptions are the consequence of an individual's point of view, which is why it's important to have a variety of views.

"We are met here to consider means for rectifying the imbalance we recognize and to consider ways of modifying the existing system, which we want to go on performing," he concluded.

Oteifi then observed that "what we say regarding planning may lead to control by the state. There's no mention of the situation in the Third World where there are restrictions and repressions on journalists."

Pronk (Netherlands) was worried that the Commission had now deleted so much of the Interim Report that there would not be enough left for member states to react to. "I don't feel that the Secretariat has encroached upon the commissioners' prerogatives; it should continue to make bold statements. There *is* a problem about domination and inequities and those parts of the text should be deleted."

Somavia (Chile) objected to the labeling of statements about domination and the power structure as being pejorative and rubbish. It would be deforming the ideas to change them, he thought, because there is no objection to the language in which they are posed.

Zamiatin replied that a phrase like "we see a domination trend emerging" is language he might approve but others would object to. "We will need to say that some people feel there's domination in news but others don't agree."

He complimented the Chairman and the Secretariat on the draft Interim Report: "A document the commissioners challenged, but after all, that's freedom of communication."

Zamiatin thus had the last word at this third meeting of the Commission--the longest and most confrontational of the sessions so far. Omu was the most disputatious of the commissioners, making a number of blunt accusations against Western journalists as deliberate distorters of news. He also tried repeatedly to get the main points of Masmoudi's NWIO paper integrated into the text of the Interim Report, but was overruled by Chairman MacBride.

Verghese, Lubis, and Oteifi, though from developing countries, were moderate in their interventions and inclined to point out the validity of arguments on both sides, for example, differences between developed and developing countries were not deliberate but were due to differing perceptions. Both Lubis and Verghese stressed the need to give attention to the free flow of information at the national level if there is to be improvement in media internationally. These remarks were immediately deplored by Masmoudi and Somavia, who insisted that the focus must be kept on the international situation in communications.

Oteifi, a lawyer, contented himself almost entirely with criticisms of the form rather that the substance of the draft. He objected to the length and organization and also to the inclusion of footnotes.

Pronk, an economist, had a thing about "secret information" being transmitted by transnational corporations without the knowledge of government or public. He kept returning to this topic again and again.

Beuve-Mery, the distinguished founder of *Le Monde* and the oldest of the commissioners, sat quietly listening for the most part until provoked by Masmoudi's attempt to delete the paragraph cautioning against monopolies. He made an eloquent statement on the dangers of any kind of control over the press and denounced an article by a Moscow University dean[8] asserting that media must be instruments of government. "Such an attitude," Beuve-Mery said, "was a total refusal of pluralism." Zimmerman and Abel were assiduous in pointing out a number of inaccuracies and false assumptions in the text about broadcasting and newspaper operations. Abel was especially vigilant that misstatements in the text of polemical pronouncements from Third World spokesmen did not go unchallenged.

Much of the time at the meeting was given over to group editing with Abel and Zamiatin leading the denunciation of pseudoscientific terminology and foggy writing.

---

[8] Yassen Zassoursky, Dean, Faculty of Journalism, Moscow State University.

Chapter 6

THE INTERIM REPORT

The Interim Report was a voluminous document, seventy-nine pages in length and another example of the UNESCO Secretariat's indulgence in pompous prolixity. A mere listing later of the various sections reaffirms this observation.

The report is in two parts: Part I is a description of the progress of the Commission's work and activities carried out since it started (presumably a factual account of the proceedings unanimously adopted by the Commission). Part II contains an outline of the problems raised or likely to arise, certain of which it had already begun to examine (reviewed in a preliminary way but with no decisions actually taken.)

The report also indicated that the Commission gave consideration to two memoranda concerning the New World Information Order prepared by Commissioners Masmoudi and Osolnik, copies of which were annexed.

In his letter of transmittal, Chairman MacBride stressed that the Commission had not reached decisions on any of the matters discussed in Part II. So far, the Commission had just surveyed and identified problems. "The major task of formulating recommendations in regard to the problems raised still remains," he wrote. Unfortunately, many never accepted this reservation, as we shall see, and persisted in treating the text in Part II as though it had been officially adopted by the Commission.

Without going into exhausting detail, here is part of the table of contents for the report--enough to afford ample notion of the contents.

CONTENTS OF THE INTERIM REPORT

I. A major issue
    The paradigms of the problem
    Criticisms and repudiations
    The functions of communication
II. Communications: Its structures and actors
    A. Established structures

      1. traditional and interpersonal forms
      2. institutionalized communication
      3. communication on a planetary scale
    B. Actors involved
      1. role and function of private groups
      2. collectivity and society
      3. transnational companies

III.   Socioeconomic,   sociopolitcal,   and   sociocultural   effects   of communication
    A. Social aspects and implications
      1. socialization and influence
      2. a factor in integration or disintegration
      3. homogenization
    B. Cultural aspects and implications
      1. vehicles of the cultural message
      2. mass communication and mass culture
      3. vehicles of educational messages
      4. alternative approaches to the learning process
    C. Economic aspects and implications
      1. a variable governed by economic factors
      2. communication and development
      3. communication as a political tool
    D. Politic aspects and implications
      1. as a political force
      2. as a political tool

IV. Communication Problems Today
    A. Freedom of information; its significance and constraints,
    B. Accuracy and distortion of information
    C. Balance and imbalance
    D. Professional conduct and responsibility
    E. Specific situations and social groups
    F. Material imbalances and inequalities
    G. Technology: Implications and contradictions

V. Communications tomorrow: Trends, prospects, ambitions
    A. Strengthening national capacities
    B. Redressing the qualitative balance
    C. Democratizing communication
    D. Towards a new world information order

    The above outline omits many of the subheads, but this is sufficient to indicate the substance of the Interim Report. As the Director-General told the Commission at its initial meeting, "It is essential to submit a preliminary report describing the progress of your work and containing a detailed plan of the final report as it will then seem possible and desirable to you to conceive it."

INTERNATIONAL REACTION

When the Interim Report was released in the fall of 1978 it produced highly mixed reviews from both East and West: from member states, media organization, and individual professionals, including members of the Commission.

It restated many of the free press principles contained in the UN and UNESCO charters and resolutions (with the Soviets dissenting), but at the same time it opened the door to controls over the media (with the West objecting). A main objection of the Soviets was the reaffirmation of the right of free access. Western spokesmen objected, among other things, to what they considered new and restrictive concepts, such as, for example, "the right to communicate," "democratization" of the press, "developmental journalism"--all of them ill-defined and subject to self-serving interpretations by authoritarian regimes.

Third World spokesmen, on the other hand, praised these concepts while deploring various omissions and calling for expansion of some segments. Elie Abel was distressed that large portions of the report had been written by the Secretariat without submission to the Commission. He had never seen, much less approved, them.

Chairman MacBride seemed undisturbed by the whirlwind of reaction. He said that the Interim Report did not attempt to offer recommendations or solutions, but was designed to stimulate widespread comment. "The reactions, criticisms, and concrete suggestions that are provoked by this report will assist the Commission in formulation of its Final Report," he commented. He assured Abel and other commissioners that they would have ample opportunity to reshape the document and it would be far different in its final manifestation.

The Interim Report, translated into six languages, was distributed to all member states of UNESCO and its NGO members, as well as to members of the United Nations system, intergovernmental and nongovernmental organizations, and media specialists. Responses were received from 32 countries, with papers from 137 organizations and individual professionals.

Since the contents of the Interim Report were drastically changed by the time the Final Report was issued, no useful purpose would be served in analyzing these responses in detail. It will suffice to give a sampling of the comments to indicate the tone of the international reaction and thus, the vast diversity of views and the enormity of the task that confronted the Commission in trying to take all of these ideas and suggestions into account.

Some of the comments are extracted from papers submitted, but most of them are taken from the debate on the Interim Report when it was discussed at the UNESCO General Conference in Paris in November 1978.

WESTERN RESPONSES

The United States submitted a 27-page set of recommendations: one-third of it consisting of comments on the Interim Report and the bulk of it suggestions for the Final Report and the New World Information and Communication Order (NWICO).[1]

The first Interim Report comment concerned biases in the issues covered (problems were surveyed but without recognition that nations with diverging philosophies about communications would perceive problems differently).

The second comment dealt with largely neglected trends: the history of cooperation with and among Third World governments in applying media to development problems and the inadequate coverage of the emergence of increasingly productive and affordable technologies for broadcasting, telecommunications, and computing.

The third comment related to the implications of the emerging technologies (potential applications of both high and low technology for accelerating development did not receive adequate attention).

In the much longer section on suggestions for the Final Report, the United States made several proposals. It believed that it would be important to analyze the cultural, political, and economic situations of different countries as factors in the development of their communication systems and their approach to international communication issues.

The United States also recommended that there should be acknowledgement of the communication roles of individuals, communities, private institutions, public institutions, and governments.

The paper went on to argue that, because there were so many issues that were not subject to negotiation, compromise, or consensus, the Commission should address itself to analysis and proposals of concrete and practical measures such as telecommunication tariffs and postal rates.

---

[1]New nomenclature adopted at UNESCO's 20th General Conference. Reason: information refers to *content*, communication to the *process* of transmission and presentation.

The U.S. paper concluded, in effect, with an essay on the New World Information and Communications Order (NWICO). It began with an analysis of the political and technological trends in world communications. It also discussed the need for collaboration between developed and developing countries to assist in building communications capacities. It concluded with a discussion of the promise the information age holds for increased productivity of information in economics and social services and increased diversity of news coverage along with cultural and political expression within and between nations. In this way, the paper asserted, trends in communication might begin to ease rather than inflame the more difficult transitions underway in the economic and political spheres.

The European Broadcasting Union (EBU) judged the Interim Report a remarkable synopsis of communication problems; nevertheless, the EBU considered it highly questionable.

"It has the serious drawback of making it necessary to generalize systematically and to study the implications, advantages, and disadvantages of communication systems in very general terms that apply to press news agencies, radio, television, cable, satellites, and video cassettes. Accordingly, many observations cannot be anything but questionable when they are considered not as generalities but in relation to a particular mass medium, technical system, etc." Understandably for a broadcasting organization, the EBU believed that the latest modes of dissemination, all based on developments in electronics of the last fifty years, were inadequately dealt with.

The comments by the Inter American Press Association (IAPA), one of the most vigorous defenders of the free press, were typically tough and defensive of the media. "The Interim report purports to isolate the world's communication problems...[but] in some instances, does this by posing a series of questions worded in such a manner that they point to predetermined responses; in other instances, they do this by omissions." The IAPA also noted that the Interim Report was written to reinforce certain concepts and theories put forth by "so-called experts commissioned by UNESCO" about the role of the press in modern society.

"The assumption implicit throughout is that the media are responsible for all the ills of the world. Therefore, there must be national communication policies or international norms to use the media to further economic and cultural development, to close the gap between developing and developed countries, to endure peace and universal brotherhood, to eliminate the blight of racism and apartheid and to achieve all manner of other worthy goals sought by thinking humanity for centuries."

COMMISSIONERS' RESOLVE

Because of the widespread critical reaction to the Interim Report and the confusion and misunderstanding created by too many technical terms and unsupported claims and assumptions in a text written largely by staff, the commissioners were determined to take a more active role from that point on in the writing and review of the text. Scattered around the world as they were, however, it was difficult for them to have a close, active involvement--a condition some suspected was not altogether displeasing to the Secretariat. As it turned out, they were no more successful in their participation in writing the Final Report, although as this telegram attests, some tried:

> ELIE ABEL   STANFORD CALIFORNIA   2/5/80
> THANKS YOUR COMMENTS PART ONE STOP ALL EXCEPT ONE INCLUDED SINCE THEY REPRESENT IMPROVEMENTS TO TEXT STOP PARA ONE WRITTEN BY VERGHESE DISTRIBUTED TO ALL MEMBERS NOBODY REACTED UNFAVORABLY AND THUS INSERTED STOP EYE DELETED FIVE LINES PARA 104 SO YOUR COMMENT NOT NECESSARY -- DELEON.

EXAMINATION BY THE 20TH GENERAL CONFERENCE

During the vigorous debate in Commission IV (Communication and Culture) at the 20th General Conference of UNESCO sixty-one statements were made by fifty-four delegates of member states and seven observers. The discussion took place on November 14 and 15, 1978 in Paris.

The Secretariat's account of the debate is divided into Favorable Judgements, Critical Observations, and Priority Topics. In accordance with UNESCO practice, no identifications of the delegate or country was associated with the comments.

Favorable comments began with the ritualistic congratulations to the president and members of the Commission. Several delegates regarded the Interim Report as a realistic document, neutral and balanced in its arguments. Two of them considered that it covered, if not every aspect of communication, at least the most important ones. In the view of another, the report provided proof that progress had already been made to achieving a world approach to communication problems. Other delegates expressed the hope that the Commission's work, which had already fostered a new awareness of the problems, would give fresh impetus to UNESCO's activities in this field and would pave the way to encourage members to adopt policies and plans designed to improve the situation of communication in the world. Others noted that they assembled a large amount of data that had previously been scattered. Recognizing the scope and complexity of the issues raised, most delegates considered that the Report constituted the first serious attempt at a comprehensive review of what the Secretariat called "the innumerable qualitative and quantitative aspects of information and communication seen in the context of political and cultural aspirations as well as in the context of development at both the national and international levels, and that it provided the basis for a systematic and operational approach."

Many delegates qualified their favorable judgements with suggestions and critical comments. Several speakers, for example, regarded the Interim Report as a juxtaposition of data and observations, placing more emphasis on description than on interpretation, and reflecting confusion and ambiguity, particularly in the definition of basic concepts. Examples included distinctions between media and mass communication and between information and communication. Others thought that, while the Interim Report identified may issues, a number of matters had been overlooked and neglected. Some delegates believed that the document was lacking in a basic unity of conception.

One delegate regretted that the Interim Report, in place of a detailed plan for the Final Report (which it should have contained), had substituted "a staggering statement of problems that would take fifty years of research to solve."

Several delegates had misgivings about the vocabulary used, which in their view referred too frequently to the harmful effects of the media. One of them considered the Interim Report no more than a collection of theories, which, far from being universally accepted, might even become instruments of oppression in the service of authoritarian governments. One observer equated in a pejorative and ambiguous fashion and the defense of permanent values with conformism. Two other observers noted that the Commission should stop discussing what had already been done and concentrate on what could be done.

The Secretariat's account of this segment concludes with the observation that there was general agreement that the Interim Report provided a good starting point, despite its preliminary character, for studying the "very complex process of human communication."

The concluding section on Priority Topics consisted of eight parts, each of which will be summed up briefly--no easy task because it occupies nine closely typed pages.

SUMMARY OF THE EIGHT-PART PRIORITY TOPICS SECTION

Freedom of Information

Most of the delegates addressed the issue of freedom of information, whose meaning differed from one country to another. Several from the West stated that freedom of the press and of information had been won by their people as the culmination of a long historical process, that it was a part of the cultural heritage of their countries, and that it could not therefore be called into question. Freedom of opinion and expression, which was fostered by the plurality of information media, constituted a fundamental right; it was therefore inalienable and could not be limited, restricted, or subordinated to any regulation whatsoever, except in order to safeguard the legitimate rights of third parties or to comply with accepted moral standards; freedom of information and free access to many and varied sources were components of a democratic, free, and pluralistic society. They concluded this argument by stating that, since freedom of information was the most reliable and effective means of correcting errors and achieving objectivity, it was vital to eliminate all obstacles impeding the full exercise of this freedom.

While many delegates considered that the Interim Report gave prominence to the concept of freedom of information, some were of the opinion, on the contrary, that it had not been adequately highlighted. One delegate even reached the conclusion that the report tended to favor a regimented press.

The Soviet and Third World delegates were not prepared to swallow this concept to that degree. Even when freedom of expression was total, they pointed out that it should not operate to the detriment of decency and respect for the truth. The right to communicate, in their view, implied the right *not* to communicate and the right to respect of privacy. On par with freedom, *responsibility* was an essential element; freedom of information should be so consonant with ethical concern as to make it unnecessary to choose between sacrificing freedom to morality or sacrificing morality to freedom.

Several delegates declared themselves in favor of honest, fair, and responsible reporting and free flow of ideas and opinions, so long as it did not promote the dissemination of half-truths and distortions. Some pointed out that there was no freedom where information was monopolized. Another speaker was of the opinion that if, in the name of human rights and freedom, the enormous technical and material resources of the developed world were deployed in order to dilute or to undermine the intrinsic significance of the values and cultures of other societies, turning individuals into automators reflecting alien, stereotyped attitudes, and destroying priorities that were the product of age-long experience, such principles should be resisted.

Others observed that freedom of information was too often bound up with individual ownership of the media, and that the imperfect concentration of powers and privileges in the hands of a few made a mockery of freedom. From this point of view, it had to be acknowledged that freedom implied equality, or at least a certain measure of it. In the view of another delegate, the state should be entitled to call the offending party to order when freedom of information took the form of an act of violence against the human conscience. Another wondered whether freedom or aggression was the appropriate term when consumer countries received information that was quite irrelevant to their needs.

Under UNESCO rules, observers may only take the floor when all delegates who wish to speak have been heard. On this occasion, one observer maintained that it was up to the Commission to prescribe the conditions of the free flow of information that would reconcile requirements both of freedom and responsibility, taking account of the institution of the new relations between media and their audiences, which should function as true partners and learn their responsibilities through the exercise of their freedoms. The other observer said that there were responsible and irresponsible governments, the capacity of the latter to do harm being infinitely greater.

Imbalance of News

It was generally recognized that there remained a need for a concerted international effort to reduce quantitative and qualitative imbalances in the flow of news. As might be expected, the delegates' views were pretty well divided along ideological lines, particularly with reference to the role of government in the media.

At the national level, several delegates thought it preferable to rule out all forms of government control and censorship in view of the distortion entailed (which in turn created imbalance) to keep news dissemination the sole responsibility of the media. In the opinion of others, state support for development of the media constituted the sole possible alternative in many countries, and in the absence of state intervention, the information vacuum would automatically be filled by distorted values from developed countries.

At the international level, the imbalance, which operated principally but not solely along the North-South axis, was claimed by some to be a sequel to colonialism, allegedly "maintained by those with the will to dominate by possessing both the word and the sword." This imbalance derived from the virtual monopoly of the major international news agencies, which distributed nearly three-quarters of the news generated in the world, and from the data banks controlled by the transnational corporations.

In the view of several speakers, the imbalance resulted essentially from the inadequacy of the human, technical, and material resources of the developing countries. The problem was one of infrastructures which could be solved by concerted technical and financial efforts, provided that each country developed a communication system adapted to its own needs.

A few delegates considered that the real, deep-rooted causes of imbalance were still little known and that it was the Commission's responsibility (in UNESCOese) "not only to identify and study them--in particular by showing how these intranational and international phenomena influence one another--but also to suggest ways and means of creating new conditions in which communication would no longer benefit only those countries possessing the know-how, in which access by all to true, impartial, and responsible reporting would be encouraged, and in which integrated, balanced, and organized national systems open to international exchange and facilitating the safeguarding of cultural identity, could be developed."

National Policy and Interdependence

A third set of problems concerned standard-setting instruments that would be universally binding in the field of communication. Some were persuaded that any study of the problem must be based on the principles of the sovereignty of each state to lay down its own communication policy. In the opinion of one delegate, it was for the developing countries themselves to promote a national policy that would (1) put an end to dependence in matters of information, (2) develop a system that would satisfy the needs of the population and that would place information within the reach of everyone, and (3) put information in the service of development by ensuring the participation of all citizens.

While some delegates believed that the sovereignty aspect had been underplayed in the Interim Report, others regretted that scant attention had been paid to the interdependence of states and peoples, of which communication is an essential part. Similarly, whereas several speakers objected to any attempt to establish universally binding standards, since the decision as to what constituted appropriate information was not a matter for laws and regulation, others thought it necessary to provide legal controls or ethical standards to govern exchanges of information.

Content of Information

The discussion of content highlighted the basic differences in news values. In the developed, market-economy countries, this value was generally bound up with commercial criteria, even when the profit motive was attenuated by the free flow of ideas and information. In the developing countries, the media were essentially a means of projecting trends and reporting processes of development, rather than just events. They had a "duty," some said, to provide information useful in everyday life, to revitalize folklore, to foster cultural mobility, and to evolve a country-wide independence for culture and information.

Others were convinced that the state should refrain from interfering in the content of messages and from compelling individuals to adopt their own way of seeing things. Deciding whether an item of good news was as worthy of interest as an item of bad news was the responsibility of journalists and their readers, and not of governments, even though for those media organized according to the laws of the market, profitable news was good news.

Journalistic Training and Professional Ethics

The point of issue here was whether journalists should or should not be subject to rules or codes of conduct, while at the same time providing them with safeguards in the exercise of their duties, and whether such codes should or should not be freely accepted by those concerned. It was pointed out that a system of safeguards did operate in a number of countries and journalists enjoyed a status similar to that of certain professions. Others considered nevertheless that journalists should not represent a class of people or an institution distinct from society and be placed above the law.

A number of delegates and one observer emphasized the importance of training and refresher courses for journalists, recommending that such courses in developing countries should be organized to enable communicators to become familiar with new situations by correcting habits that "stultified the imagination." Training courses should also be given to acquaint journalists from the industrial countries with the realities of the Third World.

Several delegates, in a show of pride that would have done credit to their native chambers of commerce (if they existed), described the journalist training courses established in their countries and the positive results achieved.

New World Information Order

In a debate that pretty well mirrored the discussions in the Commission, Third World delegates approved the arguments and aspirations implicit in the concept of a New World Information Order (NWIO), and some commented favorably on the documents by Masmoudi and Osolnik, which accompanied the Interim Report. Several delegates indicated that the Commission's most important function was to define the NWIO implications and identify specific provisions that should be undertaken to establish it.

Other delegates and observers emphasized ed that the demand for an NWIO was in keeping with the determination of developing countries to achieve complete independence; accordingly, the new order should foster the expansion of media in the developing countries, ensure a freer and better balanced flow of news, and "provide a vision of the world which measured up to mankind's present-day situation and the problems confronting him."

One observer regretted that the Interim Report had presented the new order as being an act of negation and rejection. In the opinion of several, the aim of the new order should be to improve the distribution of the media and the information channels. Eastern bloc speakers stressed that the new order should serve as an instrument of solidarity, a force for harmony, and a natural extension of the effort to bring nations closer to one another so they might work together for the elimination of war, poverty, ignorance, and prejudice.

Attention was given by some to the connection between the New World Information Order and the International Economic Order. Two delegates thought the first was both the essential component and the precondition to the second. Another speaker said that a parallel between the two should not be taken too far, because the economic order was based on existing economic theories, whereas the information order was still independent of theories relating to communication.

Other Issues and Comments

Several delegates held the opinion that the Interim Report did not deal adequately with the experience of the socialist countries. Two cases in point, they said, were (1) the balance to be maintained between the freedom of expression and the responsibility of information professionals and (2) the participation of the people at large in the "elaboration" of information from the sociopolitical context.

Others pointed out that the report did not make sufficient reference to the situation in those countries where the state totally controlled the media. Other questions raised by one or more delegates related to the following:

- theory of communication and of culture,

- computerization of society,

- commercialization of information,

- propaganda and advertising,

- linguistic aspects of communication,

- electronic research, and

- relationship between communication and illiteracy.

Form and Content of the Final Report

Finally, a number of delegates expressed concerns about what would come out of the Commission's work. Two feared that it would not be able to complete the task assigned to it and suggested that the deadline be extended. Another was concerned about the time available for distribution of the Final Report as well as what measures might be taken at the national and international levels to effect the conclusions and recommendations of the Commission.

The majority of delegates indicated they were in favor of maintaining the global approach adopted in the Interim Report: "considering information as power and communication as a process and as a major political, economic, social, and cultural phenomenon operating at the national and international levels, deserved to be studied in all their complexity."

Certain delegates recommended that the scope of the study be restricted by establishing priorities, making choices and selecting particular topics of inquiry. Several were persuaded that this selection should be based (on the one hand) on a determination to eschew all generalization and (on the other) on the possibility of achieving practical results, including specific measures, operational recommendations, and even a program of action. Another delegate expressed the hope that the Commission might formulate its proposals in sufficiently flexible terms for them to be adapted to the particular sociopolitical circumstances of each country, in order to enable the main lines and priorities of the needed technical cooperation to be determined.

Several delegates expressed concerns regarding the limitations of the themes to be dealt with in the Final Report. Some thought that the Commission should restrict itself to the study of information proper. Others urged that it concern itself primarily with the mass media and other means of communication, while another wished to stress the role of new technologies. One delegate proposed a list of priorities covering codes of ethics and problems connected with news agencies, television networks, and the press. Another asked that a more thorough study be made of problems raised by censorship and the monopoly of information.

Several delegates expressed the hope that the Commission, in seeking to make a comprehensive review of the problems, would avoid the danger of attempting an artificial synthesis of concepts that were, in fact, conflicting. Irreducible differences should be taken into account wherever they existed. Care should be taken to avoid taking hard-and-fast positions on the ideal information and communication systems. Some suggested that the Commission provide fuller data to justify each proposal, drawing on the findings of empirical research undertaken in the different countries.

The Secretariat ended its account of the debate with this vain hope: "By eschewing all doctrinal polemics, and by bearing in mind that objectivity calls for both realism and balance, it should be possible to reach optimal understanding of the various problems and experiences involved."

In conclusion, Chairman MacBride expressed his appreciation for the "extremely constructive and rewarding" discussion to which the Interim Report had given rise, and said he agreed with many of the suggestions put forth by various speakers. He requested that member states provide the Commission with further information on the projects for training journalists and communicators that had been mentioned in the debate.[2]

---

[2]The preceding was extracted from three UNESCO documents in "Comments on the Interim Report by Specialists, National Institutions, and International Organizations." These are in Working Document No. 3, Fourth Session Part I, Dubrovnik; Working Document No. 2, Fifth Session, New Delhi; and Working Document No. 2 Add 2, Sixth Session, Acapulco.

Chapter 7

MEETING IV
DUBROVNIK, YUGOSLAVIA
JANUARY 8-12, 1979

During the week-long meeting, the Commission discussed such topics as whether there should be an international code of ethics for journalists, what concrete steps should be taken towards the establishment of a New World Information and Communication Order, and how to achieve a greater democratization of communication. In addition, it examined reactions of governments, nongovernmental organizations, and private institutions to its Interim Report. With the cooperation of specialists from Yugoslav universities, press, and broadcasting organizations, the Commission also held two roundtable discussions, one on communication and society and the other on cooperation in communication among developing countries.

FIRST SESSION (JANUARY 8)

The meeting opened with brief ceremonial speeches by Chairman MacBride, the Yugoslav Secretary of Information, the secretary of the Yugoslav National Commission for UNESCO, and the President of the Assembly of Dubrovnik. The Commission members began with a discussion of comments on and reactions to the Interim Report (IR).

They next debated the format of the Final Report and took a closer look at the list of topics and issues that might be considered.

A number of suggestions were made, particularly with regard to reactions to the IR. Verghese (India) felt that a free and balanced flow of information was important *within* each country as well as internationally and that this idea had not been sufficiently reflected. He also believed that the IR concentrated too heavily on the print media at the expense of broadcast media and traditional means of communication.

Oteifi (Egypt) reported that reaction to the IR in his country had been generally good, but that there tended to be a confusion in the text between information and communication. For the Final Report, a clear distinction should be made between the two.

Zimmerman (Canada) argued that the IR had not clearly expressed the main task of the Commission. In addition, there had been little attention to the distinctive role of women in the mass media.

Several members of the Commission agreed with the Chairman that more time would be required in order to produce the Final Report and suggested that the mandate of the body should be prolonged by from three to six months.

The Secretary of the Commission (Deleon) reported that little reaction to the IR had come from the Socialist countries, from the Arab states, or from Africa. Oteifi (Egypt) suggested that insofar as the Arab states were concerned, this was because Arab translation of the text had only been received in the latter half of December.

It was generally agreed that despite the Chairman's efforts to make a clear distinction between Part I of the report, on which the Commission had agreed unanimously, and Part II, which was simply an outline of problems it intended to study, many readers had tended to confuse the two.

It was also generally agreed that sharper definitions would be required in the Final Report, that the language required improvement both in English and in French, and that a connecting thread should be established between the various parts.

SECOND SESSION (JANUARY 9)

Should there be an international code of ethics for journalists? If so, who should be responsible for drawing it up and administering it? What are the responsibilities of those who own or control the media? Should there be a code of ethics for them, as well? And what are the interests of the public, the "consumers" of mass media, in all of this?

These were a few of the questions raised by the Commission as it began a debate on the concrete measures to be taken toward the establishment of a "New World Information Order" (NWIO). Two members (Masmoudi, Osolnik) argued in favor of setting up a code of ethics, but Nagai (Japan), citing experience from his own country, warned of the dangers of too much restriction on freedom of foreign correspondents. In Japan, he pointed out, where the press (although powerful) was not as free as it might be, citizens often relied for honest reporting upon the reports of the unfettered foreign correspondents.

Commission members noted that the subject of a code of ethics had been previously discussed at the seminar that the Commission sponsored in Stockholm last April, and in which news agencies, newspapers, and broadcasting organizations had been widely represented. There had been no unanimity on the question however.

There was general agreement that codes of ethics were widely accepted at the national level, although their specific content differed considerably. One speaker suggested the possibility of regional codes as well. Masmoudi (Tunisia) recalled that the United Nations had struggled with the problem since 1952 without success but thought that UNESCO might do better in this respect.

Osolnik (Yugoslavia) believed that the question of an international code was more urgent now because of the information explosion and the fact that technological developments had made the world smaller. A code was necessary, he thought, to protect journalists from tyranny and dictatorship.

Most of those who spoke felt that any code that was established should be drafted by professionals in the information field, and that it should be administered by them as well, although other interests should be represented.

Losev (USSR), sitting in for Zamiatin, referred to the "misinformation explosion" in the world today. The Commission's Final Report, he said, should be inspired by the recently adopted UNESCO Declaration on the Principles Governing the Contribution of the Mass Media to Peace and International Understanding.

The Commission asked its Secretariat to do a comparative study of national codes of ethics or conduct, press councils, advertising codes, ombudsmen, and other ways of setting standards, in order to see what common elements might be distinguished as a basis for a possible international code. It also agreed that three of its members (MacBride, Masmoudi, Osolnik) would make a first draft of a recommendation in this respect, to be referred back to the Commission at a later meeting. (It was never done.)

Before this decision, two members (Abel, Nagai) expressed strong reservations about the idea of an international code of ethics, although agreeing that such regulations might be useful at the national level. In any case, they argued, it was a mistake to assume that the drafting of a code automatically solved problems of professional misconduct. Even the medical profession was not regulated on an international basis, they added, although this would be far easier than journalism.

It was recognized, however, that freedom and responsibility are two sides of the same coin and that one could not be separated from the other. Osolnik suggested that a new definition or a new vision of freedom needed to be developed to meet modern conditions. Oteifi (Egypt) added that, ideally, a code of ethics would enhance rather than restrict the liberty of journalists.

The Chairman compared the present situation regarding journalistic ethics to an earlier period in the struggle for human rights, when international standardization of human rights was regarded as anathema. The European Convention on Human Rights might serve as a model, he added, for regional codes of ethics for journalists. Other sources for such instruments might include the Universal Declaration of Human Rights, the two United Nations covenants on human rights, the Helsinki agreement, and the recent UNESCO declaration on the mass media.

In this discussion on democratization of communication, several aspects were stressed. They included access to news sources, access to and participation in the mass media, democratization of management and professional decisions in the mass media, and the right of reply. In this connection, Masmoudi suggested that the Commission might see what was needed to bring the UN Convention up to date on the Right of Rectification and Correction, adopted 25 years ago, but ratified so far by only four countries.

THIRD SESSION (JANUARY 10)

A further discussion of democratization of communication focussed mainly on ownership, control, and financing of the mass media. There was general agreement that many nations, particularly the poorer countries of the Third World, had no option but public ownership, and it was suggested that the Commission should examine various models of state financing that allow for autonomy of operation. Examples were cited from Japan, Canada, United Kingdom, the Federal Republic of Germany, India, the United States, and Egypt to demonstrate the wide variety of experience available, particularly insofar as broadcast media are concerned.

Two speakers (Abel, Nagai) were of the opinion that assuring autonomy despite government financing or public financing was probably easier for radio and television than for newspapers. In this connection, there was also considerable discussion about the role of advertising and the influence of advertisers on privately owned media. Reference was made to the dangers of monopoly or concentration in the media field.

Verghese (India) deplored the fact that the media were essentially regarded as vehicles for entertainment, even in the developing countries, and stressed the need to reinforce their role in the development process and in the mobilization of public support for social change. He also stressed the need for appropriate technology in the media field as in other fields, and warned of the dangers of cultural shock from the importation of highly sophisticated equipment and programs.

Most of the afternoon's discussion centered on ways and means of managing technical and financial assistance to the developing countries within the framework of a new international information order.

It was generally agreed that assistance was necessary in order to strengthen and improve information infrastructures in such countries, to help train professional personnel, and to provide them with appropriate equipment. Somavia (Chile) insisted that the means and institutions for the transfer of technology were all important, because the wrong kind of assistance could work against democratization of communication in the beneficiary countries and could, in fact, increase their dependence on the industrialized countries.

One crucial problem was that of the choice of appropriate technologies, Somavia noted. An independent body was required, he said, which could evaluate the different technologies available and advise developing countries on their choices.

Communication was viewed also as a field in which technical cooperation among developing countries themselves could be improved, either on a regional or an interregional basis. This was particularly true with respect to the training of journalists. Insofar as possible, this should be done in their home countries or at least in their regions. Regional broadcasting unions could play a leading role in this respect. There was also a suggestion that journalists from industrialized countries be given some training in Third World countries before being assigned as foreign correspondents in those countries.

Noting the great variety of technical assistance programs now being carried out through United Nations agencies, the Commission expressed the need for a better picture of what is actually being done. To this end, the Secretariat was asked to provide documentation on the subject for its next meeting.

In the evening a panel discussion was held in which Yugoslav specialists discussed "Interaction between Society and Communication Media."

FOURTH SESSION (JANUARY 11)

Several aspects of the relations between communication and education were explored as the Commission continued its examination of democratization of communication.

Should "communication appreciation" courses be developed in secondary schools, similar to the "art appreciation" or "music appreciation" courses now offered?

In any case, members of the Commission argued, communication is such an important part of modern everyday life that understanding of it must be taught in primary and secondary schools, not for those who will become specialists in the field, but for everyone. Access to and participation in the mass media, as part of the process of democratization of communication, required first of all a knowledge of how those media operate. Furthermore, if citizens were to participate effectively in the formulation of communication policies, they must know what the options are. On the one hand, there was the need to teach communication in the schools. On the other hand, there was the role of communication media in school and out-of-school education, and above all in continuing life-long education. The role of communication in civic and political education was also mentioned.

Other points touched upon in the morning's discussion included the exploitation of women by the media and the problem of censorship. Somavia (Chile) reported on a study currently being concluded of women's magazines in six Latin American countries. While they did not deal specifically with political subjects, the analysis showed, the orientation of both advertising and editorial content tended to produce a conservative image of the role of women in society. Abel reported, however, that there had been a radical change in women's magazines in the United States over the past decade, and that they tended to deal much more now with real problems rather than with fantasies.

There was general agreement among the commissioners that political censorship was unjustified except in time of war or extreme national emergency.

Verghese reported that recent attempts at censorship in India had had disastrous consequences and had produced the very opposite result of what was intended. In the end, the government had realized that it had simply driven the opposition underground and produced a wave of rumors far more dangerous than factual reporting.

There was less agreement on the question of censorship involving violence or pornography. Abel argued strongly in favor of citizens' action rather than government controls.

In the evening, representatives of TANJUG, the Yugoslav news agency and broadcasting organization, held a panel discussion on regional cooperation among developing countries.

FIFTH SESSION (JANUARY 12)

The Commission devoted its last two morning and afternoon meetings to a brief review of topics that had been mentioned only in passing or not at all, but which, it was thought, deserved some mention in its Final Report.

These included the role of women in the mass media and the role of the mass media with respect to women, the question of postal rates and telecommunication tariffs for the transmission of news or other forms of communications, the viewpoint of major world religious bodies on communication problems, the development of appropriate communication technologies for developing countries, informatics and telematics, the relation between communication and the establishment of a new international economic order, and the place of the creative arts in communication.

On virtually all of these subjects, the Commission expressed the need for further information and documentation, and in-depth discussion of them was put off until the next meeting in New Delhi. Assistance was sought either from the Secretariat or outside bodies, and in some cases Commission members themselves were asked to prepare memoranda. Pronk (Netherlands) was asked to contribute a paper on a new international economic order and Garcia Marquez (Colombia) one on the role of creative arts in communication, with special reference to literature, theater, poetry, and cinema.

The final action of this session was a determination that mass communication research itself should be the subject of a section of the report. Several research organizations would be asked to prepare material for the new section.

PERSONAL OBSERVATIONS ON THE MEETING

The nonaligned countries, led by Masmoudi (Tunisia), were pushing the New World Information Order (NWIO)[1] and intended to make the MacBride Commission and its Final Report a major focus of their efforts. Masmoudi repeatedly emphasized that the resolutions passed at the General Conference and in the United Nations General Assembly mandated the Commission to concentrate its efforts in formulating its Final Report on how to establish the NWIO. "This is the Commission's sole mission. The whole world awaits our answer."

---

[1] Although the term NWICO was adopted by UNESCO in 1978, the commissioners did not use it in debate; it was, however, used in the Final Report.

The nonaligned group intended to insert in the Commission's Final Report all that they had to forego in the UNESCO Declaration on the Media. Osolnik (Yugoslavia) hailed the Declaration as a great achievement, but then went on to detail the cost to the nonaligned countries in participating in the consensus. He listed a series of points they had forfeited, but with no mention of the term NWIO, the responsibility of journalists, the State, code of professional ethics, national sovereignty, and interference of the media. "In seeking a consensus we had to forfeit some concepts. From this we have a lesson. In our Commission, we will have to seek consensus, but we must not give up important considerations."

The politicizing of the Commission was more apparent at this meeting than ever before. There had been previous evidence of bias in the selection of the commissioners, in the commissioning of research papers, and in the choice of authors for drafting the Interim Report.   In this meeting, the "line" was very obvious in the Masmoudi (Tunisia) to Osolnik (Yugoslavia) to Somavia (Chile) play in behalf of the NWIO.   Oteifi (Egypt) and Verghese (India), while generally supportive of Third World interests, were not doctrinaire. They expressed more objective views and occasionally questioned the Commission's activities in the relationship of Somavia to the Executive Secretary (Deleon). The alliance between this exiled Chilean radical and this Yugoslav socialist was close, confirmed by the fact that Fernando Reyes Matta (Somavia's assistant in the Institute for Study of Transnational Institutions) was hired by Deleon to write Section C of the Interim Report on "Socio-Economic, Socio-Political, and Socio-Cultural Effects of Communication."   Chairman MacBride's secretary confided that Somavia and Deleon were in frequent phone contact.

The slanting of the Commission became so clear that Elie Abel began giving serious consideration to resigning. He felt so alone that he wondered if it would not be wise to separate himself from the Commission in order to manifest his disagreement with the way things were proceeding and thus disassociate himself from the Final Report, which, he was certain, would represent a majority view definitely at odds with his own.

He did not rule out the possibility of resigning at the next meeting in New Delhi, but he was somewhat reassured by a decision of the Commission that the Final Report would provide for the inclusion of attributed dissents. He told Osolnik that if the nonaligned group in the Commission kept pushing so hard for the NWIO, it would drive him into a position where he would have to resign. Osolnik begged him not to and observed that the Interim Report was subject to criticism for not recognizing the pluralistic nature of the world, and the title of the Final

Report might well be changed to Communication Problems in a Pluralistic World (instead of "in Modern Society"). He said that perhaps there were some aspects of the NWIO that were a bit extreme and he conceded, for example, that the attacks on advertising were overdone. After all, he said, Yugoslavia is increasingly using advertising.

Abel also had a frank talk with Deleon. He documented his assertion that the Interim Report was "repetitious, redundant, rhetorical, and tendentious" by citing various paragraphs and phrases. He then said bluntly that he was sick and tired of UNESCO's predilection for imposing controls on the media, which lead inevitably to state control, and that this continued thrust was pushing him into a corner that gave him only two alternatives: resign or initiate an explosive dissent with worldwide coverage. Why, when there were so many areas of commonality, did the Commission devote so much time to ideological arguments that get in the way of consensus?

Deleon's response was to charge Abel with dereliction. "You should speak up more and more forcibly. You are the only voice the West has," he said--an interesting acknowledgement of the biased selection of the Commission members.

Abel was also unhappy at the Chairman's seemingly perverse insistence that this was a very successful meeting and that, despite some differences, it would be possible to resolve them all. Abel was certain that there were some basic differences that were irreconcilable; certainly there were some principles on which he would not compromise. Abel now agreed that he should prepare some aggressive interventions of his own, rather than counter-punching or correcting misstatements. Abel was pretty much alone. Beuve-Mery (France) was old and frail and spoke only when the chairman coaxed him; Zimmerman (Canada) was a nice lady but no debater, and she limited her comments to broadcasting and women in the media; Pronk (Netherlands) was a leftist politician and economist; Oteifi (Egypt) and Lubis (Indonesia) generally followed the Third World line; and only Nagai (Japan) spoke up for press freedom in the Western sense of the phrase. At this meeting the two Africans, Ekonzo and Omu were absent, but when they were present, they took a hard anti-Western line.

The friction between Chairman MacBride and Secretary Deleon, evident from the first meeting, had, if anything, increased. MacBride had recently written two letters to Deleon in which he ordered that no member of the staff was to accept a speaking engagement or travel outside Paris on Commission business without his approval. Furthermore, Deleon was forbidden from commissioning any more papers without the Chairman's consent. MacBride's secretary felt sure that certain information coming to the Commission is being held back from the Chairman or, at the least, intentionally delayed, such as invitations to conferences or for speaking engagements.

At Dubrovnik, the chairman introduced Mary Holland, a noted Irish journalist who, he said, would be acting as an editor for the Final Report to insure a uniform writing style and standard. Her appointment, however, was strongly resisted by Deleon, who delayed processing her papers and made it obvious to her that she was not welcome. The hostility was so manifest that it appeared that Ms. Holland would likely refuse the assignment.

The USSR, as represented by Commissioner Zamiatin, had consistently assumed a negative posture toward the New World Information Order. Zamiatin had frequently ridiculed the idea as ill-defined and "mere sloganizing." He was not present at Dubrovnik but sent Sergei Losev, the deputy director general of TASS, to sit in for him. Although Commission regulations prohibited substitutions, Losev was allowed to sit at the table as an observer and on two occasions, by consent of the commissioners, allowed to speak.

It is significant that, following a long intervention by Masmoudi regarding the Commission's mandate to focus on the NWIO, Losev spoke at length on the Draft Declaration on the Media and how it alone should serve as guidance for formulating the Final Report. He barely mentioned the NWIO and then only in the exact words of the Declaration, i.e., the Soviet Union is "conscious of the aspirations of the developing countries for a new, more just and effective new world information and communications order."

The other intervention that disproved the contention that the NWIO had universal acceptance came from Elie Abel. It was provoked by Somavia's assertion that, as the result of the development of a consensus draft at Nairobi, there was a new spirit of cooperation (in support of Third World communication concerns) in which even the United States joined. To document this claim he read a portion of Ambassador Reinhardt's plenary speech at the Nairobi UNESCO conference about U.S. reaction to the Interim Report--but only the pro part. He stopped short of the sentence indicating that there were parts he disapproved. Accordingly, Abel said he felt obliged to correct a misimpression. He then read the next sentence of Reinhardt's address and added a section from Dalley's speech at the United Nations General Assembly in which he said that there were alarming aspects of the NWIO concept that were totally unacceptable.

Two major thrusts opposed to U.S. interests were developing in the Commission. The first was to recommend an international code of ethics for journalists. This was being pushed by Masmoudi as a part of his NWIO concept calling for an "international deontology"--a kind of moral obligation governing information and communication. This proclamation of ethical principles would be accompanied by accountability of those in control of information along with penalties for violations of these principles. Chairman MacBride was in favor of an international code for journalists and he appointed Masmoudi, Somavia, and himself to develop a recommendation in this respect for the upcoming New Delhi meeting.

The second major thrust was toward the socialization of communications. This was done under the rubric of "Democratization," but is in keeping with the doctrine that true Socialism is the extension of the democratic idea beyond the political sphere of life into the economic, i.e., into the work place to overcome the "tyranny of capital." This effort was being rationalized under the guise of greater public participation in the communication process, but the debate frequently veered into involvement in the ownership and the management of the instruments of communication. This pressure came most strongly from Somavia, who ran an institute devoted to revealing the sins of transnational corporations, but it was also in keeping with the Masmoudi-Osolnik-Deleon line.

Chapter 8

MEETING V, NEW DELHI, MARCH 25-30, 1979

This meeting was much less politicized than the previous one in Dubrovnik; the rhetoric was more restrained, the quality of debate higher, and a start was made at focusing on specific issues. This change was due to two factors: a different mix in the personnel and the impact of the Elie Abel paper distributed at the start of the meeting.

On the question of codes for protection of journalists and journalistic ethics, the West picked up more support than anticipated. The feud between the chairman and the executive secretary continued, despite the Director-General's intervention, and was exacerbated by the Chairman's hiring of an outside writer to edit the Final Report. Soviet participants continued to "get in bed" with the United States on some issues.

NEW MIX OF PARTICIPANTS

Absent from this meeting was Somavia (Chile), who had been wont to lecture the Commission on the need for democratization (socialization) of the media.

Absent also was Beuve-Mery (France), ill in Paris, who was represented by Jean D'Arcy, former director of the French Television System and former head of the UN Office of Radio-Television. Since Beuve-Mery virtually never spoke, D'Arcy's insights into communication issues--satellites, WARC, UN/UNESCO media matters, and the like--provided a substantial plus. Zamiatin (USSR) did not appear for the second time in succession; he was represented by Professor Yassen Zassoursky, Dean of the Faculty of Journalism at Moscow University. His presence was another moderating factor: whereas Zamiatin was apt to indulge in ideological cant and dogmatic assertions of traditional Soviet positions, Zassoursky, who was a scholar and a media communications specialist, was much more analytical in his approach and made a number of reasonable comments and suggestions. Nagai, the Japanese journalist and a staunch U.S. ally, was ill in Tokyo but Lubis (Indonesia), who had not attended the Dubrovnik meeting, was present and gave support to the Western views. Masmoudi (Tunisia), while repeating the same material from his NWIO paper, nonetheless was more restrained than previously.

The result of this altered makeup of the Commission at New Delhi was to produce a much more relaxed atmosphere and general spirit of reasonableness.

THE ELIE ABEL PAPER

Abel's paper, called "Communications for an Interdependent, Pluralistic World," summarized the general views of the Western media and government spokesmen. It dwelt on the desirability of diverse information sources and a multidirectional world system, destroyed the "myth of passivity" (populations of nonaligned countries were not "passive recipients" of unwanted foreign information because their governments control the news they receive), discussed the nature of news, argued against the adoption of a single standard for control of communication, and listed the general areas in which he felt the Commission could find agreement as well as those that could not be solved by consensus.

The distribution and subsequent discussion of this paper had a primarily salutary effect on the Commission's deliberations. It was generally praised by the commissioners, particularly for pointing up for the first time the likely areas of agreement and disagreement. Criticisms were made of certain details, but overall, the paper was well received and Abel was quite "bucked up" by its reception.

Above all, Abel's paper served to start crystallizing points of view. Previously, the debate has been rather general, without any sides being taken. Then, all of a sudden, a commissioner from the West came forth with a straightforward presentation of his personal views and put them on the record. Until then, the only comment had been the views of the nonaligned, as reflected in papers by Masmoudi and Osolnik. Now the Western view point was out in the open in black and white and became a basic Commission document.

THE MACBRIDE - DELEON FEUD

The tense relationship between the Chairman and head of the Commission's Secretariat did not diminish. MacBride was still furious at the way Deleon sabotaged his attempt to bring Mary Holland (the writer) on board to edit the Final Report. When Holland withdrew in the face of Deleon's hostility, MacBride chose Mervyn Jones, a British novelist and journalist, to be the editor. Deleon tried to oppose this move as well, but it appeared that Jones was prepared to stick it out and contend with the Secretariat's opposition to hiring an outside writer.

Because of the feud, the Director-General (M'Bow) dispatched the "Smiling Indonesian," Makaminan Makagiansar (Director-General for Communications and Culture) to New Delhi to try and smooth tempers; he failed. Among other things, he tried to get MacBride to agree that Jones should report to Deleon. No deal!

Apparently MacBride, though furious with Deleon's highhanded methods and independent behavior, decided that it was too late in the day to replace him, so he tried to work out some sort of *modus operandi* that would get the Commission's work done within the present staff organizations.

M'Bow's problems in trying to heal the breach were complicated by the apprehension that if pushed too far, the distinguished chairman might resign, thereby creating an international brouhaha.

THE PROTECTION OF JOURNALISTS

On this issue, Abel picked up some support within the Commission, but there were storm signals ahead.

MacBride told the Commission about two meetings he had convened recently in Paris regarding protection of journalists. The first was a meeting with representatives from the International Organization of Jurists. He followed this up with a meeting of representatives from several media organizations to whom he presented a paper that the jurists had formulated. He now proposed holding a much larger meeting in Paris on May 2 and 3, to which a group of media associations, unions, and other interested parties were to be invited. The recommendations of this meeting would then be submitted to the Commission, which would thus be confronted by a proposal that presumably had the backing of the majority of professional media organizations in the world.

MacBride seemed to have been playing his own little game here. He organized these meetings without the sanction (or even the knowledge) of the Commission and financed them outside of the Commission's budget, apparently with funds furnished by M'Bow.

The paper shown the media people at the first meeting was not circulated by MacBride, but he did give it to the U.S. State Department, and copies were being bootlegged among U.S. media groups. And they didn't like it. It appeared to be an attempt to gain acceptance for an international code of journalistic ethics by tendering a code for the protection of journalists. But this trade-off would be at the expense of such undesirable conditions as the licensing of journalists and the acceptance of a set of responsibilities the West had labored to excise from the Draft Declaration on Use of the Media.

When MacBride introduced this topic at the meeting of the Commission at New Delhi, Abel spoke out strongly against the need for protection of journalists, especially if tied to an international code of ethics. Lubis, the Indonesian journalist, said he had suffered harassment (he was jailed for twelve years by Sukarno), yet he agreed with Abel that journalists should not be entitled to any more rights than those of other citizens. Zimmerman (Canada) agreed. Zassoursky (USSR) said he did, too, saying "If I were a journalist in a foreign country I wouldn't want to be protected, because that would mean I would be protected by government."

Furthermore, he said, Zamiatin had instructed him specifically to oppose any code of protection of journalists. Oteifi (Egypt) joined in, saying all that was needed was to accord a journalist in a foreign country the same rights accorded any citizen of that country.

These views, plus the assurance given privately by Osolnik (Yugoslavia) that he saw no possibility of there ever being an international code of journalistic ethics, gave Abel the feeling that "maybe this international code business may not turn out to be a problem in the Commission after all."

SOME SOVIET VIEWS

In addition to the expression of opposition to a code of protection of journalists, Zassoursky (representing Zamiatin) made some other comments inside and outside the Commission that were supportive of Abel's views. In his critique of Abel's paper, he agreed that Abel was correct in asserting the pluralistic nature of the world and, therefore, there should not be any one model of communications.

In a breakfast meeting the next day (which Zassoursky had sought with Abel), he enlarged on this point saying, "We don't want UNESCO saying go this way or that way--it's not their business." Moreover, he continued, since we recognize these differences among us we must not create a situation that requires dissenting opinions "by trying to force extreme positions." When Abel said he thought they should try for consensus but was not sure how far one could push the developing countries, Zassoursky expressed his disdain in the best Zamiatin manner, responding "Oh, those people are foolish!"

ROUNDTABLE DISCUSSIONS

Roundtable discussions were held during the meeting on two topics: "Communication and Development" and "Impact of Future Technological

Developments." In addition to the commissioners, the participants included Indian officials, academics, and journalists. An American technologist from the FCC, A. M. Rutkowski, also participated "as a consultant to UNESCO."

In the technology discussion, Rutkowski argued that the emerging communication systems would be so capacious and flexible that technology would cease to be a dominant limiting factor in man's ability to access and exchange information and thus, "concerns represented in the demands for an NWIO will largely be satisfied by the development of global communication systems which allow ready access by all peoples and nations."

The Soviet participant, M. I. Krivocheev, of the Moscow TV-Radio Research Institute, stressed the importance of television as a mass medium and the need for its tight control by the state. Yash Pal, from the Indian Space Application Center, deplored the congestion in the geostationary orbit and the likelihood that developments would tend to increase the gap in communication infrastructures between developed and developing countries.

Much of the discussion concerned "appropriate technology" with Less Developed Countries (LDC) spokesmen indicating that in some instances equipment and systems must be designed to comply with LDC conditions in mind; they objected to equipment that smacked of "consumerism."

In the development roundtable, the Indian participants took a generally Third World/partisan view. D. R. Mankekar from the Ministry of Information and Broadcasting insisted on the inevitability and desirability of a New World Information Order (NWIO) and a New International Economic Order (NIEO). He also described his plan for a World Press Institute. Masmoudi, predictably, reiterated support for the NWIO as well as his conviction that it ought to be the sole subject of the MacBride Commission's work.

Abel, also predictably, expressed his opposition to the institute idea and the notion that the circulation of information and ideas must be brought under control by proclaiming a new world order. Zassoursky continually emphasized the "effect of the mass media" and the need for state involvement and control, whereas Jean D'Arcy stressed the need to focus on "infrastructures."

Other Indian participants repeated points from papers they had prepared on Indian national policy on communication in support of development.

PRONK'S PERSPECTIVE

Johannes Pronk (Netherlands) revealed himself at New Delhi as a full-fledged socialist. This was reflected in his paper,[1] (prepared at chairman MacBride's request) comparing the New World Information Order to the New International Economic Order, in his oral presentation of the paper, and in his comments about the roundtable discussion on the new technology. Running throughout was an attack upon the market place (whose operation needed to be redirected for the public good) and a repeated identification of transnational corporations as malevolent manipulators.

---

[1]"Relation Between the New International Information Order and the New International Economic Order," No. 35 in the Mauve Series (see Appendix I).

Chapter 9

MEETING VI, ACAPULCO, MEXICO, JUNE 4-8, 1979

FIRST SESSION (JUNE 4)

Two commissioners were represented by substitutes: Toskio Harikawa for Nagai (ill in Tokyo) and Sergei Losev for Zamiatin (USSR). Losev had just been named Director General of TASS.

The initial session was devoted to comments on the agenda and on the predraft of Part I of the Final Report. Osolnik (Yugoslavia) proposed that the item on Protection of Journalists should be discussed in connection with an international code of ethics, because the two were closely linked. The Chairman disagreed and ruled that they would be discussed as separate topics.

Leading off the discussion of Part I, Somavia (Chile) said there was not sufficient analysis that links past communication developments to present problems such as colonialism, the role of religion, and communication as an instrument of liberation and change. The text was a glorification of technology whereas it should have been considered in the context of its control for social purposes. "A future shaped by technology may not be what we want."

Lubis (Indonesia) said the historical approach was useful to point out how communications had been part of colonialism but that approach had also been important in nationalistic movements to throw off the yoke of colonialism.

Zimmerman (Canada) declared that it was important to consider the flow of information (and barriers to its flow domestically), before turning to its international aspects. No attention had been given to language, which of course was a major factor in communications at all levels. Masmoudi (Tunisia) said that in Part I "our point of view (nonaligned) was largely expressed." Nevertheless, he had general criticisms about length, accuracy of certain dates, and the need for greater elaboration of some points.

Osolnik suggested that too much importance was being accorded the new technology. The draft ignored the role of economics, which was the overall driving force in communication development in the world.

SECOND SESSION (JUNE 5)

Losev said the text did not correspond fully to the Soviet point of view, but it was impossible to reflect all views of the sixteen commissioners. He suggested that greater attention should be given to the role of communication in world policy. Further, there was not enough about advertising. He agreed with "Comrade" Osolnik's remarks about the primary role of economic forces in communication development and quoted from "an American," Herbert Schiller, on freedom of the press and information. He noted that pluralism is a relative term and has two sides; it can provide false information as well as truth. Oteifi (Egypt) and Lubis (Indonesia) both objected to the difficulty of understanding much of the language, and Verghese (India) said it was more obtuse than need be. Abel agreed that the language was inappropriate and that its writers appeared unable to make up their minds as to the target audience. The language lacked grace and style. The text contained a good many sweeping and unsubstantiated statements and unattributed quotations, much pseudo-scientific language, and paragraphs that were not only inelegant but also badly expressed. (He pointed out numerous examples.) Verghese was not persuaded that technology was overemphasized but found that there was insufficient attention to the role in communications' evolution of religion, alphabets and numbers, books, education, language, and understanding. Somavia (Chile) maintained that greater emphasis should be placed upon the organization of political action. One should not confuse freedom of the press with freedom of expression, he said. Freedom of the press was for those who have the access to the press; it does not mean that individuals necessarily have access to the means of publication. Moreover, he thought the report was too soft on colonialism and transnational corporations.

As to the language, Somavia argued it should be simple but still presume an understanding of certain technical knowledge. After all, it was to be produced in the context of the UN system. MacBride agreed that the Final Report should be written for an informed public but certainly not in the UN/UNESCO gobbledygook. Although the Interim Report was deliberately provocative, the Final Report should be more solid.

At this point MacBride introduced Mervyn Jones, a professional British writer retained to do the final editing. Jones made a number of critical comments on the predraft, including the observation that lack of precision in writing usually derived from lack of clear thinking.

Abel then raised the question of Mr. Jones' status, noting that a partial rewrite he had done on the predraft had been rejected by the Secretariat. Somavia was of the opinion that the fact that the basic text was to be in English did not justify inserting Mr. Jones into the situation. MacBride contended that Jones was necessary to insure grace and style in the writing. He was tired of defending the writing in the Interim Report, and he wanted a competent editor for the Final Report.

In the afternoon session, Masmoudi (Tunisia) expressed the view that the impact of colonialism was not sufficiently stressed and that mention should be made of the power of communications and how they must be therefore regulated and codified.

Oteifi (Egypt) mentioned a number of points that were neglected in the predraft, including the difference between ownership and management, the disparities between developing countries themselves as well as between developed and developing countries, the use of media for propaganda purposes, and the question of whether right of reply applies to both print and broadcasting media.

A discussion ensued of provisions for the right of reply and how universal they were. Masmoudi asserted that there were such provisions in twelve countries and it was time to update the Universal Declaration of the Right of Rectification, adopted in 1952, which was signed by twelve countries and ratified, he said, by ten (including France, Cuba, and Yugoslavia).

Turning to part II, Verghese (India) mentioned a number of missing elements such as literacy, the role of women, postal services, and the military. Somavia (Chile) added that data on the location of data banks and computers, distribution of investment in communications, research and development in the field, and the use of media for intelligence purposes was lacking. Abel cautioned that care should be taken to ensure that all the data in the Final Report was up to date at publication time.

Abel revealed that the growth of media conglomerates in the United States was more the result of tax policy than of the alleged drive for power, citing as an example that family newspapers are being sold to corporations to avoid inheritance taxes that would force the papers out of business.

Losev (USSR) objected to the fact that most of the information in Part II concerned developed countries (data on Cuba was missing) and it was therefore not a balanced report. Reducing media imbalance was the most important task of the Commission he said. UNESCO had an important role in helping developing countries improve their communications and the Commission should work in close cooperation with the Secretariat in order to fulfill its mandate.

THIRD SESSION (JUNE 6)

Masmoudi (Tunisia) said he had already summarized for the Commission all of the main problems, so he had no need to repeat them. The role of international agencies, however, needed to be spelled out, to complement the activities of the developing countries in compliance with the decisions of the UNESCO 20th General Conference. The Commission should propose a world mechanism to insure the coordination of the activities of international agencies with the development activities of the Third World he continued, and this mechanism should be entrusted to UNESCO.

Chairman MacBride reminded everyone that there are already four enterprises involved in this sort of activity: UNESCO, ITU, the UN Information Committee of 41, and the Washington consulting conference, which was designed to deal with this matter. Abel observed that these various UN agencies did not welcome interference from outside organizations. Proposing such a body would need to be done with recognition that each agency had its own leadership and purposes. Moreover, he was not sure if these agencies were necessarily the chief actors in these matters and, thus, such a mechanism as Masmoudi proposed might not be able to come to grips with them.

Pronk (Netherlands), absent the first two days, observed that the chief fault with part I was that it was too optimistic. It was based on Western societies and did not provide sufficient analysis of the relation of communications to economic bases. He said these six questions should be raised in Part III:

1. How can we guarantee that communications technological development will benefit the people?
2. Are we not too optimistic about technology?
3. What is the function of freedom of communications?
4. How can we guarantee that communication becomes a two-way process?
5. What is the relation between the New World Information Order and the New International Economic Order?
6. What are the possibilities of changing the imbalances in access to communications?

Losev (USSR) expressed the view that the most important consideration was the role of the media in combatting apartheid, racialism, and war propaganda. This was related to developing media balance because it relates to world peace and security. If this role of the media was emphasized, all the other problems would be solved. Garcia Marquez (Colombia) noted that Pronk's (Netherlands) six points could only be considered within a general political context asking what the Commission's position was on these matters? Abel expressed the fear that the Commission would loose sight of problems that concern journalists, citing the example of the gap between urban and rural areas, worldwide such as the lack of rural newspapers, the lack of interest by urban journalists in rural affairs, and the like. He specified radio as the cheapest way of reaching out to rural populations, but added that there are other techniques that should be explored. There was not much sense in mobilizing nations' communications with each other when large segments of the population within those countries can't be reached, he said.

Lubis (Indonesia) agreed with Abel, and Zimmerman went on to stress the importance in national development of both radio and television as the only assured communications media for much of the population of developing countries. Nevertheless, Losev (USSR) stressed the importance of defining the lines along which assistance should be provided. He cited a number of declarations of nonaligned meetings that claimed that the cause of imbalances was colonialism and the Commission's purpose should be to liberate the developing countries from such dependence. Somavia (Chile) agreed that there must be a recognition of guidelines that already exist, "but we are proceeding without knowing what we believe collectively. Since up until now our individual views are not attacked, we assume there is assent and that our views will be incorporated in the Final Draft. But this is not necessarily so."

He then listed a number of questions and asked the Commission to respond "so we can decide on what we agree."

Chairman MacBride objected, saying that at this time they were attempting to ascertain all views and needed to discuss all topics before determining their collective opinion. "We must proceed topic by topic and, where we can, suggest a way to deal with a problem," he said. "I will not try to force anyone to a commitment on any issue at this stage." Pronk and Somavia argued the matter with the chairman and then Abel observed that he doubted that they were so much in the dark about their respective views. He for one was ready to stand up and be counted at any time, but he would be bound by the decision of the Chairman as to when that should occur.

Later in the afternoon, the Commission attended a roundtable organized by Mexican authorities on "Culture and Communication." In general, the Mexican participants supported the thesis with which Flores Olea, the Mexican ambassador to UNESCO, opened the meeting: culture and communication are irreconcilably opposed. They joined in attacking mass media for standardization of thought, threats to cultural identity, propagation of impersonalized and conformist life styles and so on, "so as to militate against man's cultural and creative capabilities." For the most part, participants were literary, liberal types selected by Garcia Marquez (Colombia). The only panelist to defend mass media and capitalistic enterprise was Tony Ornes, substituting for his father, German Ornes, president of the Inter American Press Association (IAPA).

FOURTH SESSION (JUNE 8)

The Chairman began by announcing that the discussion of Protection of Journalists would be postponed until the next meeting, because he planned to prepare a comprehensive paper on the subject. Somavia (Chile) urged, however, that Osolnik (Yugoslavia) be permitted to present the paper he had ready on this topic.

Osolnik, giving an oral digest of an eighteen-page document, said there were two main views, namely, that (1) freedom of journalists must not be limited by rules of behavior of any kind and (2) freedom of information must be linked to the responsibility of journalists for the consequences of their activities with respect to individuals and society. He then went on to review the discussion of this topic as it had been previously addressed in the Stockholm seminar, the Interim Report, the Draft Declaration on the Media, and the May seminar in Paris of representatives of media organizations.

Osolnik expressed the hope that, when the Commission's Final Report was read by journalists, they would not feel they have been betrayed and that the proposals will be seen by them not as restrictions, but as elements of freedom designed for their protection.

Losev (USSR), referring to Pronk's (Netherlands) paper on NWIO and NIEO, said that Pronk's notion of analyzing the former as a "subsystem" of the latter seemed a reasonable approach. So far, he observed, progress on NIEO is not encouraging. Regarding Masmoudi's proposal for an Institute for Research, Losev said he doubted if it is needed since it would appear to duplicate activities already under way. Masmoudi replied that the plans for an Institute for Research were not frozen, but the objective was to respond to the need to mobilize resources for establishing the

NWIO. Losev conceded that an International Press Institute (as proposed by the nonaligned countries) might be useful.

Ekonzo (Zaire) asserted that protection of journalists, especially in Africa, was needed when they told the truth. When they do so they are often put in jail, so journalists don't always have the freedom to say what they would like. Newspapers and radio stations go along with the regime for fear of being eliminated. It is hard to find good people for journalism, he said, because they prefer to go into vocations where they don't get into conflict with the government. The work of the Commission will be meaningless unless account is taken of the role of national legislatures and unless governments change their attitudes toward the journalistic profession.

Abel thanked Ekonzo for drawing attention to this situation and pointed out that several of the commissioners had themselves been sent to prison for writing criticisms of a regime. His dilemma, he said, was proposing concrete measures for dealing with the problem. He doubted whether creating a special category of human beings (journalists) was the way to go about it. "I see journalists' vulnerability reflected in that of all citizens," he continued, "but imprisonment of journalists is more conspicuous and we don't hear about the other citizens. I feel grateful to Ekonzo for stressing that journalists are often punished for telling the truth rather than for making a mistake."

Garcia Marquez (Colombia) pointed out coincidences between Ekonzo's description of press treatment and treatment of the press in his own country. In his view, one could no longer make a career of journalism in Colombia (nor in much of Latin America) so there was constant movement out of the profession. It is a matter of complying (and not going to jail) or risking starvation. He agreed with Abel that journalists should not be considered privileged human beings, and he urged the Commission to denounce the conditions in which journalists work. Lubis (Indonesia) echoed Ekonzo, Abel, and Marquez. "In many countries, if a journalist really practiced the ethics of his profession, he would risk jail or greater danger," he said. Somavia (Chile) expressed the view that the question of protection of journalists should be related to the rights and responsibilities of the enterprise, not of the individual editor or reporter, but of the entrepreneur. What people fear is government or commercial enterprises, he said.

Jean D'Arcy (France) dropped a bomb into the final session by proposing that the Commission take the position with WARC '79, opposing the use of shortwave frequencies for international broadcasting. He said such transmissions constitute a continuing aggravation in international affairs and were a constant source of discord among nations. There was a moment of stunned silence, and then MacBride suggested that this proposal be brought up at the next meeting. (It never was.)

Chapter 10

MEETING VII
PARIS, SEPTEMBER 9-14, 1979

FIRST SESSION (SEPTEMBER 10)

The opening session of this meeting was devoted largely to a procedural debate arising from the fact that the Commission was confronted by two drafts of Parts I and II of the Final Report: a version prepared by the Commission's Secretariat and a rewrite of the Secretariat's draft prepared by Mervyn Jones, the journalist employed by the chairman to serve as editor of the Final Report. The Jones draft, the chairman announced, would be the basis for discussion.

Osolnik (Yugoslavia) joined by Masmoudi (Tunisia) and Somavia (Chile), questioned the advisability of having an outsider (Jones) prepare the final draft. Somavia proposed that the Secretariat's draft of Parts I and II (168 pages) be used as the basis for discussion, with Jones' text (68 pages) used for whatever benefit it could provide. Oteifi (Egypt) reminded everyone that at New Delhi the employment of Mr. Jones as an editor had been approved by the Commission, authorizing him to redraft the Secretariat's original draft, which had come in for strong criticism. "The two versions are not incompatible; if some ideas are omitted in the Jones version, we can stir them in," Oteifi maintained.

Omu (Nigeria) expressed the view that Mr. Jones' draft did not "reflect the perspective of the Commission."

Losev (USSR) agreed that important elements had been dropped from the Jones' version, "which has been put into better English with a translation of Western mentality." Verghese (India) suggested that, because there had been insufficient time to read the two versions of Parts I and II, the Commission should proceed immediately to look at the drafts of Parts III, IV, and V, then go back to I and II later in the week after Jones and the Secretariat had collaborated in producing a single "married" draft of their separate versions.

128

Chairman MacBride pointed out that he had hoped from the beginning that Jones and the Secretariat could collaborate, but Mr. Deleon did not wish to proceed in that way.

Abel expressed concern that the Commission had been meeting for two years and had yet to agree on a single paragraph. "We are now in September and time is running out. Let's at least finish up on Parts I and II," he urged.

Losev seconded Somavia's suggestion that the Secretariat's version should be the basis for discussion.

The Commission adjourned to devote the afternoon to individual reading of the drafts.

SECOND SESSION (SEPTEMBER 11)

The entire day was devoted to an examination of the separate drafts of Parts I and II. Osolnik (Yugoslavia) led off with a long analysis of sections of the Secretariat's report that he said were not reflected in the Jones rewrite.

Lubis (Indonesia) asserted that the Jones text was "Eurocentric," drawing its illustrations from English or European Societies and claiming that English as the *lingua franca* of the world. It also failed to show that the language aspect of colonialism had slowed African development.

Ekonzo (Zaire) observed that the Jones draft, though elegant in style, was lacking in important respects. For example, it treated precolonial Africa as though it had no communication, whereas there were a variety of nonverbal and traditional forms in use.

Oteifi (Egypt) criticized both the Secretariat's draft (for failing to cite sources and statistics) and the Jones version (for nondescriptive titles).

Omu (Nigeria) made suggestions for various segments of the two drafts that should be omitted or modified; he echoed the Ekonzo criticism of illustrations solely from English history, whereas this was supposed to be an international document.

Somavia (Chile) suggested that no effort be made now to finalize the Introduction, since it was impossible to determine all that should be included until the Commission has discussed parts III, IV, and V. He then commented on specific paragraphs, observing that: (1) communications began as an ideological process via papers of independence and liberation, with the commercial process later imposed on top of this historical process; (2) communication structures follow the flag of colonial powers; (3) the tone of the drafts still suggested a belief in technological determinism; and

(4) greater stress should be placed on the link between advertising and the present communications structure.

Masmoudi (Tunisia) said the Jones draft did not seem to reflect what had been decided at previous meetings; on the other hand, the Secretariat's version had an antiprofessional bias. In some cases, it drew conclusions without building the case, noting for example that radio and TV did not necessarily "follow in the steps of the press." The text failed to give attention to the entertainment aspects of broadcasting, he said. This was the primary demand of many people and yet it was treated as something too frivolous to mention. Moreover, the role of creative people--writers, TV producers, film-makers--was slighted.

Abel pointed out that there is confusion over terms in both drafts. It might be well to define "communication" as a "process" whereas "information" is "content." He agreed with Zimmerman (Canada) that entertainment is what sells radio and TV sets and the Commission must not be too snobbish toward it. He urged that all statistics be completely validated and suggested (as one way of decreasing the dependency of developing countries upon imported programming) that they simply reduce the length of their schedules and thus offer a higher proportion of local programs.

Abel also thought that the indictment of advertising was too sweeping. Certain forms of advertising provide information that people want and need. In times of newspaper strikes, what many American readers miss the most are the advertisements. He also pointed out that a plurality of sources allows for checking one against another to determine accuracy and that there was a need to stress imbalances between urban and rural areas. Abel also believed that the Jones draft was written in a cool style, whereas the style of the Secretariat was a bit emotive.

Verghese (India) drew attention to several omissions in both papers. He noted that: (1) not enough attention was paid to freedom of speech, which preceded freedom of the press; (2) first attacks were on the presses themselves, which may have implications for new technology; and (3) in discussing languages, there was not enough attention to script and languages without a keyboard adapted for typewriter or computer. He added that (4) the role of religion and education in communication needed more elaboration; (5) advertising had both a positive and negative role (certainly social advertising) and as a means of supporting media was important to developing countries; (6) remote sensing (by satellite) fears were exaggerated and this development should not be inhibited by fears because it had enormous potential for developing countries; and (7) communication imbalances at the national level should be stressed. Verghese also proposed that the Final Report include a glossary, to which all agreed.

Garcia Marquez (Colombia) thought the Secretariat's draft was more complete and should be used as the basis for the Final Report, but because this could be unfair to Mr. Jones, the Commission should spell out his role.

Losev (USSR) was of the opinion that all these complex issues, in the last analysis, were political problems. Remote-sensing, for example, concerns national sovereignty. Countries are concerned about what is done with information picked up by foreign aircraft or satellites like the U.S. plane over South Africa that gave information about Praetoria, so countries may have to take steps to prevent remote-sensing satellites from passing over their borders. He then listed a number of omissions in the Jones draft: the ignoring of socialist countries in certain paragraphs; insufficient mention of the role of colonialism in creating imbalances; and not enough explanation of the New World Information Order. He observed that the size of a newspaper does not represent its value, citing Western papers that he claimed were stuffed with pornographic pictures and advertising.

Somavia (Chile) agreed that there is an information component to advertising, but often it goes beyond that to transform cultural style and transfer cultural models. He agreed that advertising was used as a mechanism for supporting media but asked why this had to be. He argued, "We should note that that is the way it is, but maybe we should note also that it should play a less important role." Diversity should be used, he added, as a means of checking truth, but one must distinguish between diversity of *sources* and diversity of *outlets*.

Abel pointed out that only a paper that has a large advertising revenue can afford to be truly independent of government or other pressures. He related the experience of the magazine *PM*, which tried to make a go of it without advertising; after plowing in millions of dollars, it folded.

Nagai (Japan) said his paper (*Asahi Shimbun*) was dependent for fifty percent of its support from advertising, fifty percent from subscribers. The paper has a department that checks on the validity of advertising claims before they are accepted, and there is constant consultation between editorial and business sections; otherwise the paper could not preserve its independence.

Masmoudi (Tunisia) conceded that newspapers need advertising in order to survive, but their independence could be threatened by pressures from advertisers. He recited a series of charges against advertising:

promoting use of alcohol and cigarettes; stimulating consumption at the expense of savings; and so on. "Advertising can be positive and negative and we should encourage only its positive aspects. We might use advertising to discourage consumption," he concluded.

Beuve-Mery (France) said that the Secretariat draft seemed to be almost a manifesto. The use of democratization was used in a slogan-like manner, which gave the text a certain skew. He added that he saw no need for a glossary if one used terms that could be understood.

Abel observed that the glossary should be limited to technical terms, and the text should use language precisely, which argued for having it pass through the hands of a competent writer.

THIRD SESSION (SEPTEMBER 12)

Osolnik (Yugoslavia) again led off with proposals for a number of structural changes that involved rearranging certain paragraphs and sections; this provoked an extended discussion on the distinction between transnational corporations, multinational corporations, and international corporations.

Somavia lectured at length on the topic, and it was finally decided that the UN definitions could be used.

Verghese (India) suggested that Part II should make mention of electronic translators, the increase of vertical integration of media ownership, the fact that the new technology has not replaced but carried the old traditional communication techniques with it (folk music on records and tapes, drama on TV, and the like), the growing problem of paper shortage, and the role of the mass media in fostering national cohesion. He suggested the inclusion of a graphic showing the present table of allocations for the electronic spectrum and, if available, the one to emerge from WARC.

There was general agreement that the problem of paper shortage was an important one. Beuve-Mery described the experiment in France of recycling newsprint and Abel mentioned the experiment being carried on in the United States by the American Newspaper Publishers Association to make newsprint from kenaf, a plant that thrives in many developing countries.

Verghese and Lubis (Indonesia) reiterated their concern that the Final Report did not stress the need to correct the imbalances on communication at the national level. Of the many internal imbalances, they cited ethnic majorities and minorities, urban elite and rural ignorant and others.

Garcia Marquez (Colombia) suggested that perhaps the Commission should explore the role of telepathy in communications. He observed that the Final Report was filled with definitions and they could be better off using fewer, because criticism always starts with the demolition of definitions. Nagai pointed out that the Japanese are always lumped with the West and the developed nations; Japan is Asian and he maintained that although it was industrialized, it was not developed. Masmoudi challenged some statistics on the world's population of illiterates (835 million), which he thought was too low. He asked that the Final Report devote more attention to direct satellite broadcasting, international broadcasting, and the new disc recording of sound and image. Ekonzo (Zaire) argued that there were many more languages than those identified in the Final Report and suggested that illiteracy should be shown on a country-by-country basis. Oteifi (Egypt) pointed out that concentration was not only in the hands of capitalists, but also in the hands of governments, political parties, trade unions, and others. Also, he said, there was no mention of the closed shop as a factor affecting freedom of information. Abel pointed out a number of errors of fact regarding cable, U.S. public broadcasting, and so on, and objected to a phrase implying that the purpose of any country exporting news and programs was to stir up unrest in another country. He also deplored the repeated pejorative use of "alien" in connection with all imported media materials.

FOURTH SESSION (SEPTEMBER 13)

Losev (USSR) began by asserting that too little attention was paid to TV in the Jones draft, that it was too soft on the dangers of concentration and transnational corporations, and that the paragraph on the Chinese revolution should be excised.

Garcia Marquez (Colombia) pointed out confusion in the use of America, North America, Central America, and Latin America. The Commission should decide on the terminology for the regions and be consistent in the usage.

Masmoudi (Tunisia) added that the term "developing countries" was preferred to Third World. He then gave a brief report on the Non-Aligned Summit Meeting in Havana (September 3-8), from which he had just come.

Losev (USSR) reported briefly on the 46-nation International Seminar of Journalists and Mass Media Experts, held under Soviet auspices at Tashkent, September 3-8. He then gave a lengthy exposition of Soviet views. They supported the establishment of NWIO and democratization of information as an integral part of NIEO while still respecting national sovereignty, assistance to developing countries (which should be multilateral, relate to endogenous needs, and be channeled through UNESCO), and news cooperatives. Also, an international code of conduct for the media should be developed that would make the media responsible to the international community.

Masmoudi (Tunisia) observed that public financing of media is not a way of controlling but of adding variety. Public financing avoids monopolies and adds diversity, as has occurred with trade unions, political parties, and religious groups. Mostly this has been in broadcasting, but in Sweden and the Netherlands there are publicly-supported newspapers, he said.

Transnationals not only produce but control the distribution of news and also sell hardware, he added. The trend toward media conglomerates should be offset. Different channels do not necessarily provide different content if it all comes from the same source.

Zimmerman (Canada) began the discussion of Part III and observed that the tone was intemperate and marred by the constant use of "battle words."

Abel supported Zimmerman in deploring use of "battle words"; this was supposed to be "a responsible document by thoughtful adults," he said. "This treatment is unworthy. We have standards of probity to uphold. If we want to be taken seriously in the world, this report needs to be written in mature and sober language." The Chairman agreed that the work of the Commission would be weakened by intemperate language and "overemphasis."

Lubis (Indonesia) questioned the sentiment that there was "a marked improvement" in the conditions of international news exchange, but Abel responded that this was an impression many have. He cited the efforts of the *Washington Post* and the *Los Angeles Times* to improve their coverage of developing countries.

Somavia (Chile) observed that the exchange had not improved but the dialogue had.

Verghese (India) cited some omissions in the final draft, namely references to the fact that war and defense are the most important sources of communications development. He also mentioned intelligence operations, the impact of automation on unemployment, education that builds ethnocentricity in the young and the shortage of paper for books and magazines. He observed that a distinction should be made between laws that are justifiable and those that are not. He also noted that there are other forms of censorship, such as trade unions refusing to print something they don't like, banning books by seizure, and threatening to stop plays or films, all of which are forms of communication.

Oteifi (Egypt) commented that self-censorship is a serious problem. In Egypt there is no censorship because the editor is appointed by the government, "so this is a sham of freedom and democracy." He added that customs control (forbidding importation of foreign publications) is another form of censorship, and that one can have freedom of the press practiced *within* a country, but the citizens of that country have no access to *outside* materials.

Masmoudi identified several points in Part III that he felt unnecessarily placed the developing countries in an "accusatory posture." In talking with representatives of world press agencies there was the impression of improvement in coverage of Third World news, but he believed that it was not so much a matter of an improvement as merely an *effort* at improvement. Real progress has yet to be made.

Deleon, responding to a question from Abel, said it would be inappropriate to disclose who wrote what, because the Secretariat worked as a team and every page reflects the cooperative approach to composition of the four authors.

Osolnik (Yugoslavia) insisted that style was not so important as substance. Losev (USSR) said that Abel did not give enough examples to prove his points and suggested that what Abel objected to was the substance, because the tone only reflects the arguments.

Losev then went into a long denunciation of Western media: the free flow of information is a cover for perpetuating domination; the barriers created by capitalistic enterprises are more important than any others; the one-way situation makes free flow a mockery--it is a catch word for exploitation and cultural imperialism.

Osolnik (Yugoslavia) thought there should be a section on Public Opinion in the Final Report and a greater elaboration of the section of Democratization of Communications, including new opportunities afforded by new technology, the link between communications and labor, and the possibilities of workers having access not only to information and facilities but also to decision-making.

Zimmerman (Canada) complained again that there is no concern for women, which should be included in the section on Democratization.

Nagai (Japan) objected to a statement that TV can completely alter people's lives. Some studies show children have been stimulated to do more reading from watching TV. Abel agreed it was dangerous to generalize in this area. The data so far had not been very conclusive.

Regarding comments about failure of the West to report development news, Abel observed that the developing countries do the same thing themselves. "It's against human nature to expect other people to do better what we don't do ourselves," he said, adding that market demands are one reason for news selection, but ideological reasons are also a factor.

Nagai (Japan) cited a Wilbur Schramm research paper, which he claimed showed that sixteen Asian papers did not present much news of developing countries, but tended to carry sensational news. Nagai made several additional points: it's wrong to suggest that remote-sensing can be conducted only by satellites, because it can be done by airplanes and thus by small countries: new technologies allow new nations to make a quantum jump in technology; and education itself is being democratized by the media.

Masmoudi (Tunisia) supported Zimmerman regarding women in the democratization process and also argued that there should be a paragraph on television's influence regarding pornography and crime.

Somavia (Chile) asserted that one of the control issues in the free flow of information was the control of transnational enterprises and the disclosure of ownership. Access to news sources should not be limited to journalists, he said.

Abel commented that it is a mistake always to think of free flow in international terms rather than national. Enterprises that impede information flow can be dealt with via national laws.

Somavia observed that an obstacle to international free flow is the varied concepts of news values. He added that the section on interpersonal communication should include the freedom of assembly, freedom to organize unions, etc, and that building facilities won't necessarily eliminate imbalances.

Regarding cultural invasion, Somavia said, the question of why the developing countries buy foreign materials should be asked. The answer relates to dominance and dependence. He added that the private structure, which represents the same elitist political group promoting the same view of the world, produces products cheaply because they are made for the market. They are used because local alternatives would be expensive and difficult to produce.

Zimmerman (Canada) asked if he thought the Commission should advocate not giving people classical and artistic material.

Abel observed that the BBC uses a great deal of imported material and no one ever gets the notion that the BBC is not serving the masses. In the United States, public broadcasting has attracted a small but significant part of the general audience. Most of the people of the world, however, prefer entertainment.

Somavia (Chile) responded that there are no instruments for expressing peoples interests and tastes. What people are watching does not indicate what they want. Zimmerman contended that the CBC audience research did provide answers.

Abel objected to the implication that self-management could circumvent most of the constraints to participation. "Where is the evidence?" he asked.

Turning to Part III, Osolnik (Yugoslavia) said more should be made of ethics in journalism. Lubis (Indonesia) found the text to be overly defensive (regarding the attacks on the Interim Report). He questioned whether the Commission should support a UN world broadcasting service. Abel agreed with Lubis on both counts, but Masmoudi (Tunisia) thought the "defensive paragraphs" should stay. Verghese (India) said he thought a UN news service might be a good thing.

Masmoudi thought that there should be more on human rights, not for man as an individual but as a collective animal. Regarding public opinion, he believed that polls did not reflect reality and it is up to the newspapers to change the attitude of the public.

Verghese said the section on women in the media should be stronger. He also thought that a section was needed on public opinion at the national level because people were unaware of their rights. These, he stated, were fundamental, grass-roots matters.

Abel closed the day's discussion by reminding his colleagues that the Declaration on Use of the Media was finally adopted after changing the vocabulary until it was acceptable. He observed that we are slipping back if we impose obligations on the press. "In my country," he said, "the government can't tell the press to do anything, and I feel obliged to note this." Regarding the part of the text discussing the role of the press in inciting war, he said, "In my experience, war crises are not provoked by the press but by governments; they reflect what governments decide. So I think the treatment here is greatly exaggerated."

FIFTH SESSION (SEPTEMBER 14)

At this meeting Masmoudi had a number of suggestions about the text of the Final Report. He recommended that Part V should be devoted to a "summary of consensus"; a section of Part V should indicate views not shared by everybody or about which the Commission was not sufficiently informed, and that a final section should list issues that ought to be considered in the future. He also wanted the section on UNESCO to be expanded along with a Commission recommendation that *communications* now linked with *culture* should be made a separate bureau within UNESCO. Furthermore, while stressing the important work of UNESCO in relation to development, he was convinced that the Commission should underline UNESCO's difficulty in working with other international organizations who have a role in development, because of the lack of coordination among them.

Somavia (Chile) also had ideas about reorganizing the Final Report. He recommended that different sections be written to appeal to different audiences, for example, government officials, scientists and technicians, and the general public. This, he insisted, was the only logical way to organize such complex materials.

The Commission members then turned to an analysis of Part IV-Institutional Frameworks and Professional Parameters. The remainder of the meeting was devoted to comments on minor points in the text and to a discussion of the schedule for the final meeting.

The Commission did not get to Part V, "Conclusions and Suggestions." This was left as the first order of business for the next meeting.

Chapter 11

MEETING VIII, PARIS, NOVEMBER 19-30, 1979

This final meeting of the Commission was the most heated and disruptive of the all, marked by charges of manipulation, a walk-out, and threats of more walk-outs. The Western faction was defeated in its efforts to fend off a proposal to establish within UNESCO an International Center for Study and Planning of Information and Communication. Much of the disarray was caused by the fact that the Commission did not have a complete Final Report to consider, just a stack of five stapled bundles; hence, almost the entire meeting had to be focused on Part V, the Recommendations. The Commission approved only Part II and the other parts of the report were never reviewed in final form, including Part III, which was distributed at 6:45 P.M. The Commission adjourned *sine die* at 7:45 P.M.

THE MASMOUDI SNIT

Masmoudi (Tunisia), who insisted that the term "press councils" meant councils for "the coordination of the press," kept pushing for a long list of recommendations which he maintained had never been given proper attention by the Commission and had to be included in the Final Report. These included a law to regulate rights and responsibilities of the media, an international code of journalistic ethics, and compulsory regulation of advertising. When the Commission refused to accept his recommendations, he "picked up his marbles" and went home. He returned to the meeting the next day when the Secretariat assured him that these proposals would be tacked on as an adjunct to the Report. (These recommendations, which had never been approved by the Commission, were added to the Report as Part B, "Issues Requiring Further Study" (see pages 152-154). This was to cause great confusion, because people (especially Western critics) insisted on lumping this section with Part A as an integral piece of the Report.

DISPUTE OVER THE CENTER

On the eve of the final meeting, the Western group held a strategy meeting in the apartment of Jean D'Arcy, the French substitute for Beuve-Mery. The purpose of this caucus was to rally the Western forces to oppose the anticipated move by Masmoudi to vote the establishment of a UNESCO center that would organize national communication systems in developing countries, monitor media developments, and address communications in general.   Abel (U.S.), Zimmerman (Canada), Nagai (Japan), and Lubis (Indonesia) attended the session. All seemed in agreement when the meeting adjourned, but the next day when the Commission met, the coalition broke apart. Lubis was absent, Nagai was silent, and Zimmerman voted for the proposition, explaining privately that Canada doesn't want always to appear to be dominated by the United States. (However, in a footnote in the Final Report she wrote that while she agreed "that a coordinating body in the field of communication could serve a useful purpose," she could not "support this precise recommendation." Her reasons: the Commission never had an opportunity to discuss the advantages and disadvantages of such a body, and a UNESCO conference on this topic was to be held in 1980.)

Abel argued that proposing establishment of such a center was clearly outside the Commission's competency and lacked the involvement of other international agencies. Moreover, he believed that such a center that would promote "balances and reciprocity" and would slide into unacceptable regulatory approaches to this issue. "What kind of possible ideological slant will the center adopt for training researchers and journalists?   The very existence of these potentialities will serve as a disincentive to cooperation by the industrialized countries." The whole idea, he said, was "premature, unnecessary, and unwise." Oteifi (Egypt) warned that state coordination would lead to control of information. Masmoudi, Osolnik (Yugoslavia), and Losev (USSR) spoke in favor of the proposal. And for one of the few times in the Commission's sessions, Chairman MacBride felt obliged to put the question to a vote. Masmoudi won.

GENERAL DISCUSSION

Much of the discussion related to what was not included in the final version of the Final Report. Masmoudi, for example, expressed dissatisfaction with the Secretariat's draft because three important issues, from his point of view, were not included: international languages, an international code, and the role of roundtables.

When the discussion turned to the question of supporting free access by journalists to "official as well as unofficial sources," Osolnik tried to add the proviso, "with due respect for the laws and sovereignty of all countries." MacBride replied, "A journalist cannot fulfill his function if he is limited by the laws of a tyrannical regime." Losev thereupon said he would resign if the recommendation on free access was approved. (It was, but he did not resign, contenting himself with a reservation on this item as a footnote in the Final Report. Incidentally, Losev, unlike his predecessor Zamiatin, who apparently was high enough in the Soviet hierarchy to articulate policy in his own right, often phoned Moscow for guidance.)

Osolnik argued that a "legally elected government must not be destabilized," to which Beuve-Mery (France) replied, "Alas, Hitler was legally elected."

The arguments over free access were virtually the only substantive item discussed in this final meeting; the rest of the time was devoted to wrangling over the language and organization of the Final Report.

CONTROVERSY OVER THE UNFINISHED REPORT

When the Commission adjourned for the last time at 7:45 P.M. on November 30, 1979 (the time limit set by the interpreters' hours), no clean copy of the Final Report existed. Part V was a patchwork of changes, substitute drafts, and relocated paragraphs. The Commission members had never received the promised redraft of Part I, which was to have been mailed to them along with a revised version of Part V. Some commissioners, scattered as they were around the globe, said they had not received any versions, some had seen some parts, and some other parts. Nobody had seen new versions of all the parts.

When Secretary Deleon, at the final session, tried to get Abel to sign off on the Final Report, he refused, saying he was not about to put his name on "stuff I've never seen."

Returning home, Abel engaged in lengthy and disputatious corres-pondence with Secretary Deleon over portions of the draft of the Final Report. Some of his concerns were semantic or related to matters of emphasis or omission; in other cases an elaboration or fuller explanation was needed. Frequently he insisted on correcting mistakes or misrepre-sentations. Deleon argued back and forth, occasionally accepting Abel's suggestions, but often staunchly defending the text as drafted.

Abel was particularly distressed by the addition of Section B (the Masmoudi add-ons) to Part V, and he got support (by phone) from Commissioners Zimmerman, Lubis, and Beuve-Mery on the need to make a clear separation of this addition from the primary text. He wrote Deleon that a distinction must be made between the recommendations in the two sections--one formally approved by the Commission, the other never reviewed, much less approved. As the result of his intervention, wording was added preceding Section B that read: "While they have not been formally approved nor was consensus reached upon them by the Commission, some of the members made concrete proposals for additional consultations and investigations." Despite this "warning," many people persisted in lumping the two sections together when the Report came out and treating the Masmoudi add-ons as part of the Commission's official recommendations.

The commissioners were given until January 5, 1980 to make corrections or reservations. Abel made demurs on the treatment of advertising, press monopoly, and market economy; Losev objected to the segments on censorship, right to communicate, and freedom of access for journalists; Zimmerman disagreed with the handling of international codes of journalistic ethics; and Chairman MacBride disapproved aspects of the text concerning protection of journalists.

Thus the Commission, after two years of holding eight meetings in five countries, came to the end of its work. All that remained to complete its mandate was the publication of its Final Report and its submission to the Director-General and the 1980 UNESCO General Conference in Belgrade.

Chapter 12

THE OUTCOME:
THE REPORT OF THE MACBRIDE COMMISSION

CONTENTS

The so-called Final Report, when its various parts were eventually assembled, turned out to be a voluminous publication of more than 135,000 words. It was later published as a book of 274 pages and 25 pages of Appendices. Its title: *Many Voices, One World: Communication and Society Today and Tomorrow*.

The structure of the Report was twofold. Parts I through IV were essentially descriptive and analytical, situating communication in the historical, political, economic, and social context. The segments were titled "Communication in Society," "Communication Today," "Problems and Issues of Common Concern," and "The Institutional Framework." Part V, which was titled "Communication Tomorrow," brought together the conclusions along with 82 recommendations that the Commission had formulated unanimously, plus twelve additional suggestions (not approved), which in the opinion of certain members of the Commission, warranted further study.

The lengthy Annex contained indexes of a variety of relevant documents that in themselves are worthy of study by communication scholars.

The first section described the Commission membership, mandate, and work methods and included copies of the Director-General's and the chairman's addresses to the inaugural meeting, a selected bibliography on communication, and an essay on freedom of information.

The second section contained monographs describing the various news agencies of the world, three essays on the nature of transnational news media and their operation, a digest of the Stockholm news seminar discussions and conclusions, and extracts from journalistic codes of ethics.

The third section consisted of extracts from national legislation concerning different aspects of communication, and the final section listed the titles of 63 monographs prepared by individuals, organizations, and institutions at the Commission's request.

The Final Report was given to Director-General M'Bow in late January, 1980. The Director-General then prepared a lengthy analysis, which accompanied the submission of the Report to the 21st UNESCO General Conference. This group met in Belgrade during September and October of 1980.

THE REPORT'S FIVE MAIN CONCLUSIONS (emphasis mine):

1. "Our review of communication the world over reveals a *variety of solutions* adopted in different countries--in accordance with diverse traditions, patterns of social, economic, and cultural life, needs, and possibilities. This diversity is valuable and should be respected; *there is no place for the application of preconceived models...*" (p. 439).

2. "The review has also shown that the utmost importance should be given to *eliminating imbalances and disparities* in communication and its structures, and particularly in information flows..." (p. 440).

3. "Our conclusions are founded on the firm conviction that communication is a *basic individual right*, as well as a *collective* one required by all communities and nations. Freedom of information--and, more specifically, the right to seek, receive, and impart information--is a fundamental human right; indeed, a prerequisite for many others..." (p. 440).

4. "For these purposes, it is essential to *develop comprehensive national communication policies* linked to overall social, cultural, and economic development objectives..." (p. 440).

5. "The basic considerations, which are developed at length in the body of our Report, are intended to provide a *framework* for the development of a new information and communication order. We see its implementation as an ongoing *process* of change in the nature of relations between and within nations in the field of communications..." (p. 441).[1]

---

[1] "Many Voices, One World." Report of the International Commission for the Study of Communication Problems, UNESCO, Paris, 1980.

SUMMARY OF THE COMMISSION'S RECOMMENDATIONS

Although it is impossible to include a digest of the Report in this book (it runs to some 312 pages), it is necessary to provide a summary of its recommendations in order that the reader may have some idea of what all the shouting was about in the following section devoted to a critique of the Report. For this purpose, I have borrowed an excellent summary published in the New Delhi *Indian Express* (7/14/80).

A better, more just and more democratic social order in the realization of fundamental human rights can be achieved only through understanding and tolerance gained in large part by open and balanced communication.

Utmost importance should be given to eliminating imbalances and disparities in communication and its structures, particularly in information flows.

Communication is a basic individual right and freedom of information, a fundamental human right. It is essential to develop comprehensive national communication policies linked to overall social, cultural, and economic objectives. National governments should recognize the urgency of according communications higher priority in planning and funding.

Communications can no longer be regarded merely as an incidental service and its development left to chance; recognition of its development warrants by all nations, and particularly developing countries, formulation of comprehensive communication policies.

Strong national new agencies are vital for improving each country's national and international reporting; where viable, regional networks should be set up to increase news flows and serve all the major language groups in the area. Nationally, the agencies should buttress both urban and rural newspapers to serve as the core of the country's news collection and distribution system.

National book production should be encouraged and accompanied by the establishment of a distribution network for books, newspapers, and periodicals.

The development of comprehensive national radio networks, capable of reaching remote areas should take priority over the development of television, which, however, should be encouraged where appropriate.

There should be a major international research and development effort to increase the supply of paper. The worldwide shortage of paper, including newsprint, and its escalating cost, imposes crushing burdens upon struggling newspapers, periodicals and publication industry, especially in the developing countries.

The technological explosion in communication has both great potential and great danger. The outcome depends on crucial decisions and where and by whom they are taken. Thus it is a priority to organize the decision-making process in a participatory manner on the basis of full awareness of the social impact of different alternatives.

The concentration of communications technology in a relatively few developed countries and transnational corporations has led to virtual monopoly situations in this field. To counteract these tendencies national and international measures are required, among them reform of existing patent laws and conventions, appropriate legislation, and international agreements.

For the journalist, freedom and responsibility are indivisible. Freedom without responsibility invites distortion and other abuses. But in the absence of freedom there can be no exercise of responsibility. The concept of freedom with responsibility necessarily includes a concern for professional ethics, demanding an equitable approach to events, situations or processes with due attention to their diverse aspects. This is not always the case today.

Codes of professional ethics exist in all parts of the world, adopted voluntarily in many countries by professional groups. The adoption of professional codes of ethics at the national level, and in some cases, at the regional level is desirable, provided that such codes are prepared and adopted by the profession itself without government interference.

All countries should take steps to admit foreign correspondents and facilitate their collection and transmission of news. Special obligations in this regard, undertaken by the signatories to the final act of the Helsinki conference, should be honored and, indeed, literally applied.

Free access to news sources by journalists is an indispensable requirement for accurate, faithful, and balanced reporting. This necessarily involves access to unofficial as well as official sources of information; that is, access to the entire spectrum of opinion within a country.

Conventional standards of news selection and reporting and many accepted news values need to be reassessed if readers and listeners round the world are to receive a more faithful and comprehensive account of events, movements, and trends in both developing and developed countries.

All countries should adopt measures to enlarge sources of information needed by citizens in their everyday life. A careful review of existing laws and regulations should be undertaken with the aim of reducing limitations, secrecy provision, and other constraints on information practice.

Censorship or arbitrary control of information should be abolished. In areas where reasonable restrictions may be considered necessary, these should be provided by law, subject to judicial review and on line with principles enshrined in the United Nations charter and the Universal Declaration of Human Rights, and in other instruments adopted by the community of nations.

Developing countries have a primary responsibility for undertaking necessary changes to overcome their dependence in the field of communications. The actions needed begin at the national level, but must be complemented by forceful and decisive agreements at international, subregional, regional, and interregional levels. Collective self-reliance is the cornerstone of a new world information and communication order.

The establishment within UNESCO of an international center for the study and planning of information and communication has been suggested. Its aim would be, among other things, to promote the development of national communications systems within developing countries and the balance and reciprocity in international information flows, and to mobilize resources for that purpose and manage funds put at its disposal. It should also keep under review communications technology transfers between developed and developing countries so they are carried out under the most suitable conditions.

National communication should be consistent with adopted international communication principles and should seek to create a climate of mutual understanding and peaceful co-existence among nations. The media should also be encouraged to refrain from advocating racial or religious hatred, incitement to discrimination, hostility, violence, or war.

It should be noted that the foregoing summary does not include the recommendations in the Report against the licensing of journalists ("accreditation procedures tend to foster government intervention") and the rejection of the need for international protection of journalists ("it could result in journalists being guided and watched by representatives of authority and lead to licensing schemes").

The following section is the infamous--at least in Western eyes--Part B, about which Abel, the commissioner from the United States, became so exercised. It was largely due to his intervention that an introductory explanation was finally inserted in an effort to show a clear separation from the approved Part A. Even so, many critics still insisted in lumping Part B in with the rest of the Report as though representing the views of the whole Commission.

It is included here to indicate what the controversy was about and as a summary of Third World concerns and suggestions.

ISSUES REQUIRING FURTHER STUDY

A slightly abbreviated version of Part B follows:

We have suggested some actions that may help lead towards a new world information and communication order. Some of them are for immediate undertaking; others will take more time to prepare and implement. The important thing is to start moving towards a change in the present situation.

However, there were other issues that require examination, but the International Commission lacked the time or sufficient data or the expertise to deal with them. The proposals described below have not been approved by the Commission; several were not, in fact, even discussed. Members felt free, nevertheless, to submit individual or group proposals which, in their judgement, called for study sometime in the future. While these suggestions have not been endorsed by the Commission, they may still indicate some preliminary ideas about issues that might be pursued, if and when they arouse interest.

1. Studies are necessary to define more precisely the interdependence of interests of rich and poor countries, as well as of countries belonging to different sociopolitical systems. Research undertaken to date has not adequately explored this community of interests; more substantial findings are desirable as background for eventual future measures leading to wider cooperation. Similar studies are necessary to prepare more diversified cooperative efforts among developing countries themselves.

2. For the same purpose, indicators should be worked out to facilitate comparison of the results obtained through various media in different countries.

3.   As international cooperation depends on mutual understanding, language barriers are a continuing problem.   There is a certain imbalance in the use of international languages and studies might be undertaken with a view to improving the situation.

4.   A new information and communication order cannot be developed on the basis of sporadic projects and initiatives, and without a solid research base.   Feasibility studies are needed to ensure better coordination of activities in many field, particularly at an initial stage, involving: (1) news collection and supply; (2) data banks; (3) broadcast programme banks for exchange purposes; and (4) exchange of data gathered by remote sensing.

5.   The texts of international instruments as well as draft texts that have long run up against political barriers should be reviewed in order to promote further international legislation in this area.

6.   Studies should be undertaken to identify principles generally recognized by the profession of journalism and that take into account the public interest.   This could also encompass further consideration by journalists' organizations themselves, of the concept of an international code of ethics.

7.   Studies should be undertaken on the social, economic, and cultural effects of advertising to identify problems and to suggest solutions at the national and international levels, possibly including study of the practicability of an international advertising code, which could have as its basis the preservation of cultural identity and protection of moral values.

8.   The scope of the roundtables, mentioned in Recommendation 51, could be enlarged after appropriate studies, to include other major problems related to the collection and dissemination of international news.

9.   Further studies should be made for the safeguarding of journalists in the exercise of their profession.   The possibility might be explored for setting up some mechanism whereby when a journalist is either refused or deprived of his identity card there would be a right of appeal to a professional body, ideally with adequate judicial authority to rectify the position.   Such studies should also look into the possibility of the creation of an international body to which a further appeal could be made in the final resort.

10. The concentration of the media in the developed regions, and the control of or access to them enjoyed by the affluent categories of the population, should be corrected by giving particular attention

to the needs of the less developed countries and those of rural areas. Consideration might be given, for example, to: (1) the feasibility of generalizing sound and television broadcasting and expanding telephone networks in rural areas; (2) the efficacy of possible government measures to expand distribution of receiving sets; and (3) technological possibilities and innovations.

11. The scarcity of available resources for communication development, both at national and international levels, highlights the need for further studies in three different areas: (1) identification of country priorities for national and international financing; (2) evaluation of the cost-effectiveness of existing investments; and (3) the search for new financial resources.

12. As far as new resources are concerned, several possibilities might be explored: (1) marshalling of resources deriving from surplus profits on raw materials; (2) establishment of an international duty on the use of the electromagnetic spectrum and geostationary orbit space for the benefit of developing countries; and (3) levying of an international duty on the profits of transnational corporations producing transmission facilities and equipment for the benefit of developing countries and offer the partial financing of the cost of using international communication facilities.

FINAL COMMENT BY THE COMMISSION AS A WHOLE

The Report contained these final comments:

"Responding to its wide mandate, the Commission has sought to identify major problems and trends and has recommended certain lines of action. Apart from recommendations coming from the Commission as a whole, some of its members made additional suggestions, considering that the interest for new issues will continue to grow."

"It is important to realize that the new order we seek is not only a goal but a stage in a journey. It is a continuing quest for ever more free, more equal, more just relations within all societies and among all nations and peoples. This Report represents what we believe we have learned. And this, above all, is what we wish to communicate."

Chapter 13

CRITIQUE OF THE MACBRIDE REPORT

I think it would be fair to say as a general comment that the MacBride Report is a comprehensive document that provides an impressive synopsis of the world's complex communication problems, and that overall, the work of the Commission was a creative effort to reach a consensus among widely disparate points of view.

Understandably, the Report generated different reactions from countries, scholars, and the media, reflecting largely the ideological stance of the respondents.

As the person who proposed the idea for the Commission, I admit that the outcome was not all that I had envisioned. I was disappointed that the Commission failed to produce a set of enlightened guidelines for improving international communications and reducing its imbalances; I was pleased that the weight of its Report came down unmistakably on the side of freedom and diversity. Above all, I was pleasantly surprised at the way the Commission, despite intense pressure to do otherwise, refused to recommend establishment of a New World Information Order, a move that severely undercut the scheme for a single communication system for the world and a notion I had fought for years in conferences of UNESCO and later in the Information Committee of the United Nations.

A further elaboration of my views will be found in an interpretation of the U.S. reaction to this Report near the end of this book.

REPORT OF THE DIRECTOR-GENERAL

In September 1980, the Secretariat issued a fourteen-page document setting forth the Director-General's comments and suggestions on the Final Report to be submitted to the 21st General Conference in Belgrade in October.

After reviewing the rationale for establishing the Commission and the procedures it followed, the paper revealed that in the Director-General's opinion, the Commission had fulfilled its mandate to study the current situation in the fields of communication and information "so as to take into account the extent and diversity of the dimensions which communications has taken in the life of contemporary societies and in international relations."

The paper then described the worldwide nature of the debate and the widespread contributions to the Commission's work by a variety of organizations, institutions, and individuals. At four of its sessions, it had held roundtables and symposia; fifteen international and national organizations had regularly followed its proceedings; it established working relationships with specialized bodies belonging to the International Network of Documentation Centers on Communication Research and Policies; and it commissioned some 100 specialized studies of different aspects of communication. Thus, the Commission profited from a wide range of opinions and advice.

After expressing some amazement that commissioners with such a variety of professional and national backgrounds were able to reach consensus (although major differences of opinion remain), the paper suggested that the reason was the "tolerance and eagerness to do useful work constantly demonstrated by the president and members of the Commission and by all those who gave it their assistance."

A good deal of attention was then devoted to pointing out that the Commission approached its work by envisioning communication in the broadest sense and avoided tackling problems from the standpoint of the views or concerns of only certain circles or regions. Considering communication to be inseparable from social forces and relationships, the Commission studied communication both in universal terms and at the level of individual societies with distinctive characteristics but with growing interdependence.

The final section of the paper was devoted to reflections and comments by the Director-General. He began by discussing the importance that communication had acquired in the life of peoples and of our growing awareness of the imbalance and inequality in the flow of information between nations--a deficiency for a long time unknown or its existence simply denied. The Commission's work, he said, had provided a better understanding of this deficiency.

After enumerating the negative effects of the vertical flow of information without feed back or exchange, the Director-General asserted that the growing demand for more justice, equality, and freedom within international relations and within every nation was beginning to gain ground in the communication field. The challenge on this issue is that of winning a collective mastery, equally shared and freely entered into, over communication for man. And to take up that challenge, the concept of "democratization" of communication acquires a significance that cannot escape the international community, he said.

The nature of this challenge is not merely technical or economic, but also social. It requires both greater awareness and determination to act collectively and the place to start is at the national level; however, national efforts will bear fruit only if the international community supports them wholeheartedly with cooperation that will require resources out of all proportion to those brought to bear so far, according to the Director-General.

In a section called "Gaps and Shortcomings," the Director-General pointed out that within the time limits, no original research was carried out, so the Commission was unable to do more than gather (as material for its reflections) the existing knowledge at large in the world. It was not always able to gather all the data needed for its analysis and sometimes had to rely on the personal experience and the intuition of its members. This probably accounted for the relatively general nature of several of its recommendations.

The Commission dealt with a number of questions too quickly, including technology and technical innovations, data processing, relations of competition and complementarity among media, the interdependence of culture and communication, economic aspects of communication, and the correlation between the new economic order and the new communication and information order, he said.

The Commission did not give a precise and full definition of the notion of a NWICO, though it said it had provided a framework for its development, and consequently the Commission did not believe it was in a position to propose a global strategy for its installation. Hence, "though its recommendations cover a wide range of practical measures which can be applied in the short term, and actions of a general nature which will take longer to put into effect, they cannot be grouped in order around priority proposals or map out the main lines of long-term perspective."

In particular, the Director-General deplored the problem of the relationship between the sovereign rights of a nation and the rights of citizens to communicate or journalists to conduct investigations that remains in dispute, as do questions relating to professional ethics and certain aspects of protection of journalists. The same applied to the possible risks attendant upon an increasing concentration of the communication media in the hands of a few private or public enterprises.

After placing the 82 recommendations in various categories-- institutional matter, normative aspects, resources, and the like--the Director-General arrived at these conclusions:

1. The commissioners did "their best to comply with the mandate with regard for the time allowed them, the knowledge built up in the world about the Commission's problems and the variety of opinions they might represent."

2. The Report constituted "a valuable encouragement to Member States to continue the process of examining the communication situation, to estimate their needs and priorities, to formulate and implement national communication policies more in keeping with their aspirations, to identify all internal and external constraints on the development of their communications, and to help in finding ways to resolve them at the national and international level."

3. The Report was an "incentive for governmental and non-governmental organizations, research centers, professional communicators, journalists and the general public to participate...in the process of thinking and research needed for a thorough understanding of the very important problems presented by communications in contemporary societies...and in any action calculated to help in bringing the mass media to full flower so that they may serve the advancement of all peoples, take account of the needs and aspirations of all nations and open up for mankind prospects for broader understanding, mutual tolerance and genuine solidarity."

4. The Report was an "incentive to broaden and deepen the debate begun by the Commission to list those questions on which sufficient data were available, of which no satisfactory conspectus could be prepared or which are still in dispute, and to continue the study of those questions."

This study should be a continuous process, M'Bow said, since technology is in constant evolution, ceaselessly opening up new prospects.

The Director-General concluded the paper by indicating his feeling that the views to be expressed by delegates to the General Conference on the Commission's recommendations and on his own comments, without necessitating firm decisions at this stage, would be of assistance in charting some courses of thought and action for the future.

From a Western viewpoint, the paper was surprisingly bland. One seriously troublesome aspect was a paragraph implying that more work needs to be done on "the relationships between the sovereign rights of a nation and the rights of citizens to communicate or journalists to conduct investigations" as well as further study of "professional ethics" and certain aspects of the protection of journalists "and the possible risks attendant upon an increasing concentration of media in the hands of a few private or public enterprises."[1]

WHAT HAPPENED IN BELGRADE?

The 21st UNESCO General Conference in September-October, 1980 began in an atmosphere of hopes, expectations, and apprehensions: hopes by the Third World delegates that this meeting would provide the final push for establishing the NWICO; expectations by the Soviets that items eliminated from their Declaration on the Media might now be adopted by UNESCO; and apprehensions by the West that some of the resolutions might open the door to increased controls of the media. As it turned out, none of the developments occurred, because the Report was not even on the agenda.

Director-General M'Bow announced at the opening that the MacBride Commission Report had been prepared solely for his personal use, so no action was to be taken by the Conference other than noting it. He had, however, prepared his own analysis of the Report, which was available to the delegates. He then proceeded to present orally a digest of his critique--the history of the Commission, its purpose, and its recommendations--and ended by asserting that the Report was "an excellent resource, deserving study and reflection, but not a reason for immediate decisions."[2] (Had he chosen to endorse some or all of the recommendations or insisted on their immediate adoption, the Conference would have been engulfed in a long and bitter fight.)

This unexpected development came as a great relief to the West, especially to the U.S. delegates who had come prepared to debate every one of the 82 recommendations. Their relief was short-lived, however, because the G77 shortly came up with a disturbing proposal. They insisted on

---

[1]Report of the Director-General on the Findings of the International Commission for Study of Communication Problems, P1/C85, p. 11.

[2]Remarks by the Director-General at the opening session of the UNESCO 21st General Conference, Belgrade, September, 1980.

attaching to the Report an enabling resolution allowing the Conference to accept a definition of the NWICO.

Western members protested that such a move was irrelevant to the Report and Abel reminded the delegates, "You are attempting to do in a week what the MacBride Commission was unable to do in two years."

A drafting committee was appointed, however, which included a representation of the six UNESCO regions, including four members of the Commission: Abel (U.S.), Martin (U.K.), Masmoudi (Tunisia), and Osolnik (Yugoslavia). The group met four times with most of the debate occurring between the U.S./U.K. coalition and the Masmoudi/Osolnik team, supported by other Third World members, with occasional assists by the Soviet delegate. After hours of fruitless debate on the definition of the NWICO, the matter was left to a four-member subdrafting group of which Abel was a member.

It finally came up with a compromise consisting of a set of eleven principles on which a NWICO *could* be based. These included freedom of the press, plurality of sources, removal of internal and external obstacles to the free flow of information, and wider and better dissemination of news and information.

The United States felt that these inclusions permitted it to join the consensus, but it expressed reservations about parts of the enabling resolution and certain segments of the Report. The United Kingdom, whose Washington ambassador was dragged down to the State Department in the middle of the night to be persuaded, finally joined the consensus after expressing strong objections to the fact that the resolution emphasized the rights of governments as opposed to freedom of individuals.

Rosemary Righter of the *London Sunday Times* pointed out that the significance of this resolution was that all governments had accepted a document implying that it is possible to define the NWICO and, as a possible corollary, that governments are the appropriate determiners of policies for the press.

The Scrips-Howard News Service, commenting on the resolution, asserted that "Western countries opposed such proposals (licensing, policing of news agencies), but in the end, they caved in, preferring a liberal interpretation of that resolution and closing their eyes to its potential dangers."

The Oakley News Service on October 30, 1980, said the great problem with the resolution was that "for the first time an International body has legitimatized the totalitarian view that the press exists to serve the ends of government. That is certainly how it will be interpreted by socialist and other dictatorships as a pretext for closing down newspapers or jailing a publisher or kicking out a nosy foreign reporter."

Elie Abel, commenting after Belgrade, said, "We did probably at least as well as we have a right to expect, given the balance of forces in UNESCO." Indeed, the West was not only outnumbered in the Commission itself, but the Third World member states, often supported by the Soviets, constituted a strong majority voting bloc in the Conference. The other opposing factor was the Third World bias of the Commission staff member who, under Asher Deleon's supervision, did much of the writing of the Final Report.

GENERAL POLICY DEBATE

Delegates from 73 member states, the ITU, and twelve nongovernment organizations took the floor at the UNESCO General Conference in Belgrade to discuss the findings of the Commission. Since the Secretariat's summation of the debate occupies six pages of eight-point type, I have tried to reduce the substance of the debate to digestible proportions. As is the UNESCO custom, the debate is reported without attribution.

The discussion began with a general expression of thanks to the Chairman and members of the Commission, with favorable opinions on the value of the Report, but with reservations from some speakers. One delegate called the Report "indubitably bad."

Most speakers were of the opinion that the Commission had commendably fulfilled its mandate, citing its contribution to appraisal of the world communication system and its portents for future actions. A number spoke of the Report as a milestone in the on-going international discussion of communication issues and as a study that provided a framework within which to construct a new information order. Others thought that the Commission had not sufficiently elaborated the general principles of a new information and communication order, although there was no disagreement with the idea that practical solutions and small-scale concrete steps were needed to pave the way.

Some delegates thought that the idea of a NWICO had made headway in recent years, while others declared the concept was still vague and ambiguous. At the same time many delegates suggested the principles on which such an order should be based, and others referred to the "inseparable link" between the New World Information and Communication Order and the New International Economic Order.

A number of speakers, while generally approving the Report, criticized some deficiencies and faults they found in it. Among those cited were failure to analyze the experience of communication practices in the socialist countries, to describe fully the technological developments in communications and their implications for the future, to emphasize the role of broadcasting, and to provide concrete recommendations. Some speakers felt that private media were underestimated or that government intervention in information flow had received Commission sanction. Others argued that there was too much concentration on print and not enough on electronic media.

The majority of speakers underscored the need for continuing studies and research on communication phenomena and information practices. Particularly mentioned were comparative legislation in the field, the processes of commercialization of the media and concentration of ownership, and the effects of advertising on information content.

The debate revealed a surprising level of agreement on some main characteristics of world communications. Many spoke of the all-embracing nature of communication, stating that it was not an isolated sector, but an integral element of all political, economic, social, and cultural activity--a vital component of the life of each individual, each group and of the world itself.

Many speakers assailed the inequalities and imbalances in information flows at both national and international levels. Some emphasized that the free flow of information was free only for a few privileged groups or for industrialized countries. Others warned that technical advances tended to widen the gap between communication-rich and communication-poor countries.

In discussing imbalances, international corporations were cited by several speakers for the dominating role they played in the transmission of ideas, messages, and images. In this regard, many delegates spoke of the need to promote endogenous capacities for the production of messages and entertainment to replace dependence on materials from abroad.

A main theme running through the debate was insistence on the basic principles of freedom of expression and freedom of information, with the majority at the same time applauding the Commission's denunciation of censorship and curbs on information flows. This touched off a sharp debate on the role of the state in communication matters. Some delegates asserted strongly that governments should in no way intervene in media operations, others that they had a limited role, particularly in broadcasting, but should not interfere with content of information or control it in any manner. Still others maintained that government was a major factor, since in some instances, without initiatives by the state, there simply would be no media. Others said that governments had to use the media to inform and educate their citizens.

Several delegates noted the tendencies towards concentration and commercialization of the media in some places, which posed threats to their freedom and to the public. Others, however, argued that advertising income provided the revenues necessary to guarantee freedom and avoid reliance on governments, which was a greater danger. Several delegates criticized the Report's expressed preference for noncommercial forms of mass communications, saying UNESCO should not promote any single model of media operations.

In discussing all these issues, most speakers referred to the journalistic profession, some stressing the freedom they should enjoy in their work, while others insisted that such freedom carried with it a large measure of responsibility. On the subject of the protection of journalists, the delegates were divided. Many supported some form of protection, particularly for journalists on perilous missions, while others asserted that members of the profession asked for no more protection than other citizens.

There were also divergent views on the question of journalistic ethics and codes, while all agreed on the need for high professional standards, some asking that these be promoted by national, regional, or even international codes. Others countered that an international code was impossible, given the diversity of views on journalistic principles and practices. In any event, the majority of speakers recognized that any codes must be established by members of the profession and not be governments or international organizations.

The role of the media in creating public awareness regarding "solutions to fundamental problems facing mankind" was another major topic. Many delegates asserted that the media could make a powerful contribution to arousing public opinion on major issues and to promoting peace and international understanding. Several speakers said, however, that the doctrine of freedom of the press countered the assignment of particular tasks to the media, especially by governments. Other speakers spoke of "the indispensable role" the media should play in the development process as it was "vital for mobilizing political and social cohesion and motivating participation in development activities."

The trend toward democratization of communications and the right to communicate were supported by most speakers, while some thought both aspects need further analysis and definition. One delegate said that the right to communicate was an extension of all the rights currently accepted, strengthening the right to inform and be informed. Other speakers pointed out that it was a collective as well as an individual right, valid at national and international levels. As a corollary, the process of democratizing communication that many supported, basically required broader and more active public participation to expend the individual's right to inform.

Concrete suggestions were centered on the need for the development of communication systems in the developing countries. International cooperation for expanding all sorts of communication and information infrastructures was called for, leading many speakers to refer to the proposed International Program for Development of Communication (IPDC), saying it would be vital in overcoming existing gaps and disparities. Increased regional cooperation was also called for, citing the existing news agencies in Africa, as well as the news agency pool of the nonaligned countries as examples in this regard.

Two specific problems of a pressing nature were mentioned: that of telecommunications and postal tariffs and that of newsprint and paper. One delegate called for a major research effort by UNESCO and the Food and Agricultural Organization (FAO) to increase the world supply of paper by exploiting new sources of pulp.

COUNTRY-BY-COUNTRY COMMENTS[3]

In the debate at Belgrade on the MacBride Report a number of delegates took the floor. What follows is a sampling, based on hand-written notes (courtesy of Dana Bullen, Executive Director of the World Press Freedom Committee) of country comments by attribution.

Zambia   "We think it projects the Third World case very well. MacBride brings together a number of recommendations and analyses to see what could be done. In particular, Zambia needs training, mass media hardware, and establishment of Pan-African News Agency (PANA). We would have liked a stronger document. Whatever is needed to persuade the developed countries 'to do something practical'."

Iran   "The definitions are too narrow in the MacBride Report. It neglects the role of music, art, science--communication is a part of culture."

Bangladesh   "The development role doesn't seem to have been adequately stressed. Its purposes--training and equipment--are important, especially in regard to rural news agencies."

---

[3]Comments by the United Kingdom, France, the Netherlands, and the United States are treated in later pages.

Ukraine "The gap in communications flow results from colonialism. We are surprised that more attention was not paid to the role of communications in contributing to the solution of major problems."

Egypt "The NWICO has already been established, since it was included in the Declaration of the Media in '78. We do not need new slogans; what we are in need of are new programs."

Yugoslavia "The text has certain deficiencies. It would be unfortunate if there would be meddling by any group to support only its own views."

Austria "Our country has supported free flow of information, freedom to seek and receive information regardless of frontiers. There is an obligation on the part of states to protect, but any interference by states must be limited to protect the rights of journalists."

Australia "We support the Report in hopes that it will promote freer, more just, and more effective flow of information between and among countries. The Report is expressed with sufficient ambiguity, but it should not be interpreted to permit government interference with the media or with the free flow of information."

Canada "It is a delicate consensus. Many parts of the text hide fundamental difference of view. Freedom of Speech cannot be sacrificed, even in the name of other goals. The MacBride Report should be used as a reference document, with emphasis on very practical steps."

Ghana "Without infrastructures we are unable to add our voice forcefully on the world's problems."

Mozambique "We are pleased by the approval of the Report. The concepts of a NWICO expressed by the nonaligned countries incorporate the fundamental principles to achieve real democratization and decolonization of world relations."

Tunisia "It is impossible to satisfy everyone, but we hope the Report will be a good basis for the next three years. We should ask the Director-General to focus on studies that throw further light on this area, especially studies to outline clear ideas to improve work done on the NWICO."

Venezuela "This is an important event. The most important thing is we were able to reach consensus."

Uruguay "It is not perfection from a literary standpoint--some duplication, some omissions. The resolution does not claim to define the NWICO; it just says 'among other principles.' It simply lacks some of the principles on which we all agreed."

Cuba "We are pleased with the consensus and agreement on how to approach information and communication problems. The Report clearly shows aspirations of the nonaligned and implements the June 1980 Baghdad meeting of the nonaligned."

East Germany "Flows cannot be 'more balanced' without regard to content. The most important aspect of international communications is the content and implications. The MacBride Report fails to draw on the experience of socialist and Third World countries."

Turkey "The developed countries dominate if there is no control over communication channels; this causes distortion of the news. Freedom of the press is sacred and should not be tampered with."

Japan "The MacBride Report is an excellent starting point. We do not agree with everything in it."

Poland "The world has never been so interdependent while at the same time being divided by ideologies and social systems. It is a question of what to emphasize: the work that has to be done or just a few minor points we don't like. MacBride is definitely too Western-oriented, but it is useful."

Peru "We have supported democratization policy and participation of workers in newspapers and TV in Peru. It's important to spell out the social category of journalists and protect their working conditions. Regarding communications ownership, radio and TV cannot be a monopoly of state and private interests. We have just come back from a bad experience in which the state appointed certain editors and never helped the press people. There was censorship, newspapers closed, and journalists were banished from the country."

Senegal "Senegal is experiencing practically a one-way flow of news. Its cultural models are from countries that dominate the developing countries. It is necessary to develop our own services, our own programs-- and at a reasonable cost."

Nigeria "Nigeria feels the Director-General is ambivalent on the MacBride Report. The budget does not provide for implementing MacBride recommendations. More programs should be produced to lessen dependence. There should be ten seminars to implement the MacBride recommendations. There should be an international code of ethics, such as Nigeria has, developed by journalists and enforced by the courts."

Romania "The media must reflect the countries' policies, economy, and culture."

Hungary The delegate criticized the MacBride Report for softening emphasis on democratization.

Cameroon "The Report reflects an attitude of conciliation and intellectual cultural subjugation. Priority should be afforded free and balanced flow and higher professional standards. Some of the recommendations should be implemented via the International Program for Development of Communications."

Tanzania "In Tanzania, information is used for manpower mobilization, a basic function of the mass media, providing a solid tie to development."

Iraq "There is a blatant imbalance of news and information from a few centers who have power to disseminate information when and as they decide, thus keeping others in a state of under-development."

Soviet Union The delegate sounded several themes later enumerated by Commissioner Losev in the Appendices of the Report: overemphasis on technology, too much Western terminology, nonneutrality of technology. He said that the MacBride Report makes an important contribution to the New World Information and Communication Order. He added that we should develop international legislation for communications.

He took the occasion to charge that many press organizations are against the interest of peace and the interests of developing countries. As an example, he pointed to "how the Western press is distorting information on Afghanistan." Media, he claimed, are being used "for psychological war against developing countries."

Switzerland "Recent studies of the press reveal international conflicts concerning social injustices so people can bring effective pressure on political and economic systems. A free press prevents manipulating people in a way to perpetuate the existing structure."

(It should be noted that Switzerland refused to join the consensus on the action of the Conference in accepting the MacBride Report. The delegate arranged to be out of the room when the action was taken.)

Afghanistan The most electrifying moment in the entire Conference was provided by this delegate. Scrapping a prepared text at midpoint, he denounced the enabling resolution which had been introduced at the meeting, because it did not "ensure the right of the individual for communication; otherwise it only ensures the right of communications between governments...If UNESCO doesn't ensure the right of communications between individuals, this will not solve the problems of communication found all around the world." The delegate then went on to harshly denounce the Soviet Union for the invasion of his country. His bitter indictment was greeted with a standing ovation.

At the close of the debate, Chairman MacBride congratulated the delegates on their constructive discussion, noting that the atmosphere of cooperation that had surrounded the debate argued well for future progress in the field of communication. He said he was aware of some deficiencies in the Commission's Report but pointed out that their work had been but the first stage in a long journey.

REPLY OF THE DIRECTOR-GENERAL TO THE GENERAL POLICY DEBATE

Responding to several days of debate by the delegates, Director-General M'Bow made a lengthy oral response in which he considered the following to be the main points that had emerged:

- Our understanding of the concept of communication now extends beyond the idea of information alone, so that it takes account of the multiplicity and complexity of all the different forms of communication. Communication has contributed to activities conducted in all of UNESCO's fields of competence. Knowledge, collective awareness, and the exercise of freedoms and responsibilities alike are closely bound up with the importance and operating patterns of communications systems. Advances in technology have raised many hopes, but have also led to concern about the proper ways and means of using them.

- The ideas of democratization and freedom of information were dealt with at length. The parallel between freedom of information internationally and within every country was frequently drawn. Many speakers noted that providing people with capacities both to impart and receive information also involved ensuring that every person and every community could both listen and make their voices heard. Several speakers also stressed the fact that increasing the communication capacity of nations that are currently least well endowed in that regard cannot inhibit freedom of information but, on the contrary, such freedom can only find its fullest expression if steps are taken to remedy the serious imbalance now existing in the distribution of the means of communication.

- Development of communication potential and freedom of information were often considered as inseparable. Freedom of information no longer appears to be systematically incompatible with national communication policies.

- The ever-widening disparities between developed and developing countries aroused deep concern; several speakers laid stress on the dependence in which these placed their countries and suggested means of eliminating it.

- The Commission's Report was unanimously greeted as an essential contribution to the effort of reflection that has been going on in the organization for years. Naturally, the differing responses that find expression in a pluralistic world prompted delegates to make reservations to one or more aspects of the study, but nobody regarded it as being one-sided or as serving no useful purpose.

- The sum total of the criticisms, suggestions and proposals generated by the debates will undoubtedly provide UNESCO with a contribution to the exercise in thinking in which the Member States and Secretariat will be engaging for the purpose of drawing up the second Medium-Term Plan.

- The Report should be disseminated as widely as possible so that, wherever necessary, it will prompt a more searching examination of the issues it raises and will stimulate research in all areas where it appears necessary.

- By bringing together facts and figures that had hitherto been widely scattered and by making a more precise evaluation of an at times underestimated imbalance, the Commission's Report has also altered the international community to embark on tangible activities. There appeared to be unanimous agreement that instead of priority being given to endless theoretical positions, it should go henceforward to practical measures of an operational nature designed to strengthen the communication capacities of countries suffering from the present disparities.[4]

---

[4]"Report of the Director-General on the Findings of the International Commission for the Study of Communication Problems," 21st General Conference, Belgrade, September-October 1980. Document 21C/88, Items 457-488.

Chapter 14

WORLDWIDE REACTIONS TO THE REPORT

COMMISSIONERS' COMMENTS

Abel As a member of the U.S. Delegation to the General Conference at Belgrade, Elie Abel made a long intervention in which he expressed his views about the Report and the Commission's work.

He began by reminding everyone that, since the Commission reflected the true diversity of the planet, its Report was understandably less than unanimous in its approach and recommendations. Among other things, there were semantic difficulties owing to the fact that certain words (such as "information") have different meanings in different languages.

He pointed with satisfaction to certain formulations and with regret to a number of others. On the plus side, he listed abolition of censorship, removal of internal barriers to information flow, provision of diversity and choice in communication content, free access to news sources by journalists, and improved mechanisms to ensure that the media through voluntary measures are accountable to listeners and reader.

Abel was pleased that the Report rejected licensing of journalists and stressed the need for training journalists so they are encouraged to raise standards and qualify everywhere as true professionals.

He was disappointed that the Report contained relatively few concrete and practical measures, though it did include two recommendations for research: on new sources for newsprint and on ways to reduce tariffs for news transmission.

Assumptions in the Report about the immense profitability of international news agencies and the unlimited appetite of the Third World for international news, he labeled as myths, and he explained the problem of defining the word "democratizing": in the West, he explained, it means answering to the will of the people in the sense of guaranteeing equal rights, opportunity, and treatment; in socialist countries, the claim is made that the media are inherently democratic because they are owned by the people, through the state.

Abel concluded his intervention by supporting the list of recommendations that would give voice to the voiceless, including women, but disapproved of the notion that in expanding communication systems, "noncommercial forms of mass communication" must receive preference. "Only media independent of the state can serve to check excesses of government," he said.

As a sort of postscript, he regretted that the majority of the commissioners had found themselves in disagreement with its Chairman, who had tried hard to include a recommendation for protection of journalists. "The MacBride Report (its Chairman dissenting) clearly states that it 'does not propose special privileges to protect journalists in the performance of their duties'."

Several other commissioners had their comments about the Report included in the Appendices of the Report itself.

Masmoudi Predictably, the commissioner from Tunisia expressed the view that the work of the Commission "has on the whole permitted a definition of the concept of a NWICO and to bring out its guiding principles...." He was disappointed, however, that the Commission had not proposed to the Director-General a declaration and draft charter for discussion of this matter at the next General Conference.

He also thought that the text of the International Convention on the Right of Correction should have been amended and submitted for adoption and ratification by member states.

Regarding the protection problems in the field of information, "it is advisable to consider besides the protection of journalists, also that of the user...."

Since linguistic barriers constitute obstacles to "peace and progress...it is advisable to invite international institutions to give attention to the question of international languages and study adequate solutions to obviate this situation...."

Also, predictably, Masmoudi expressed the idea that a better title for the Report would have been "For a New World Information and Communication Order," because, he wrote, "it reflects the major objective of the text."

Sergei Losev The commissioner from the USSR said that, though the Report was useful, it had "definite shortcomings and failures," ten of which he ticked off.

His initial concern was over the lack of a proper definition for the word "communication" (too wide) and consequently the problems of "information" were not adequately dealt with.

He believed that the position of the developing countries has been eroded, especially their sovereignty in the field of information and communication. Moreover, a proper place in the Report was not given to the problem of "cultural invasion" and the "role of the Western mass culture in damaging cultures of developing countries."

Also, the Report did not take into consideration "the achievements and experiences of the socialist and developing countries in setting up their national systems of communication and of achieving self-reliance." As a result, he concluded, "the Report is a little bit too Westernized in its terminology."

Losev also deplored the tendency to employ old-fashioned language and "trite formulas such as the notion of free flow of information."

The Right to Communicate, he judged, had not gained international recognition, not by any countries represented on the Commission. At the same time, he continued, the problem of developing international laws in the field of information and information exchange had not been adequately dealt with.

Losev thought that the "very notion of a NWICO has been eroded in the process of compiling the Report" and he urged that still more efforts be made "to develop a NWICO which is so needed by the world today."

He concluded by complaining that the Commission was only afforded the opportunity of a first reading of all but Part V of the Report and this prevented a thorough discussion on points in the other parts.

Gabriel Garcia Marquez and Juan Somavia   The thrust of this joint comment concerned the manner in which certain issues were presented.

The two commissioners from Colombia and Chile began by underlining the significance of the issue of "democratization," which "is particularly crucial in the Third World countries dominated by repressive regimes." This included "access of participation, decentralization, open management, and the diffusion of power concentrated in the hands of commercial or bureaucratic interests."

They stressed that communications "is a determining factor in all social processes and a fundamental component of the way societies are organized." The approach taken in the Report "permits a more ample and equitable understanding of the problems involved and gives individual issues a more global perspective."

Garcia Marquez and Somavia objected to the tendency in the Report to "glorify" technological solutions to contemporary communication problems, warning that "technological promise" is neither neutral nor free, and that, while there is a need to develop infrastructures in the Third World countries, it should not be overstated.

Insufficient acknowledgement was made (in the Report) in general, of the importance of the research that had been done in making communications an issue in contemporary debate and in underlining a number of the Commission's statements.

In conclusion, the two commissioners admitted that the Report was "lacking on occasion a fully systematic and coherent style" and as such, "it is more of a negotiated document than an academic presentation." This fact, they added, "enhances its practical and political value.

MacBride   The Chairman did not include a comment in the Appendices, but he did reflect on the document in his Preface to the Report.

"When the final draft of the Report came before us, I felt impelled by a desire to rewrite it from beginning to end. I am sure my colleagues and members of the Secretariat felt the same impulse.

"The style of writing varied, parts were prolix. Apart from the fact that we did not have the time necessary to undertake such a task, we felt that despite stylistic imperfections, the Report conveyed our views.

"The reader must bear in mind the many linguistic, cultural, and philosophical strands that were woven into the vast mosaic on communications.

"There will be many steps, strategies, and facets in the patient step-by-step establishment of the new structure, methods, and attitudes--which are required. Thus, the NWICO may be more accurately defined as a process than as any given set of conditions and practices. The particulars of the process will continually alter, yet its goals will be constant: more justice, more equity, more responsibility in information exchange, less dependence in communication flows, less downwards diffusion of messages, more self-reliance and cultural diversity, more benefits for all mankind."

The chairman's bitterest disappointment with the Report was the fact that it did not include his recommendations regarding the protection of journalists. When the Commission failed to follow his lead in this matter, he had even convened a special conference of diverse media groups in Paris in May of 1979 on the protection of journalists and their duties and rights for the purpose of passing along the group's views to the Commission. The conference was in some agreement on the need to protect journalists on dangerous missions, but not on the duties and rights of journalists. The Commission stuck to its view that journalists should not be treated in any way different from other citizens.

This recommendation prompted the following footnote from Chairman MacBride:

I consider this paragraph quite inadequate to deal with what is a serious position. Because of the importance of the role of journalists and others who provide or control the flow of news to the media, I urge that they should be granted a special status and protection.

Mochtar Lubis In an article in the *International Herald Tribune* (10/7/80), the commissioner from Indonesia began by observing that the Report had received a mixed reception from enthusiastic approval to total rejection. This was not surprising in view of the composition of the Commission, which ensured from the beginning that consensus could not be reached on issues of press freedom, freedom of information, and related problems.

"I approached the work from my point of view as a citizen from the Third World, where in many countries today freedom of communication is either severely curtailed or does not exist at all. From the beginning, I insisted that the Third World countries could have the moral right to demand a new world information order only after they established and guaranteed freedom of information in their own societies.

"They are not really interested in the free and balanced flow of news and information within their own societies. What they really want is access to the international information and communication network (which they can control) to feed the world with what they term 'positive news and information.'

"The Report reflects the contradictions already inherent in the communication situation at national and international levels, just as the debates reflected the same contradictions. I am sure all members of the Commission feel unhappy with the end result considered from the perspective of each one's convictions.

"But if you want to find something positive about the Report, then it must be its almost exhaustive identification of problems in our communication system today. One may disagree with its recommendations (a number of the Commission's members, including myself, noted their disagreement with some passages), but it is obvious that one would not expect solutions from the Commission, or UNESCO, or the United Nations itself."

Lubis concluded the article from which these excerpts have been taken with this admonition: "National and international communications should be free from tampering by all kinds of power, political or economic. And all citizens of the world should have free access to all kinds of information and opinions."

Michio Nagai Writing in his own newspaper the *Asahi Evening News* (1/23/80), the commissioner from Japan began by observing that though the Commission's work was a long, prolonged study, it was still too short for a debate on the difficult questions involved. "However," he said, "in this world where more than 150 nations are seeking coexistence, the only way to avert war, to narrow the North-South disparity in wealth, and to guarantee a proper life for all is to reform communication throughout the world so that people can talk and respond to each other as human beings."

He said the problem of communications in the world may be summed up in three ways:

"First, there is international disparity." (Although abundant information on the West is available in Japan, little information on Japan is transmitted to the West; shortage of information on developing nations is unfair to people living in those countries and information on the petroleum-producing nations is indispensable to the people of developed countries in today's world of economic interdependence.)

"Second, the principles of communication, such as freedom of expression and freedom of the press, are being shaken in various parts of the world." (24 journalists were killed and 57 injured from 1976-1978; bombs were placed in 13 newspapers within that period; communications are hindered in many countries due to martial law and authoritarian suppression.)

"Third, imbalance and oppression not only make international communications difficult, but threaten the very right of communication which is a basic human right in many countries. (The basic problem is how best to secure the right of communications for all people both internationally and in each individual country.)"

"To smooth the international flow of information, it is essential to strengthen the foundation of information in the nations of the South and to cooperate to that end. Japan accounts for only 1 percent of Asia's population. But its share in Asia is as large as 66 percent in the circulation of dailies, 46 percent in the number of radio receivers, and 63 percent in the number of television sets. These figures vividly attest the inadequacy of the foundation of communications in Asian countries. Therefore, Japan and other developed industrial states must and can do a lot more to help reform the status quo....

"So far Japan has been a reticent giant in the international community. Though a big economic power, it has been principally a receiver of information. Until recently, moreover, Japan was a developing nation. For these reasons, it is in a position to understand the wishes of the nations of the South, which are seeking a new information order....

"Japan is already a big information power so far as the domestic situation is concerned. Can Japan not direct this power outward to assist the construction of peace in the world? The problem of the new world information order seems bound to become a big task in the 1990s for Japan as well."

Jean D'Arcy   Although he was not one of the commissioners appointed by the Director-General, this French count attended several of the meetings as a stand-in for Beuve-Mery and contributed to the discussions. As a former chief of the Television Office of the United Nations, he was an authority on telecommunications and the acknowledged leading expert on the issue of the "right to communicate." He had this to say about the Report:

> It seems to me that the MacBride Report made all delegates adhere to a new awareness of communication problems. Because of the Report, there was an increased awareness of the need for an endogenous development of communications infrastructure in developing countries and the need for national communication policies...while the Report should be seen as an important contribution to the study of worldwide problems of communication and information, it does not solve the problems. It should be seen as a stage in the elucidation of a major problem area that occupies a crucial place in current international relations.

I have been unable to discover other public statements by commissioners on the Report, but their views were telegraphed by comments made during Commission sessions when discussing parts of the draft. Commissioner Zimmerman (Canada), for example, thought insufficient attention was given to the role of broadcasting and, particularly, to the importance of women in the communications industry. Verghese (India) believed that there should have been more attention to oral communications and to the need for the development of small, inexpensive equipment for developing countries. Both he and Lubis (Indonesia) agreed that the Report put too much attention on communications flow at the international level and not enough at the national level. Osolnik (Yugoslavia) seconded Masmoudi in his promotion of the NWICO and indicated that he, along with Ekonzo (Zaire) and Omu (Nigeria), certainly would be in agreement with the Group of 77's resolution on the Report.   Commissioner Pronk (Netherlands), an economist and liberal politician, sided with Somavia (Chile) in his distrust of transnational corporations and probably deplored the absence in the Report of any linkage of the need for a NWICO to the need for a New International Economic Order, about which he wrote one of the Mauve Papers.[1]

PRESS COMMENTS

News reports, columns, and editorials in the world press followed predictable lines, with the Western journalists expressing alarm over directions perceived as leading toward controls. Third World papers, however, claimed that the Report proved the need for establishment of a NWICO, while the Soviet press hewed to its concern that the sovereignty of each state must be protected by requiring the press to abide by national legislation.

Here are some random samples:

Editor and Publisher magazine, a trade paper of the U.S. newspaper industry, carried a column in its February 1990 issue that began, "The mountain labored and brought forth a mouse. So far, that's all that can be said about the highly-touted Report of the MacBride Commission.

"Apparently the Report has been written and rewritten. It has turned into a monumental boondoggle.

"The suggestion has been made many times that the Report is the creature of Marxist-oriented personnel at the Secretariat.   MacBride addressed the Inter American Press Association in Toronto last fall and did not respond with an emphatic denial when asked about it at that time.

"The danger is that the negative aspects of the Report will be used by the governments of developing nations as a reason, or an excuse, to limit the exercise of press freedom in their countries. The world does not need more restraints on freedom, now or ever."

On October 3, 1980, the *Chicago Tribune* editorialized that UNESCO seems to have learned what can (and cannot) be achieved in the contentious

---

[1]"The Relation Between the New International Information Order and the New International Economic Order," No. 35 in the Mauve Series (see Appendix I).

area of international communications, because this time "the Director-General wisely decided not to submit for debate a controversial 292-page report of world causes and news flow."

The Report, the *Tribune* said, "called for elimination of censorship and for free access to news sources. But it also proposed measures that were included for protection of journalists, but could be used by repressive governments to justify licensing journalists."

The World Press Freedom Committee, located then in Miami, Florida, represented 34 free press organizations around the world. As such it has been a constant watchdog over free press values everywhere in the world, but especially over the activities of UNESCO. In its November 4, 1980 *Newsletter* it led off with the comment, "There were a number of items in the Report objectionable to the media, but on balance, it is not a bad resolution."

After acknowledging that it affirmed a number of principles of freedom and diversity, the *Newsletter* added that "it also contains some points that are indeed troublesome. These include the statement that the NWICO must be based on 'the freedom of journalists and all professionals in the communications media, a freedom that is inseparable from responsibility.' Advocates of such control interpret 'responsibility' to mean duty to the state."

The other troublesome point in the Report was its insistence that the people must be afforded access "to the functioning of the mass media. Opponents of the free-flow principle will interpret that to mean that 'the people' shall be directly involved in the editorial process."

The Los Angeles Times September 20, 1980 editorial, picking up M'Bow's statement that the "concept of democratization has acquired (because of the Report) a significance which, it would seem, cannot escape the international community," remarked that such a statement is an ideal view of what should prevail in the world, but does not. "It is worth noting that some two-thirds of the 146 member-governments of UNESCO have demonstrated a strong bias against democracy. Their conception of a free press is a press that exclusively serves the interest of the state, a press that in fact is only a tool of the state."

Associated Press reports written by Paul Churkow from Belgrade during the conference included a number of references to the Report:

October 18 - "The MacBride Report contains recommendations that appeal to both the communist preference for government-controlled media and the developing countries push for a greater role in news distribution and communications."

October 19 - "Many of the nonaligned nations are trying to turn the recommendations in the MacBride Report into a blueprint for the new information order, and Western governments are opposed to allowing proposals such as these from becoming part of UNESCO's operating philosophy."

September 26 - "Far from representing the moderate compromise some UNESCO officials had promised, many of programs (in the budget) revive some of the sensitive issues that had been negatived out of the final recommendations of the Commission."

September 22 - "292-page Report by the 16 member journalists and government information specialists has been billed by its creators as the most advanced document ever published in favor of a free press. Others, particularly the Western press, have criticized a portion that calls for national legislation to 'limit the process of concentration and monopolization' in the media and to 'circumscribe the action' of the international news organizations."

The Wall Street Journal on September 19, 1980, editorialized "in March, the Commission produced a book-length Report loaded with masterful jargon and gobbledygook. Its recommendations weren't uniformly pro-Third World as many Westerners had anticipated...but the Report is also loaded (in addition to the anticensorship and pro-access provisions) with ominous conclusions and recommendations: The media must 'contribute to promoting the just cause of people struggling for freedom and independence'; steps are needed to 'reduce the negative effects of advertising and other commercial considerations on editorial policy and broadcast programming'; and 'transnationals (meaning Western news organizations) must comply with specific criteria and conditions defined by the national legislation and development policies'."

In an editorial in the *Columbia Journalism Review* (July-August, 1980), which responded to allegations that the Commission proposals would virtually deliver the free media of the world into the hands of various governments, it said, "Such statements hardly seem justified by a close reading of the Report, which in many cases rejects proposals that might more truly have been causes for alarm in the West. For instance, the Commission voted not to endorse a proposed code setting out the rights and responsibilities of journalists, a measure which Western observers feared would be used by governments to put reporters on a short leash. So leery was the UNESCO group of possible government controls that it recommended against special legislation to protect journalists, noting that such safeguards would increase the dangers entailed in a licensing system, since it would require some body to stipulate who should be entitled to claim protection. In fact, the Commission forcefully urged all nations to insure admittance of foreign correspondents and to guarantee them free access to the entire spectrum of opinion within a country. The Report also bluntly calls for the abolition of censorship."

The British *Economist* (4/1/80) began its critique in this blunt fashion: "Could have been worse. That is the best that can be said about the Report by UNESCO's MacBride Commission...."

The article then listed what it considered to be the three main troublesome recommendations: (1) the formation of an international center for the study and planning of information (this could lead to a repressive world press council); (2) the reduction of 'commercial' considerations on national and international communications (consider the alternative to 'commercial' news); and (3) the desirability of international news agencies conforming with the 'development policies' of the countries where they work (more stories about hydro-electric power, fewer about dissidents' power).

"But the 16-man commission achieved a balance in the list of 82 recommendations...Many are unpalatable to the Soviet block, others to the Third World. In that sense, MacBride...justified his own nicely balanced qualifications--both the Nobel and Lenin peace prizes...What the Russians have accepted is the Report's statement that to seek, receive, and impart information is a basic right of the individual. Their delegate balked at the majority's recommendation for the abolition of censorship and the right of journalists to tap unofficial news sources, but it is there.

"The Third World also has been deprived of a remedy for its main complaint that there must be a new and balanced information order. What they have got instead are rather obvious proposals for the creation of strong national news agencies and broadcasting networks in developing countries.

"When will UNESCO decide to stay inside its educational and cultural bounds and abandon the politically explosive issue of news and the press? UNESCO's general conference would probably do best to bury the MacBride Report at Belgrade."

Another British paper, the *London Financial Times*, was no less blunt. "The Report is nonsense. It confuses information with propaganda and prefers the latter. In attacking the idea of profit-making media, it is attacking the diversity of information and opinion that one would have thought a Commission, including at least one journalist, would have sought to defend. There is basic prejudice throughout the Report against the market economy.

The subject is, in any case, beyond UNESCO's competence. The price of going along with nonsense is to get more nonsense for the international community...The Foreign Office should say so."

The Inter American Press Association, strongly free-press oriented, commented in its January 1980 newsletter that "Western spokesmen have objected, among other things, to an International Center for the Study and Planning of Information and Communication; the fear is that it could turn into an international press council intended to control the flow of news...The Commission's conclusions and recommendations also contain some new and potentially restrictive concepts, such as "the right to communicate," "democratization" of the press, and "developmental journalism"--all of them undefined and subject to interpretation by authoritarian governments."

The American Newspaper Publishers Association (ANPA), in a six-page analysis, found segments of the Report "encouraging," but was "troubled by others and would strongly oppose implementation of some concepts we believe would undermine press freedom."

ANPA welcomed the recommendations supporting abolition of censorship and the importance of free access to news sources, but it was concerned about the general tone and tenor of the Report. "One feels that even in cases where sentences are carefully constructed so as not to be arguable, that the drafters nonetheless carried a bias against private enterprise and in favor of government controls on the press. We fear much of the report will encourage national government officials seeking to control the press in their own personal interest. We are even concerned over the suggestion which seems to underlie much of the report...that the media should be enlisted in 'just' causes."

Other concerns expressed by ANPA included the concept of "right of reply and correction" (it will lend impetus to someone other than editors and publishers deciding content), "issues requiring further study (especially any effort to license journalists in the guise of offering them protection), language that tends to disparage commercial advertising (support from many advertisers is safer than depending on government as a single source), and the suggestion that "effective legal measures" be designed to limit "concentration and monopolization" of the media (government itself is a monopoly and the greatest concentration and monopolization exists in countries in which the government runs the press).

Incidentally, MacBride believed that commercial concerns may explain what he called the "outrageously hostile and unbalanced coverage of the Report." "There has been a very strong campaign organized by some of the news agencies," he told *Advertising Age* (12/13/82). "In many cases the reports were published by people who hadn't read the Report."

PRESS COVERAGE

In reviewing news stories of the Report, John Massee, on the staff of the Commission, rated 37 clippings as reflecting fair-minded or balanced coverage and called them "a blend of praise and consideration of various sections of the MacBride Report."

Fifty-five stories were put in the category of "negative, hostile, and/or defamatory." All 30 clips from *Tanjub* (Yugoslavia), which operates a news pool for nonaligned countries in addition to its regular news service, were judged by Mr. Massee as "favorable."

Leonard Sussman of Freedom House reported that of 63 news accounts of the Belgrade conference, 60 percent were unfavorable, 32 percent were balanced, and 8 percent were favorable. Of the editorials, 92 percent attacked the work of the Conference.

Joseph Mehan, Chief of Information for UNESCO in New York, found 229 editorials in the U.S. press concerning UNESCO on communication issues, and out of 302 press clippings from U.S. publications, not one dealt with any UNESCO activity other than communications.

NATIONAL ASSOCIATION OF BROADCASTERS CRITIQUE

Despite a protest from Commissioner Zimmerman of Canada, backed by Elie Abel, almost no attention was paid to the role of radio and television while developing the Report. It is not surprising, therefore, that broadcasters, unlike the print media practitioners, paid little attention to the work of the Commission while in progress or when it was completed. It is also true that broadcasters never interested themselves in the communication debates that raged for a decade in UNESCO. The only in-depth critique from this branch of the media that this writer has discovered[2] was made by the U.S. trade association, the National Association of Broadcasters (NAB), with a membership of more than 4,600 radio and 650 television stations and all of the major networks in the United States.

The NAB comments began by observing that there was much in the Report with which to agree (maintenance of diversity, free flow, freedom of information, free access, and right to communicate, for example), but it is

---

[2]The European Broadcasting Union (EBU) did file a comment on the Interim Report.

disturbed by the fact that the Report suggests "that there is something socially dangerous or inherently evil about commercial communications systems...The Commission has not justified its strong preference for noncommercial media...In nations where listeners and viewers have been given a chance to choose between the two, information consumers have tended to vote with their tuners for the broader free market of ideas offered by the commercial and other overseas broadcaster."

The NAB also objected strongly to the Commission's urging that transnational communication organizations be subjected to exacting legislative and administrative regulation in each locale they serve, saying, "We cannot imagine any arrangement better designed to inhibit and discourage free expression than to subject the financing and content of communication to government control."

REACTIONS OF INDIVIDUALS

Western journalists, in general, found little to praise in the work of the Commission and much to deplore. The Report did not overcome their continuing suspicion of efforts by UNESCO to achieve a resolution of international communication issues and, in fact, raised the question of whether the organization had any business involving itself in these matters at all. Moreover, they were alarmed by what they found in the Report that seemed to point to future UNESCO activities that might jeopardize press freedom.

Mort Rosenbloom, then editor of the Paris *Herald Tribune*, called the Report "deceptive and double-edged" and wrote:

It appears that UNESCO and authoritarian governments acting behind it see an increasingly assertive role. The MacBride Report, over Western objections, suggests that UNESCO form an International Center for the Study and Planning of Information and Communication. Given the organization's record, this is like asking a timber wolf to watch over a plate of steak tartare. This whistle has been blown time and again, but diplomats and news executives from democratic societies continue to lose ground.

William Rubury, writing in the *Washington Journalism Review* (10/80) sounded the same theme:

Free-press supporters are worried most about the paragraph naming UNESCO as the favored instrument in deciding international communication issues and about a proposed Center for Study and Planning of Information and Communication. The center would train Third World journalists, but Leonard Marks of the World Press Freedom Committee said it would decide 'what is news.' Its creation would institutionalize UNESCO interference in the global news media.

Gerald Long, managing director of *Reuters*, was perhaps the most blunt critic of the Report among important journalistic executives. In numerous speeches he denounced it as "filled with ill-founded judgments on matters about which most of the Commission members knew little or nothing" and as "destined to be one of the great unread documents of the world." For good measure he expressed his view that "it is a gallimaufry of undigested ideas about information and ideas in general, mostly written by the UNESCO Secretariat from the viewpoint of those who do not believe in freedom of the press...MacBride adds nothing useful and it's full of dangerous nonsense."

Another newspaper executive, Harold Andersen of the *Omaha Tribune*, speaking on behalf of U.S. newspaper publishers at a meeting with U.S. Secretary of State Edmund Muskie (6/10/80), expressed concern with aspects of the MacBride Report, especially the prospect of UNESCO programs flowing from it that, it was felt, could tilt toward control of news content and government manipulation of the press for social and political purposes.

Rosemary Righter, then writing for the *London Sunday Times*, has, over the years, been the leading critic among journalists of UNESCO. Concerning the Report, she charged that, though it was the formal responsibility of the sixteen experts, it "had been largely written by a special UNESCO Secretariat," and though it "had come out in vigorous support of the principle of free reporting, it had also produced a series of recommendations encouraging state regulation of the media, saying that reporting should serve a bewildering number of just causes, and inviting UNESCO to give priority to the 'elaboration of international norms' in its communications programs."

She also observed that "the outcome of these negotiations (on the enabling resolution) certainly gives the MacBride Report, indigestible as it is, a longer shelf life than it might otherwise have had. Even after two years' discussions, the members of the Commission had stopped well short of defining a 'new order.' But it is now clear that the efforts of others will be linked to the Report's more controversial recommendations as well as the reflections that appear elsewhere in it." (from *Intermedia*, Special Issue)

Leonard Sussman, then Executive Director of Freedom House and another of the most prominent long-time critics of UNESCO, wrote a long article on communications in the June issue of the *Washington Journalism Review* (6/81). In the segment about the Report he said, "Reflecting the diversity of its membership, the Commission repeatedly gave equal weight to the 'collective' as well the 'individual' right to communicate. In most countries, this will be regarded as support for governmental dissemination of news and information...The resolution on the MacBride Report asked the Director-General to continue studies 'which did not receive sufficient attention' from the Commission or 'which deserve attention.' This suggests concentration on a series of issues...included at the end of the MacBride Report. These were issues that the Commission in two years had either rejected, could not agree on, or had never considered. They include some of the most controversial issues that divide a pluralistic world--issues that can never be compromised by those who hold stringently to the independence of journalism from government."

Percy Qubozo, Editor of the *Johannesburg Post*, who had known suppression only too well, sounded a warning note. "At no stage in the history of its exciting fight to survive has the media been so endangered as it is now. The solution offered in the MacBride Report is not the kind of solution any self-respecting journalists could live with. To give governments the right to determine press standards would be like giving the accused in a trial the right to take over the proceedings." (from News World (10/80)

Leonard Marks, a former Director of the U.S. Information Agency, said in the *Washington Star* (10/5/80) that the Commission had identified the ideological difference between advocates of state control and the champions of a free press. "Sergei Losev of the USSR objected to free access to news sources and to abolition of censorship. He argues that these problems are to be 'solved within the national interest of each country.' Elie Abel of the United States dissented from the recommendation that measures should be taken to 'reduce the influence of advertising on the editorial policy and broadcast programming,' labeling the proposals 'symptoms of ideological prejudice'."

Marks noted that, though UNESCO actions had no binding effect on its members, "a resolution limiting access, applying censorship, and requiring licenses for journalists will put the international stamp of approval on those practices and act as a stimulus to developing countries to adopt them."

A representative of the developing countries, the Zimbabwe journalist Cen Chemulengwenda, emphasized that the urgent needs of development must take precedence over the "luxury of critical press. Its role must be strictly defined for maximum contribution to development. A nation in a hurry to develop is like a nation in a state of emergency; freedom to criticize must be restricted by the government according to its priorities" (from *Time* magazine 10/6/80).

Dana Bullen, Executive Director of the World Press Freedom Committee, in a speech at the Fletcher School (11/20/80), said that the MacBride Commission had completed a massive study of the media that fueled much of the debate at Belgrade. "Along with a batch of highly mischievous proposals, the Commission's Report supports some good ideas, such as opposition to censorship and advocating free access to news sources for journalists." He noted that the Soviet commissioner had deplored the tendency of fellow members to use what the Russian termed "already old-fashioned and trite formulas such as the notion of a free flow of information."

An Asian journalist, S. M. Ali (later a UNESCO Regional Director in Asia), after summarizing factors that caused attacks on the Commission by Western press and misgivings on the part of others, added, "Then there is Mr. MacBride himself--a wonderful but difficult personality with a few deeply held convictions--doing his own loud thinking before journalists who were only too happy to interpret it in the way they liked."[3]

Cushro Irani, an Indian publisher representing the International Press Institute, said, "Here we have the MacBride Commission in effect saying that communications are synonymous with all human activity, past, present and future. It is a safe catch-all proposition. It also leaves governments so-minded free to grab as many of the levers of control over the press in their countries as they can. The Report claims to have achieved a remarkable synthesis of different opposing points of view, hedging ideological dimensions, political chasms, and assorted pitfalls in various directions...It is rather like Shakespeare, you can go to it for any appropriate quotation to support any position on almost any issue!...There is no synthesis possible between freedom and the lack of it by whatever name called."

T. A. Margerson, a United Kingdom diplomat who had previously likened the Interim Report to a bad egg, said, "We are disappointed in the Report. This egg...is less addled than it was two years ago, but it is still undebatably bad."

---

[3] S. M. Ali, Manila "Depthnews" column, March 13, 1988.

After listing "those parts that are palatable," he gave as a major concern "the underlying attitude that solutions should be imposed be governments from the center...The centralist policies UNESCO openly promotes and which are strongly echoed in the MacBride Commission Report are exactly those which a totalitarian government uses to gain control of its people and to conceal the truth from them. Lurking behind the Report, and indeed implicit in UNESCO's own program, is a striving after some unified global answer to communication problems. The Report seems to delight in theoretical and political argument rather than practical solutions."

Another Britisher, Chairman of the Royal Commission on the British Press, Lord McGregor, speaking in Parliament (12/8/80), said that the Report "is a statement of familiar themes drawn from the so-called 'media sociology' produced by the radical left in recent years. From their point of view, the main function of the means of communications is to maintain the established order. They regard such concepts as freedom of the press and freedom of communication as mere fig leaves which conceal the real interest of the multinational capitalist owners of the instruments of communication."

From India came two articles in *Mainstream*. The first by C. Raghavan (1/19/80) asserted that the major thrust of the Report is "democratization of Information and Communication, and freeing them from the twin evils of government controls and restrictions flowing from concentration of media ownership or commercial influence."

He continued, "The Report is basically a negotiated document and compromises (in language) to accommodate East, West and South. Inevitably, the compromise language will be cited in the future by protagonists of different views to suit their own purposes...As the MacBride Commission sees it, the public's right to be informed and to inform, is now subject to constraints flowing out of government and state actions, and also out of the growing commercialization of the media and of the growth of monopolies and concentration of media structures. Progressive commercialization of the media has distorted the exercise of the right of Information by coupling it with the obligation that, for a person to be an informed citizen, he must become a privileged target of advertising."

D. R. Mankekar, also writing in *Mainstream* (3/22/80), suggested that while the Western media would find it difficult to object to the Report's basic recommendations, the Report fully vindicates the Third World countries' stand on the handicaps they suffer in the realm of communications and media and on the imperative need to eliminate them."

He himself, however, has several objections. The Report "stops short of recommending institution of an international code of ethics or a machinery to monitor international reporting," he says, and thereby "the Commission bows to the strong reservation to such devices by the Western media." In addition, "the Commission is inclined to support the doctrine of the right of reply and rectification but is content to leave the matter to the moral obligation felt by individual newspaper editors or to the prevailing practices in different countries."

Both of the Indian writers, overall, were commendatory in their reviews.

Another Indian view was reflected in an editorial from *The Times of India* (12/11/79):

The MacBride Report does not unequivocally declare what it believes its purpose to be; instead it takes refuge in ambivalence. It does, for instance, condemn censorship harshly. At the same time it makes journalists responsible for promoting national integration, development, and peace.   Such "responsibilities" can cause journalists, at least in open societies, to collide directly with officialdom, since their idea of how to further these laudable objectives may not coincide with those who are in control of the state. Again, the Report upholds "access to unofficial, as well as official, sources of information...At the same time, it does not seem adverse to a proposal to concede the international 'right of reply and rectification' to governments, groups, and individuals, a 'right' which, if granted, would clearly infringe editorial freedom. Decisions on many other dangerous proposals in the Report have been similarly put off, like those for a permanent UNESCO-blessed body to supervise reporting, an international code of ethics, steps to make the media work within certain stipulated conditions, and so on.   The fate of such recommendations, destined to reduce the media to official public relations units, will be known when the Report is officially released in March. In the meanwhile, the battle to have them removed must go on."

Still another view from India was set forth by S. M. Ali in an article on the Report in the New Delhi *Deccaan Chronicle*, which took a generally supportive approach: "Despite a few notes of dissent from the U.S. and Soviet members, it is a unanimous Report, by and large positive and constructive, reflecting the vision of a better world than has influenced the lives of many members of the Commission...."

Two lengthy critiques of the Report were carried in a special issue of the *Human Rights Internet Reporter* (1/81). The first was by Frank Barber, who covers the Third World countries for the *News Chronicle* and the BBC; the second was by Raphael Mergui, a Moroccan journalist writing for *Jeune Afrique*.

After admitting from the start the difficulty in forming a committee competent to deal with the international communication problem, Barber proceeded to tick off a number of places where he believes the Commission was wrong, including: (1) its view that the communication gap as a "reflection and legacy of the colonial past" is a misconception ("it began much earlier"); (2) the spread of Western values becomes "cultural domination," which is largely created by "a few transnational companies;" and (3) when the rights of minorities "excluded from the normal communications channels" are examined, there is no hint that anybody on the Commission ever heard of Soviet dissidents.

Barber reserved his particular pique for "UNESCOese," which he said is an international language largely drawn from American sociology and whose moral assumptions have been provided by Soviet double-think. "It is hard to believe that the journalist members could have expressed themselves in such a style. The turgid opaqueness bears the stamp of the functionary who is no longer required to speak to ordinary folk and so need not make himself understood...Quite apart from the gaps, distortions, questionable assumptions and the persistent anti-Western bias, the Report is also rambling and repetitive. It is by no means certain that Mr. MacBride and his fifteen colleagues knew for sure what they were supposed to be investigating."

Raphael Mergui began his critique by asserting that "UNESCO has fallen into the trap of setting itself objectives that lie outside its competence, simply because it has been too ambitious...It has just produced a monument to theoretical concepts that are void of all cultural content--the MacBride Report on Communication...[is] a document, hundreds of pages long, full of platitudes and incoherent argument. Taken together, they offer the best possible justification for restricting the activity of the media."

In his concluding paragraph, Mergui says, "The authors of the MacBride Report stand condemned for having offered, in their vulgar and facile vision of communication, as an instrument, a means of legitimizing the fusion of the media with the state--even though their intentions, or that of most of them, were quite different from the result they achieved. By its very nature UNESCO cannot appreciate the vital necessity of resisting as vociferously as possible of the maximum separation of State and the media. Frankly, it would have been better if it had kept completely silent."

In addition to the views of individual journalists, there were statements from three officials, who may or may not be reflecting the official views of their respective countries.

Mr. Cyril Townsend, speaking in Great Britain's House of Commons (8/12/80), deemed the Belgrade conference a defeat of "catastrophic proportions" for Britain and the West, and he did not agree with UNESCO's solutions, which he characterized as "medicines 10,000 times more dangerous than the disease."

After quoting criticisms from Rosemary Righter and Gerald Long, Mr. Townsend claimed the Report "left out such fundamental principles as the right to freedom of thought, opinion, and expression, that frees circulation of information and ideas, freedom of movement, freedom from censorship and arbitrary Governmental control and access to all sources of information, unofficial as well as official."

Lord McGregor, in a speech to the Commonwealth Press Union (CPU) (8/9/80), said he wanted to make three points clear about the Commission, "that its purpose was ill-conceived, that even if its purpose had been well-intended, its organization and procedures were not appropriate to achieve the purpose, and that it represented a danger to the free press wherever such a press existed."

He observed that the Chairman saw himself as "conducting an investigation into the whole of human society." Most people, he said, "would regard this as an insane endeavor, but it was worth considering from the point of view of Tallyrand, who observed that many people used words to conceal rather than to reveal meanings."

Continuing in this vein, Lord McGregor also charged that the Commission "attempted to explore impossible terms of reference which no sane body would ever have addressed themselves to. It was badly organized and improperly administered for the task. The membership shared very little in common and brought to the Commission widely conflicting points of view. No one could undertake the task the Commission set itself, and to appoint a high-powered body for such a purpose was a waste of time and resources."

The Dutch ambassador to the Council of Europe, Mr. Jan Breman, in an article in the organization's journal (5/28/80), described the Report as "a study in escapism and hypocrisy" and summed up the work of the Commission "as a mountain that had born a mouse."

He claimed that the Commission recommended an NWICO, "but the remedy for existing shortcomings can never be slogans, playing with words and arm-twisting which, never mind the perorations to the contrary, would inevitably lead to state control and its ugly twin sister, censorship."

The ambassador concluded by asking why the Report failed to give proper attention to the real problem of imbalances in the flow of information caused by the expulsion of foreign correspondents and the closure of foreign news agencies by totalitarian regimes.

"How can there be talk about 'balance' when one side is composed of pluralist societies, and the other of one-party countries with state-controlled information? How can there be a balance when one part of the world's press is free to gather facts and treat them as it chooses, and the other part is not?"

Mervyn Jones, a British journalist, was brought in by Chairman MacBride to give the writing of the Report a bit of style and polish. He was never able to accomplish much because of the violent resistance of the Commission's staff. He did, however, as an insider, develop many insights into the workings of the Commission and its task, some of which are reflected in a long and witty article he wrote for *The Guardian* (12/30/79), shortly after the Report was finished. Here are a few examples:

Earlier this month, the Commission...left on the table five stapled bundles labelled Draft of the Final Report. This opus totals 133,000 words, of which a remarkably large number have four or more syllables.

The actual writing of the Report was entrusted to four UNESCO professionals. As the basic text was to be in English, the fact that only one of them could write this language wasn't exactly helpful.

A quote like this is typical of what emerged from the team's struggles: "Promoting conditions for the preservation of the cultural identity of every society is necessary in order to enable it to enjoy harmonious and creative interrelationship with other cultures. It is equally necessary to modify situations which suffer cultural dominance in many developed and developing countries."

When I think of the potential readers whom I know and respect, I must say the Report insults their intelligence. Not only is it virtually unreadable, but its intellectual level is pitiably low; few of its chapters would be accepted as papers by a first-year student in the world's worst university.

"UNESCO," one of the staff said to me in a moment of frankness, "was never equipped to write a report on communication." It's a strange admission, for UNESCO has had a Communications Division for years and years, but the outcome shows that it's true. Perhaps those who were responsible for the failure would be well advised to keep out of the business and stick to such little matters as education, science, and culture."

COMMENTS OF UNESCO MEMBER STATES

The Netherlands   In its response, the Hague applauded the priority given in the Report to the free flow of information and the explicit rejection of restriction on freedom of information. It endorsed some points including the recommendation that "all countries should take steps to assure admittance of foreign journalists and facilitate their collection and transmission of news."

While noting that developing countries have a legitimate wish to preserve their own culture, this wish "should not become the pretext for restricting the free international flow of information." Policy, therefore, should be focused on creating conditions in which the media can function without restrictions.

Objection was raised to the implication in Chapter V that national communication policies should serve and be subordinate to overall social, cultural, and economic development objectives. "This could mean that freedom of information would only apply to the extent that the flow of information was consistent with and directed towards the realization of these objectives."

The proposal to establish within UNESCO an "international center for the study and planning of information and communication" elicited the criticism that the word "planning" could be taken to mean "the formulation of international norms for the substantive regulation of information and communication flows."

The response added in conclusion that, while considering that the Report contained many positive elements, there was a feeling that "a number of the conclusions and recommendations are liable to conflicting interpretations....Final judgement will therefore depend heavily on the content of the concrete policy proposals formulated in response to the Report."

The United Kingdom   This summary of the United Kingdom views on the Report begins with its reservation about the enabling resolution, passed at Belgrade, which "purported to lay down a number of basic considerations on which a new world international information and communication order could be based, even though they have never been debated." The United Kingdom's principal objection was the emphasis placed on the rights or responsibilities of countries specifically, on governments and not enough on consideration to the rights of individuals.

The assertion in the chapter on Material Resources of the Report that "at the bilateral level there has to date been more planning than concrete action leading to practical results" was, as far as the United Kingdom is concerned, untrue. The British then provided a detailed summary of the record of the United Kingdom Aid Program in providing assistance in training and other facilities in communications.

The United Kingdom response noted that much of Part IV provided a serious contribution, but the same could not be said for Part V, which envisaged a dominant role for governments in either regulation or controlling operation of the media. "There is a clear expectation that national governments should play a more dominant role in communication matters, through the formulation of national communication policies, for example. We cannot accept the undue emphasis thus given to governmental intervention."

The British were also of the opinion that the evidence in the Report did not justify the bias against the commercial media. "The alternative, of media subject to government whim, is not acceptable because...the worst form of monopoly in the media is a state monopoly."

Reservations were also expressed about recommendations affecting the practice and pursuit of journalism. "We support the thesis that the media and its representatives should enjoy basic rights of access, and the right to publish without fear of censorship. But we are vigorously opposed to any proposal which discriminates in their favour by comparison with other individuals or which could, though a form of licensing, subject them to a degree of governmental control--whether domestic or international."

Finally, the United Kingdom response said, there should be no place in the main body of the Report for Part V-B, because many of the issues listed as "requiring further study" had never been endorsed in any manner by members of the Commission and therefore, "should not be granted unwarranted status by being read as a part of the main text of the Report."

France   The magazine *Jeune Afrique*, while widely distributed in French-speaking Africa, is published in Paris and consequently could be perceived as expressing a French point of view. In the issue of 11/24/80, an article entitled "L'information En Question" began by asserting that the MacBride Report's "hundred pages of platitudes and incoherent texts will remain the best justification for submission of the press by government."

"The MacBride Report keeps the Third World under the simplistic illusion that the Western media conspire and tend to a recolonization of the souls. Maybe one day it will become the breviary of some dialectical tyrant.

"The Report is eminently contradictory. Although the authors themselves are partisans of the freedom of the press and of journalists, they prescribe remedies and ask for government interventions that can only alter it substantially. One cannot at the same time ask for abolition of censorship and of the free circulation of foreign journalists and wish for the regimentation of the work of the international press. How can the Commission call for setting up an international committee for control of the press depending on UNESCO that is itself, as much as one knows, an intergovernmental organization?

"The contradiction is not difficult to explain. Dealing with a right as fundamental as freedom of the press, diplomats naturally have a tendency to forge a compromise between the three present theses: that of the West to let things alone, that of the Soviets who have nationalized all the media, and that of the Third World which champions a press engaged in the development battle. Or can there be a just medium between freedom of the press and subjection?

"The MacBride Report is in fact an authentic product of ideological ecumenism dear to international functionaries."

THIRD WORLD RESOLUTIONS AND PERSPECTIVE

The Belgrade conference was regarded by the Third World delegates as an opportunity to try and end what they considered a Western monopoly of international communication and news distribution, which, they charged, results in biased, superficial, and uncomprehending coverage of non-Western news. The pretext was the tabling of two resolutions: The first was related to accepting the MacBride Report, in which they set forth propositions that *could* be considered for establishing a NWICO, and the other an attempt to claim the Report as an international sanction of the need for a NWICO.

The second resolution was a recital of virtually all of the Third World concerns that had been expressed in the preceding decade of debate on international communication issues and what should be done about them. Because the resolution was submitted by Algeria, Cuba, Gabon,

India, Iraq, Nigeria, Pakistan, Sri Lanka, Yugoslavia, Tunisia, Venezuela, and Zambia on behalf of the Group of 77 and the nonaligned movement, it could be said to accurately reflect the Third World response to the MacBride Report.

After the routine citing of various UN resolutions and passing around kudos for the Director-General (for having created the Commission) and for its members (for their "dedication, breadth of vision, and quality of their Report and the general trends expressed in their recommendations"), the resolution quickly disclosed what they particularly had in mind, specifically, the findings of the Commission that they claimed "indicate orientation for the establishment of the NWICO." The remainder of the resolution was a list of reasons for approving the Report:

- It reaffirms that this process is inseparable from establishing a new international economic order.

- It suggests that the NWICO should replace the existing state of dependence of developing countries with relationships based on more equitable international cooperation among nations and countries, stressing the right of each nation to develop its own communication system and preserve its national sovereignty and cultural identity.

- It considers that the NWICO should be based on principles of equality of states, noninterference in the affairs of other states, social and ethnic groups, and individuals to acquire an objective picture of reality on the basis of comprehensive and true information, as well as the right to express themselves freely through culture and communication, on the right to inform the world public about its interests, aspirations, political, social and cultural values, and to protect its cultural and social identity against false or distorted information which may cause harm to itself or jeopardize friendly relations between nations, on the rights of all peoples to participate in the international exchange of information under favorable conditions in terms of equality, justice and mutual benefit.

- It emphasized that the NWICO also includes the more equitable distribution of available natural, technological, and other facilities and conditions necessary for the development of communications and the more balanced circulation of information, messages, and ideas.

- It reminds all concerned that further efforts are needed "for launching new initiatives reaching more paths for accelerating and activating the process of establishing a NWICO."

- It calls on member states to study the possibility of implementing the recommendations of the Commission, especially those which activate (1) collective self-reliance on the basis of mutual assistance and solidarity in the development of communications, (2) the democratization process of communications and facilities for transfer of information, (3) the elimination of all forms of monopoly, and (4) the betterment of working conditions of all professionals in the field on information and communication.

- It calls upon experts and professionals and non-governmental organizations to increase their participation in the resolution of communication problems, particularly by (1) promoting research and identification of critical issues, (2) expanding news circulation and giving more space in various media to news of developing countries, (3) stimulating interest of the general public in questions relating to communications, and (4) specifying measures for raising professional standards and for the protection of journalists while avoiding any licensing procedures or regulation.

- It endorses the view that UNESCO is the most qualified forum for consideration of communications issues" and calls for giving greater emphasis to that part of its program and budget dealing with communications, especially to give effect to proposals for the development of communications.

What might be regarded as a composite Third World perspective on the Report was prepared by Cees Hamelink, a Dutch communications scholar, who gathered together a number of different but mutually supporting written views of ten fellow communication specialists.[4] The following is a summary of the views of the various authors, as presented by Singh and Gross:[5]

---

[4]Cees Hamelink (Ed.). "Communication in the Eighties: A Reader on the 'MacBride Report' Rome, IDOC International, 1980.

[5]"The MacBride Report: The Results and Response" by Kusman Singh and Bertram Gross. Chapter 50 in *World Communications Handbook* edited by Gerbner and Siefert, Longman, 1984, New York.

The Report did not go far enough to meet Third World demands. It did not relate the older and the present communication orders to general historical trends (Nordenstreng, Capriles). It did not articulate the basic features of the desired new order (Capriles, Dajani) or show how efforts to attain the new order could promote the cause of peace by lessening international tensions (Nordenstreng). It "reified" the idea of 'communication' and used both "communication" and "information" without conceptual clarity (Opubor). More attention should have been given to communication research (Roncagliolo, Dajani), to training in, not merely for, Third World countries (Eapen), and to national planning as the context of national communication policies (Szecsko).

The danger inherent in new technologies was a powerful theme for many of the authors. While commending the Report for observing that "the new communications technology raises more problems than it solves," Schiller criticizes it nonetheless for urging international cooperation on technology transfer to Third World countries and ignoring "the structural realities of transnational business as the engine behind technology transfer." This could lead to "electronic utopias." Szecsko observes that the Report "leaves open quite a few doors for technological determinism to creep in," while Hamelink charges that it could "elevate technology to the degree of mystification." With support from Dajani and Becker, Roncagliolo reports that UNESCO was already, in the wake of the Report, developing a "Marshall Plan...to co-opt the idea of a new world information order by transferring it into more technology, more training, more bilateral aid, in other words, more dependency." For Hamelink, this could bring the world together in a "corporate village," thereby converting the dream of a new order into a "world order of transnational corporations."

In a more positive note, three contributors hailed the Report's call for the democratization of communication. Szecsko quotes approvingly from the Garcia Marquez-Somavia comments on promoting access, participation decentralization, open management, and the diffusion of power "in Third World countries dominated by repressive minority regimes." Roncogliolo hails the Commission for having legitimized this issue, observing that in Latin America "no subject could be more crucial." This theme links research with political practice and "leads directly to the material base" of the mass media. "It was not by accident," he observes, "that the democratization of communications has been selected by the IAMCR for its next scientific conference...." Foubert emphasizes the role of documentation centers and networks in promoting "alternate channels of communication" and "participatory media." After attacking the West German criticisms of the Report as "Marxist," Becker holds that when translated into German the Report would "fulfill a very important role within the political situation in the media in the FRG" by virtue of "its two central demands for democratization and decommercialization."

Latin American Views   As has been noted, the Third World countries do not constitute a solid political bloc and were often split along regional lines in their thinking. The following excerpts from Latin American publications differed somewhat with the views of the G77's resolutions on the MacBride Report.

An article that appeared in *CHASQUI* (2/1/82), a Latin American magazine devoted to communication issues, began by asserting that "the MacBride Report is one of the richest and fertile studies to have emerged in recent years."

The article went on to observe that many of the "modalities to achieve authentic participation of the journalists in the running of the media and makeup of content appear undoable in many parts of the world where they would not change the existing power structures and relationships."

"Also doubtful is the statement that the NWICO must be viewed as a condition for the New World Economic Order. This thesis appears to suggest that in order to push ahead with economic reforms it is necessary that the demands of the NWICO be previously fulfilled and satisfied. This is neither realistic or practical."

In Mexico, one person who had been particularly outspoken in regard to the MacBride proposals relating to press freedom and government controls was Carlos Adalid, a journalist and manager of the Mexican Association of Advertising Agencies. In an editorial in *El Universal* (7/5/82), he attacked the concept of a NWICO and called it "a carbon copy of the order created by Joseph Goebbels for the Third Reich of Adolph Hitler during the '30s or the other established by Joseph Stalin in the USSR during the '50s which denies freedom of the press."

On the other hand, the Mexican presidential press secretary (a Mr. Mathews) has said that Mexico will support the establishment of a NWICO "to put an end to the hegemonic systems of the international news agencies and create a better understanding among peoples."

An article in the Argentinean journal *El Nacional Cuero* took a "yes, but" view of the Report. "We agree on the need to guarantee the freedom of expression [and the] exchange of information as well as freedom to work and to engage in trade without establishing official models for behavior and censorship. However, the state has the obligation to prohibit abuses, all forms of manipulation, derogatory campaigns, the imposition of values, violence, vulgarity and bad taste...Freedom of expression is a noble and vital aspiration which must be maintained and respected when it is not used against the interests of the community and when it does not violate the basic principles of the social order."

Soviet Reaction In addition to the demurs made by Commissioner Losev (on censorship and access), a Draft Resolution was submitted at Belgrade by the German Democratic Republic and the USSR.

Its preamble was a recital of the usual Soviet rhetoric about "recognizing the role of information and mass media in creating public awareness regarding vital concerns of mankind, such as safeguarding peace and detente, arms limitations and disarmament, promotion of human rights, world understanding, national politico-social economic and cultural development, the strengthening of sovereignty and independence of developing countries, and national liberation of peoples subjected to oppression--and invites all member states to study the Report and its recommendations."

The Resolution went on to:

- invite Member States to take into consideration the Commission's recommendations, particularly regarding the elaboration and establishment of national information and communication policies and systems, "as well as when promoting the democratization and decolonization of communication systems at both national and international levels."

- urge the Director-General to promote discussion of the Report and to "take into account the results of the Commission's reflections and analysis in preparing the Medium Term Plan."

A further Soviet analysis was provided by two high-ranking individuals, Yassen Zassoursky and Sergei Losev, and because the former is Dean of the Journalism School at Moscow University and the latter was then Director-General of TASS, the official Soviet news agency, and the article appeared in *Pravda* (the official Soviet newspaper), one can assume that they were, in effect, speaking on behalf of the state. Moreover, both had a relationship with the Commission: Zassoursky occasionally sitting in for Zamiatin and Losev replacing Zamiatin as Soviet representative after the third meeting.

Their article was largely an expansion of the points that had been made in Losev's addendum to the Report, though there was one major difference and one added angle. The difference was in the tone, which was straight-out Cold War rhetoric applied to international communications. As such, this article provided a clear indication of what was current practice in Soviet diplomacy before glasnost. What Zassoursky and Losev did was to comb through the Report in order to identify every part of the text in which there was negative mention of the Western--and especially the United States--media and then exploit these comments in accordance with the Soviet "line."

They began by blaming Western news agencies for violating the statement in the Commission's Report that "information must become an instrument of peaceful cooperation between nations." Their "bourgeois reports" about events in Afghanistan or Iran, in El Salvador and in the Near East, they claimed, created "a situation of tension and military hysteria" and provoked "aggressive actions against the forces of progress." Moreover, these actions "show an unwillingness of the owners of the information-propaganda complex to heed the voice of international opinion."

They pointed with pride to the effective aid the USSR was extending to developing countries to set up national agencies and production centers, whereas the Commission rejected "the solicitations of American representatives who attempted to push UNESCO aside and make the mechanism of rendering aid subordinate to a certain consultative group, in which the United States controlled the International Bank for Reconstruction and Development, as well as Western regional banks, were playing dominant roles." This was an attempt to make the media of developing countries dependent upon the very transnational corporations that are the "vehicles of imperialist propaganda."

The authors then took a predictable swipe at Western commercialism and monopolization in the news media, both of which are mentioned critically in the Report. They quoted the need "to reduce the negative influence of the market place and commercial considerations on the content and organization of national and international information flows" and asserted that the Report showed "convincing facts" that the press and broadcasting "in the so-called free world" were concentrated in a few small corporations. This monopoly domination, they added, raises the question of the place of journalists within the mass media system, as well as their (the journalists') responsibility to society rather than to the owners of the media.

The new element in the Soviet response was the mention of the Report's condemnation of the practice of using journalists for espionage purposes, especially in developing countries.

The article concluded by citing certain concepts "with which it is difficult to agree." This situation was attributed to the fact that the MacBride Commission had "a rather mixed staff, which also included representatives from the West." As a result of the efforts of the Western representatives, the idea of the NWICO "was thoroughly emasculated," and the "pernicious role of Western mass culture in the destruction of national traditions of Third World countries is underestimated." Furthermore, the success achieved by socialist and developing states in development of the mass media was not fully reflected.

The authors could not forgo propagandizing in the final paragraph. After admitting that, all in all, the Report "represents a serious contribution to the cause of placing information in the service of peace and progress," the concluding sentence states:

Further efforts in using information exchange for the good of peace and progress, the formation of a new information procedure based on respect for national sovereignty in the field of information and culture, the liquidation of imperialist dominance in the spiritual life of developing countries, are of great significance in strengthening the political and economic independence of developing countries, international cooperation, and mutual understanding.[6]

A further elaboration of Soviet perspectives on issues considered by the Commission was contained in Mauve Paper 53: "Responsibility and Obstacles in Journalism." It was prepared by a group of consultants (unnamed) to the president (Nordenstreng) of the Prague-based International Organization of Journalists, generally regarded as supporting the Soviet concept of the press.[7]

The paper began by calling for "the acknowledgement of the fact that it is the right and responsibility of the sovereign state to choose the structure and limitations of those media which operate within the

---

[6]A translation of an article published in *Pravda*, 5/5/80, and reprinted in a handbook of *World Communications*, p. 460.

[7]M. L. Mueller. "Warnings of a Western Waterloo," Edward R. Murrow Center of Public Diplomacy, Tufts University, p. 1.

boundaries of that state." Following a dissertation on the social and ethical responsibilities of journalists, it supported "the general purpose that UNESCO has been designing in the well-known (Soviet) declaration on the contribution of the media."

The paper concluded with an analysis of state responsibility and cited opinions of international lawyers to the effect that no state can escape responsibility for the conduct or acts of omission of both private as well as public media.

European Community Reaction A Draft Resolution was submitted at Belgrade by the United Kingdom, Luxembourg, Ireland, France, Federal Republic of Germany, Denmark, Italy, Belgium, and the Netherlands.

After citing parts of the UNESCO Constitution regarding free exchange of ideas and knowledge, recalling the Universal Declaration of Human Rights, and appreciating the action of the Director-General in creating the MacBride Commission, the resolution:

- invited Member States to study the conclusions and recommendations, especially those contained in Part V "when considering the development, elaboration, and strengthening of their information and communication capabilities, bearing in mind the fundamental need to safeguard freedom of opinion, expression, and information."

- invites the Director-General to take into account the conclusions and recommendations in preparation for the Medium Term Plan, "having particularly in mind the need for UNESCO to concentrate its activities on those areas where it can make practical contribution to the development of capabilities to communicate and disseminate information."

Chapter 15

UNITED STATES REACTION

In its intervention at Belgrade following the adoption of the MacBride Report, the United States, represented by this writer, began by expressing a unique feeling of satisfaction "because it was at the 19th General Conference that the U.S. delegation proposed the idea which the Director-General subsequently developed into the International Commission for Study of Communication Problems.

"Understandably a report of this kind, attempting to explore the totality of communication issues of the modern world, is bound to be somewhat uneven; consequently we have strong reservations about particular parts, but feel, over all, that the Report is a testament to the universal desire for freedom and for libertarian values in which the United States firmly believes."

After detailing several aspects of the draft resolution that were "exceedingly troublesome," the intervention placed particular emphasis on three concerns in the Report itself: possible invasion of the editorial process by insuring the people access to the functioning of mass media (III-4), a paragraph (V-2d) that could be interpreted as furthering the unapproved material in Part B, and the suggestion (V-2h) that the Director-General be asked to undertake (without any guidance) studies for the establishment of a NWICO,

Despite these and other concerns, I explained, the United States had joined in the consensus because it believed it was important to gain formal recognition of the Report "as an affirmation of freedom and diversity in the flow and exchange of information and encouragement of actions toward increasing the ability of all peoples to participate in and benefit from the world's communication process."

SUMMARY OF U.S. VIEWS

The Report was a mixed bag from the U.S. standpoint. Affirmations of communication values in which it believed were preserved in the text and recommendations, but not all objectionable language and recommendations were eliminated. The Report had both positive and negative aspects.

The pluses included support for freedom of the press, communication viewed as a basic right, denunciation of suborning journalists for intelligence activities, condemnation of all forms of censorship, freedom of access to private as well as public news sources, voluntary local and national codes of ethics, and agreement that no single model be adopted for international news policies.

The minuses were the recommendation for establishing a UNESCO Center for Information and Communication, insistence on circumscribing activities of transnational media enterprises, attacks on advertising, and the call for supporting UNESCO as the favored instrument for international communication activities.

SPECIAL U.S. ATTENTION TO THE RECOMMENDATIONS

The 82 recommendations were in the first portion of the MacBride Report to be received by the U.S. State Department, and they raised an immediate concern about the pursuit of certain of these concepts when the Report would be submitted at Belgrade.

As it turned out, of course, the Report itself was not on the agenda. But the State Department, not knowing that this would be the case had to be prepared if there was a call for their immediate implementation of the recommendations. In such case, the general conference would be engulfed in a bitter fight for which the U.S. delegation should be well briefed.

Accordingly, State made elaborate preparations by establishing an *ad hoc* committee to analyze all of the 82 recommendations and develop a U.S. position for each one; thus, members of the delegation sitting in the communication sector would have prepared comments ready on any recommendation that might come up.

This committee, chosen from the Federal Communications Commission, Department of Commerce, Defense Department, and various bureaus of the State Department was chaired by this writer. We worked throughout the summer of 1980 to prepare for the expected brouhaha at Belgrade. In addition, so that every member of the entire delegation would be familiar with the issues, I prepared an extensive critique of the Report for them to take to Belgrade. In its writing, I borrowed generously from the analysis the committee had made of the 82 recommendations. This paper was never given official clearance by the government, but it was supplied to every member of the delegation for background, and since it is true to the analysis developed by all the pertinent branches of the government, the paper (although somewhat modified in this version) could be said to rather accurately reflect U.S. reaction to the MacBride Report. The critique and analysis constitutes the following chapter.

Chapter 16

AMERICAN CRITIQUE AND ANALYSIS
OF THE REPORT:
A PERSONAL INTERPRETATION OF U.S. VIEWS

To begin, one recognizes that the MacBride Commission has made a worthy effort to accomplish an impossible task: "to study the totality of communication problems in modern societies." The Report is an impressive synopsis of the world's highly complex communication problems. Understandably, considering the diversity of national views on international communications issues, there are parts of the Report that anger some and please others. In the United States, some strongly approve of certain comments and recommendations and have strong reservations about others.

Over all, the work of the Commission, I believe, has been a worthwhile effort to reach a consensus among disparate viewpoints. Most importantly, it reflects areas of common ground upon which it may be possible to construct positive programs of cooperative action. It is in a spirit of building upon mutual understanding developed through the Commission's work that the following analysis and critique has been prepared.

Despite my net assessment of the Report as affirmative, a greater share of these comments is devoted to its negative aspects than to its positive ones, since Americans are understandably more concerned with whatever implications the Report may have for adversely affecting their interests.

NEGATIVE ASPECTS

Though the editors clearly made an effort to be equitable in setting forth a range of views on the issues covered, there are some subjects that are treated with something less than impartiality from the U.S. perspective.

Indictment of Western Media

There are implications that Western domination of the international news flow causes a disequilibrium in world communication that prohibits developing nations' participation, promotes neocolonialism, disrupts national cultures, and fosters "transnationalization" of information. The free flow of ideas, branded as really a one-way flow, is seen as a veil for commercial penetration and perpetuation of the West's dominant position. Furthermore, the Western international news agencies are criticized for being insensitive to the needs and concerns of the Third World.

There is a litany of familiar charges--charges recited repeatedly by Third World representatives at various conferences for the past decade and incorporated in papers setting forth the concept of a NWICO. Some of these charges have been inspired by the Soviets who have been quick to denounce the Western media for fostering neocolonialism and cultural imperialism.

The West does not dispute the reality of the imbalance in the flow of news and information between the industrialized and developing countries. Disagreement arises on the reasons for one-way flow and imbalance and the remedies to be applied. These are the central issues in contention.

In some respects, the Report appears to be trying to convert a doctrine of free flow into one of balance by spelling out a series of reforms in the world communication system. U.S. professionals and policy makers, while recognizing the need for modifying this imbalance, reject the notion that this should be done by imposing international restraints and restrictions upon the communication activities of the industrialized countries--the apparent target for these reforms. Nor can it be done by unconditional sharing of Western information resources.

From the U.S. viewpoint, the correct approach is to strengthen the communication capacities of the developing countries. Indeed the Report calls for national efforts at greater self-reliance, building appropriate infrastructures and national news agencies, and establishing national and regional production centers. Many of us in the West have reservations about various proposals for regulations, taxes, and controls in advertising, transnational corporations, and journalistic practices, because we believe this sort of intervention in the name of balancing information flow will inevitably lead to its curtailment.

One particular implication requires special attention: the suggestion that reporters and news editors tend to be guilty of narrow ethnocentric thinking in reporting of foreign news and that press and broadcasters in the modernized world are not allotting sufficient space and time to foreign news, especially of developing countries.

The underlying question here concerns the definition of news. Clearly, in any society, news values are inseparable from national values, and editorial judgements will be made on the basis of the interests of subscribers and listeners.

Western media executives agree that they are not doing as good a job of Third World press coverage as they would like, particularly on development news. On the other hand, some recent research seems to contravene the charge that the Western-controlled media report only "bad news." In fact, some of it shows that Western-controlled media carry a higher proportion of foreign news than the Third World press carries about other developing neighbors.

The U.S. media are inclined to attribute various comments in the Report to a bias against enterprises designed to produce profit; actually, the criticisms do not appear to be of the enterprises themselves but of their effects. The U.S. is persuaded that imbalance results not from animosity but from a tendency of the Report to focus on the weaknesses or unintended social effects of private communication enterprises without giving comparable attention to the system's successes and contribution.

Misguided Perceptions

The following remarks cover some of the activities that have been treated in the Report in a manner that appears to project a perceptual imbalance of the communications philosophy of the Western democracies.[1]

Transnational Corporations

The tendency to view critically the role of private commercial institutions is especially evident in the Report's attitude toward transnational corporations (TNC), which are seemingly regarded as evil *per se*.

Two recommendations calling for information disclosure by transnational corporations and legal measures to circumscribe their actions presuppose negative TNC behavior without admitting the positive benefits of their activities. In any case, these matters lie outside of UNESCO competence. Monopoly situations warrant careful scrutiny, but this examination should be made on a case-by-case basis because in certain instances there is evidence to prove that monopolistic arrangements best maximize economies of scale and scope, and thus serve the public interest with low costs.

The need for a case-by-case analysis is also relevant to the critical comments in the Report regarding media concentration. The U.S. free-marketplace, pro-competition position is supported by several U.S. laws,

---

[1]It is interesting to note, however, that Commissioner Losev (USSR) asserts in the Appendices that the Report is "... a little bit too Westernized in its terminology and its approaches."

and the Federal Communications Commission (FCC) has long limited cross-ownership and multiple-media ownership in given localities.

Advertising

Advertising is singled out both as a pernicious influence and as a target for taxation. Although the text of the Report acknowledges that advertising undoubtedly has positive features (fostering, for instance, economic health and independence), its primary purpose is "selling goods and services so that it tends to promote attitudes and lifestyles which extol acquisition and consumption at the expense of other values."

Actually, there are many influences on lifestyles (of which advertising is but one) that operate in the world today, including industrialization, human behavior, and the universal aspiration for a better life.

Everyone is opposed to deceptive or unfair advertising, but any regulation of the industry must be done at the national level. While recognizing that further research by advertisers is needed on the effects of advertising in LDCs, I believe that the net impact of advertising can be beneficial in several ways: informing consumers of available products; stimulating industry responsiveness to consumer needs; enabling distant buyers and sellers to reach one another; and providing essential revenues for media.

An international tax on commercial advertising, suggested as a possibility, is clearly discriminatory. There is no rational basis for taxing advertising as opposed to other goods and services.

It is my feeling that much of this criticism stems not from anti-Western predispositions but from failure to understand such Western actualities as concentration, advertising, transnational influences of commercialism, or editorial and managerial independence, along with the failure to understand the separateness of these issues. Therefore, the tendency to lump all these questions together produces an aggregate negative effect that persuades U.S. media that the Report is biased.

Private Commercial Media

The most obvious of the anti-Western attitudes is contained in recommendation 31. It calls for giving preference "in expanding communication systems to noncommercial forms of mass communications." This embodies the presumption that commercial media are bad *per se*. The U.S., of course, has recognized that commercialization has some negative effects on the quality of mass media; in fact, this is why it has supported the introduction of public broadcasting as an alternative to the mass audience appeal of commercial broadcasting. But again, the U.S. is at once opposed to commercial domination and in favor of diversity and competition as safeguards of the public interest. We do not say our way is necessarily the best, only that it is best for us. Here again this is a national issue, to be decided democratically by the people (not imposed by the government) of each country. The choice and form of national media institutions are not the proper concern of international bodies.

In any case, the question to be decided is not whether a mass media system is to be supported through commercial or noncommercial funds. It is whether or not the financial support of a media system allows for diversity and competition.

Stating that noncommercial forms of mass communication are preferable appears to endorse the "noncommercial" system of the socialist states without also balancing this by pointing out that this system has led to the establishment of a press whose primary aim is to support the objectives of the governmental regimes.

Market and Commercial Considerations

A further anticommercial attitude of the Report is reflected in a pair of recommendations that propose that "ways and means be considered to reduce the negative effects that the influence of market and commercial considerations have (on) communication flows" and suggest that "consideration be given to changing existing funding patterns of commercial mass media."

Here, as in other parts of the Report, there is the assumption that there are nothing but negative aspects of market and commercial considerations--the positive aspects are virtually ignored.

No one means of funding communication systems is necessarily the only way. It is seldom that the funding model itself causes negative effects, but rather the way it is used by those (whether in the public or private sector) who control it.

Generally, the U.S. government does not interfere with market forces. The objective is to achieve a balance between effective operation of the marketplace and public interest.

The International Communications Center Controversy

One of the most controversial issues the commissioners debated concerned the recommendation that UNESCO might undertake establishing an International Center for the Study and Planning of Information and Communication. This controversy has since been overtaken by events. At the UNESCO intergovernmental conference convened in April 1980 to discuss this matter, the U.S. joined in the consensus agreeing to establish a new international mechanism (IPDC) within UNESCO that would coordinate communication assistance internationally. The outcome of this resolution, originally tabled by the U.S. at the 20th General Conference, could greatly increase the effectiveness and efficiency of bilateral and multilateral assistance programs in this field.[2]

"Bias" and Imbalance

It should be emphasized, as the Report notes, that since the U.S. has more concentration of communication activities, and is the world's largest producer and disseminator of media products, it is obviously the most visible target. Consequently, U.S. media are likely to feel that most of the criticism in the Report is directed at them. Not that they are above criticism. It is just that the U.S. is so ubiquitous and so dominant in this area that it automatically is subject to a disproportionate amount of blame without recognition of its positive contributions. This is a perspective to bear in mind in judging the "bias" of the Report.

Nevertheless, there does seem to be an assumption implicit throughout the Report that the media have failed to be properly responsive to the world's ills, and therefore should be held accountable and reformed. At the same time, the Report slights the evolution of the press, both as a significant instrument of public service and as a major contributor to the development and distribution of the new communication technology. The text in general, it must be said, however, is largely even-handed in its exposition of the issues. The slant is manifested primarily in the italicized summaries at the end of each section of the text--assertions and conclusions that in many cases the preceding discussion does not seem to justify--and in the Recommendations, which sometimes even contradict statements in the body of the Report.

Postures to Which the United States Takes Exception

At the outset of its work, the Commission made a fundamental decision: to consider communication "...in its broadest sense...as a social process to be studied from every angle, not in isolation but in an extremely broad social context."

This emphasis on the importance of the social, political, and cultural environment in the development of communication permeates the Report. Following along these lines, the Commission, in the name of social good, asserts that the media have certain restrictions and constraints upon communications at the national level. This attitude is interpreted by some to

---

[2]The International Program for Development of Communications (IPDC) was authorized by the 21st UNESCO General Conference, 1980 (see Appendix II).

sanction government controls. The Report insists, for example, that communicators have "a certain responsibility to inform the public on matters that ought to concern them" and that those in charge of transnational corporations "have a unique kind or responsibility which society has a right to insist they assume."

Journalists and media organizations, the Report goes on, should be held accountable to the public for their actions through a variety of mechanisms, such as press councils, ombudsmen, and critical journals. The United States has no quarrel with such mechanisms that are "elaborated jointly and voluntarily." But the Report continues, "Nevertheless, it appears necessary to develop further effective ways by which the right to assess mass media performances can be exercised by the public." The word "nevertheless" implies that such voluntary mechanisms may be inadequate and that governments need to involve themselves in their establishment and direction.

The United States, along with many other countries, is opposed to government monitoring or enforcement of media responsibilities and duties. The main role of government is to stimulate the largest possible diversity of media, to insure that many voices can be heard.

In the United States, to be sure, there is regulation of the concentration in media, of broadcast licenses, and diversity in programming on public issues. The intent of this regulation, however, is not to limit expression, but to ensure its diversity.

In addition to calling for increased regulation of transnational corporations, advertising, and commercial practices, the Report introduces the dangerous notion that journalists' behavior should be judged by the *effects* of their reporting. Thus, according to that view, if they are to behave responsibly, they would have to determine whether or not their reporting would foster peace, promote international understanding, enhance national identity, etc. In our view, *pursuit of truth*--wherever it may lead--is the *duty of the journalist*.

A constant preoccupation of the Report is with the relationship between power and communications. Communication is identified as a critical source of power and influence within the global system that creates relationships of domination and dependency, cultural imperialism and political disruption.

There are implications that transnational corporations (including global wire services, though they are not singled out) exert and abuse vast influence, and therefor need to be held accountable and possibly taxed and circumscribed by "effective legal action."

Not only does the exercise of such communication "power" carry with it responsibility, but also there is the implication that the concentration of too much power is not *per se* good for the world, and consequently, there should be sharing of this "power" among the developing countries--one way of reducing the information imbalance.

How the sharing of communication "power" is to be achieved is not clear, though there are recommendations that suggest directions it might take. "The electromagnetic spectrum and geostationary orbit should be shared as the common property of mankind." This same rationale is the basis for other recommendations, such as "reform of existing patent laws and conventions," "mechanics for sharing information of a nonstrategic nature...particularly in economic matters," and the fostering by developed countries of "exchanges of technical information on the principle that all countries have equal rights to full access to available information."

The United States strongly disagrees that the "common property of mankind" is a concept of legal property rights shared in common.

This label is a general term applied to depletable natural resources in areas outside national jurisdiction, in the benefits of which there is to be equitable sharing; it is not applicable to this distinct resource.

The United States supports the principle of an international free flow of information. However, given the vital significance of economics and business, scientific, and technical data, it recognizes that the proprietary rights in information must be balanced against full free-flow principles. While the free-flow principle is fundamental, it is not absolute.

The United States agrees that much more sharing of information worldwide could and should be done. However, it will require recognition that the vital interests of all states are involved, and their interests must be protected (as well as shared) as fully and freely as possible.

Incidentally, the Report does not emphasize the fact that withholding or suppressing information as a matter of policy is also the exercise of power. This is why, in the U.S. view, journalists must be free to investigate and report what they discover as a check on such power and its abuse.

Another theme flowing from the basic premise that communications must be considered in a social context is the insistence that media should be used to further economic and cultural development.

The Report brings out the need of developing countries to evolve national communication models of their own in which the media can be used as essential catalysts in nation-building. Contrary to the Western concept of journalism's role, the media, the Report says, should mobilize society behind the government program in the course of development, national unity, and cultural identity. This not only involves a search for forms of development that reflect indigenous needs and traditions, but also links national communication policies to "overall social, cultural, economic, and political goals."

The Commission does warn, however, of the danger of state-developed policies leading to state controls.

Partial Treatments and Omissions

The Report announces at the outset that it intends to deal with communications in its broadest sense; it is, however, rather narrow in its approach. It tends to dwell upon communications as though they were synonymous with mass media, particularly the press; consequently, communications are seen largely from that perspective. Radio and television are considered to some extent and films are briefly examined, but the glaring deficiency, particularly in view of their undoubted future importance, is the comparative inattention accorded telecommunications and informatics.

The underemphasis on the potential of the new technologies of communication is unfortunate, because these media can create an abundance of new channels for more and diversified messages and broader participation in the communication process. With each passing year, new breakthroughs and lowering costs multiply the productivity of communication technology, and its benefits become increasingly widespread.

Although one recommendation calls for attention to the communication needs of women, the Report fails to make a basic point: communications is the key to the full integration of women in society. Without training and access to facilities, they cannot communicate with each other and their fellow citizens and thus break out of the isolated position in which they find themselves in their own societies.

Commissioner Abel has observed that the Report "... is lacking in fresh insights or evidence leading to concrete and practical measures." This may be a consequence of the Secretariat's initial decision not to commission any original research and to rely upon existing findings.

And though the Secretariat commissioned some 100 papers, these were largely descriptive; almost none opened new horizons. It is disappointing that the Commission's two-year effort produced few fresh insights on the problems and no bold initiatives for their solution.

This may account for the fact that the Report's overall posture is backward-looking, with emphasis upon what has been done rather on what could be done. There is inordinate attention to dangers and difficulties rather than possibilities and opportunities and to the dysfunctions of communications, and not enough to its benefits.

The language leaves much to be desired, and the tone ranges from paternalistic to pompous. And at various points the Report is just plain infuriatingly vague.

POSITIVE ASPECTS

The following are some of the issues that have been dealt with in ways generally in accord with United States views. These are issues fundamental to our social and political philosophy and reality.

Journalistic Codes of Ethics

The Commission rejected pressures to recommend a universal code of journalistic ethics; instead, it endorsed the adoption of codes of ethics at national and regional levels, provided they are prepared and adopted by the profession itself, without governmental interference.

Licensing of Journalists

It also rejected the practice of licensing journalists, because this would imply government sanction and would include conditions for admission or expulsion. It warned that "accreditation procedures tend to foster government intervention in the national and international flow of news."

Protection of Journalists

Despite ardent advocacy by its Chairman of the need for international safeguards for journalists, the Commission did not agree. Special protection, it noted, "could result in journalists being guided and watched by representatives of authority, and lead to licensing schemes"; besides, "journalists will be truly protected when everyone's rights are fully recognized."

However, Recommendation 51 calls for UNESCO to hold a series of roundtables for media personnel to discuss problems related to the protection of journalists and to "propose additional appropriate measures to this end."

International Right of Reply

While noting that the Right of Reply and Correction was recognized in many countries, the Commission rejected the institutionalization of this right at the international level. It warned that if this right were so extended, "governments might be prompted to use it in order to refute criticisms that were perfectly justified...The very diversity of the systems adopted...by various countries...indicates it would be neither expedient nor realistic to propose the adoption of standard international regulations for this purpose."

Again, however, the Commission recommends that the United Nations explore the conditions under which this right could be perfected at the international level, and urges that media institutions with an international reach, define on a *voluntary basis*, internal standards for exercise of this right.

Right of Access

In the United States, this right is seen as fundamental--freedom of journalists to move about the world without hindrance, freedom to interview sources (both official and nonofficial), and to transmit their reports without interference.

This was the most bitterly debated issue to come before the Commission, and the majority sided with the libertarian view. Recommendation 44 calls on all countries "to assure admittance of foreign correspondents and facilitate their collection and transmission of news...This necessarily involves access...to the entire spectrum of public opinion within any country."

ISSUES IN QUESTION

There are a few recommendations that appear on the face of them to be totally supportable. Careful scrutiny reveals, however, that whereas the thrust of certain recommendations is laudable, there may be ramifications or unforeseen consequences that need be noted.

Right to Communicate

The "right to communicate" would seem to be one that the United States, with its long tradition of supporting human rights, would heartily endorse. This proposed right, however, goes beyond established basic rights to include such concepts as the right of access to media and participation in decision-making, the right to two-way flow of information, and the right of access to "communication resources for human communication needs."

Though the United States supports efforts to broader public access to and participation in the media, as well as efforts to improve communications in areas that lack them, it is unsure of the implications of making access and participation into legally guaranteed rights. We are not opposed to the suggestion that this concept "be further explored."[3]

---

[3]For a thorough exploration of this topic, see Mauve Papers Nos. 36 (D'Arcy), 37 (Harms-Fisher), 38 (Cocca, Richstad), and 39 (Postecka).

Democratizing the Media

Closely related to the right to communicate is the Commission's emphasis on the need for "democratization of communication."

Its recommendations in this regard advocate appropriate facilities at all levels, new forms of involvement in management, and new modalities for funding. These three objectives are accepted parts of United States national communication policy-making and facilities-planning.

The problem here is with the definition of *democratization*, a word freely (and loosely) used in international discourse. Under United States sociopolitical philosophy, "democratize" is to make "democratic," implying government by the people, the ruled having the right to rule, and equality of rights, opportunity, and treatment. Only democracies are built on the authority of the public's word, along with the right to share it by whatever means is possible and through whatever channels exist in a society. But communist nations have claimed that only in their regimes are there true "democratized communications," because the media are owned and operated for and by "the people." Those who would recommend that popular control of communications replace control that can lie with the state or with the private sector are merely endorsing one type of centralized control over another.

The underlying issues are control and accessibility of the means of communication to the members of society. In the United States, the people hold the value that the mass media, in particular, should not be under the control of government or, indeed, under any centralizing power that would interfere with freedom to speak, associate, and communicate.

Our historical experience endorses the concept of democratization as well as the fullest and the most free and democratic presumptions about the term.

Professional Integrity and Standards

There are several recommendations in the Report relating to the Commission's assertion that "for the journalists, freedom and responsibility are indivisible." The problem arises, of course, when there is a question of how and under what conditions that responsibility is to be defined and exercised.

The concept of freedom with responsibility, according to the Commission, involves (1) raising the standards of journalism so it is recognized as a genuine profession; (2) fostering professional dedication to such values as truthfulness, accuracy, and respect for human rights; (3) devising mechanisms for assuring journalistic accountability; (4) adoption of codes of professional ethics at the national and, in some cases, regional level; and (5) contributions by all media workers to the fulfillment of human rights.

All of these purposes are laudable, provided that such measures are, in the Commission's words, "prepared and adapted by the profession itself-- without government interference." The U.S. journalists strongly oppose attempts by government to set standards or impose obligations upon those working in the mass media.

In particular, in the United States, we differentiate between support for the media in voluntary efforts to foster human rights and the creation of legal structures that mandate that the media take predetermined positions on matters of social and political policy.

In America, we hold a deeply rooted conviction that even to achieve desirable social ends, independent media may not be coerced into serving as tools of social policy. Journalists must be allowed freedom of expression, even if their views are incompatible with the ideals of democracy or principles of basic human rights.

SPECIFIC COOPERATIVE STEPS

While the contentious issues listed earlier have to do with deep-seated philosophical beliefs, other issues in the Report are relatively conflict-free, and lend themselves to consensus and concrete cooperative action.

Increasing Paper Supply

Recommendation 19 calls for international research and development to overcome the worldwide shortage of paper, a shortage that impacts especially upon the "struggling newspapers, periodicals, and publication industry...in the developing countries." The American Newspaper Publishers Association is currently testing the potential for making newsprint from kenaf, a rapidly renewable crop that is found in abundance in many parts of the world. The United States strongly endorses research of this kind that may lead to reduction of critical shortage of paper that is so vital to information and education.

Lowering of Telecommunication Tariffs

High charges for dissemination of news, transport of newspapers, periodicals, books, and audiovisual materials are a major obstacle to expanding flows of information. The Report calls for a variety of national and international initiatives including cooperation of local post and telegraph authorities to adjust their tariffs "in line with larger national goals," the study of possible discounts for transmission of news, preferential rates for certain types of transmission among developing countries, and the investigation of the possibility of negotiating preferential tariffs on bilateral or regional bases.

While it is certainly desirable to expand flows of information by lowering telecommunication tariffs, it is important to note that the rates paid in developing countries are not primarily due to international decisions. INTELSAT (whose satellites transmit 65 percent of the world's international telecommunications) has a policy of globally-averaged rates designed to avoid discrimination against smaller or more remote nations. With improving technology, INTELSAT "space segment charges" have steadily decreased. The rates paid by users are set by designated telecommunication entities in the 105 INTELSAT member (and 144 user) nations that own and operate the earth stations.

In addition to earth station charges, users must also pay for land-line connections to the national networks. These charges are also set at the national level. The ultimate consideration must be the necessity for building an economically viable global communication system--one in which all nations can be full partners, each capable of transmitting as well as receiving.

Training Assistance

Recommendation 10 recognizes the necessity of adequate educational and training facilities to supply professional personnel and, in this regard, encourages "cooperation between neighboring countries and within regions."

For many years, the United States has conducted programs for training foreign journalists and other communication specialists, both in this country and in other countries. These programs have been undertaken by U.S. universities, media, and corporations. A plan for manpower training offered at the 20th General Conference is being carried forward by the United States Information Agency. Developing countries have been invited to identify regional training centers to which senior faculty members may be sent as advisors.

OTHER SUPPORTABLE POINTS

There are a number of other recommendations made by the Commission that meet with Western favor. Among these are calls for:

- the development of adequate infrastructures to provide self-reliant communication capacity;

- the development of community presses in rural areas and small towns;*

- development of national capacity for producing broadcast materials to obviate dependence on external sources;*

- greater attention to the communication needs of women;*

- abolishment of censorship or arbitrary control of information;

- condemnation of the practice of national intelligence services recruiting journalists for spying purposes under cover of their "professional duties";

- international cooperation for the development of communications, to be given equal priority with and within other sectors (for example, health, agriculture, industry, science, and education);

- utilization of local radio, low-cost small-format television and video systems;*

- the concept of pluralism and the impossibility of endorsing any national or international model of communications structures;

- having each country, within the framework of national development policies, work out its own set of priorities;*

- the communication component in all development projects receiving adequate financing;*

- effective legal measures designed to "seek and improve models which would ensure greater independence and autonomy of the media concerning their management and editorial policy, whether these media are under private, public or government ownership";

- particular efforts by journalists--both print and broadcast--to ensure that news about other developing countries within or outside their regions receive more attention and space in the media; and

- better coordination of the various communication activities within UNESCO and throughout the United Nations system.

---

*Already cited (by 1980) in UNESCO resolutions and provisions of the UNESCO work plan.

MODIFICATION OF THE NEW WORLD INFORMATION
AND COMMUNICATION ORDER CONCEPT

The MacBride Report did not provide the definitive statement on the New World Information and Communication Order. This is surprising in view of the mandate given the Commission at the outset by Director-General M'Bow and the repeated insistence by Commissioner Masmoudi (supported by Third World colleagues) that establishing the NWICO was the sole purpose of the Commission's work--its *raison d'etre*.

What the Commission *did* do was to state that the NWICO was an "on-going *process* of successive changes in the nature or relations between and within nations in the field of communications." The Commission saw its role in the end as having provided the framework for identifying and analyzing the problems and the possible solutions, and "considered the new order...but a stage in a journey."

This position is far removed from the concept of an NWICO that was articulated in papers presented at the third meeting of the Commission by Commissioners Masmoudi (Tunisia) and Osolnik (Yugoslavia), which included, *inter alia*, calls for some extreme restrictions on free flow, and demanded a rapid and drastic revision of the existing global communication system.

In fact, perhaps the major benefit of the MacBride Commission's work, from the Western perspective, may be the modifying effect it had through the ongoing recognition it makes of the *process* as outlined in its Report.

Chairman MacBride, in the Preface, also calls the NWICO a *process* whose goals are "more justice, more equity, more reciprocity in information exchange, less dependence in communication flows, less downward diffusion of messages, more self-reliance and cultural identity, more benefits for all mankind."

This observer has no quarrel with the concept of NWICO conceived in terms of these goals. The question is how they are to be achieved. This is why we approve of the use of the word *process*--an evolving, step-by-step, patient procedure to remedy acknowledged imperfections in the existing system.

Such a process provides an opportunity to move the discussion from the abstract to the concrete, so that we can focus on practical ways to work cooperatively to help all nations participate to the fullest extent possible in the production and dissemination of information.

A TESTAMENT TO FREEDOM

Above all, the Report comes across strongly in its net impact as a testament to freedom.

As MacBride himself has noted, on the application of freedom to communications, the Report is unequivocal. "The principle of freedom is one that admits of no exception and that is applicable to people all over the world by virtue of their human dignity...Obstacles to freedom and distortions of democracy are dangerous symptoms in every society...derogatory and arbitrary restrictions to the free flow of information should be eliminated straight away. There are no justifiable reasons or excuses for violations of freedom and democracy [and] in the absence of freedom (for journalists) there can be no responsibility."

SUMMARY

The MacBride Commission Report demonstrates that rationality and realism can be brought to bear on the highly sensitive communication issues. Given the diverse political and philosophical perspectives of the commissioners, a remarkable degree of agreement was achieved during the two years of their discussions. Although certain positions continue to be irreconcilable, the commissioners were able to find common ground for practical action in several areas and to agree that there are legitimate concerns and communication deficiencies that require some far-reaching changes. To a considerable degree the Commission succeeded in reflecting the strong differences in world opinion and still managed to produce findings that may have practical value in terms of encouraging effective international cooperation.

The Report emphasizes the need for a global view of communications and the need to understand how national and international aspects are so interrelated that they must be considered together if policies are to be effective.

From the U.S. perspective, the Report is important for what it did not say. It did not endorse a specific definition of a NWICO, a single model of communication systems, protection or licensing of journalists, or an international right of reply of an international journalistic code of ethics. And it does not endorse a radical or sudden restructuring of the existing world communication system.

Actually, this voluminous report is so encyclopedic that every nation can find in its pages support for its own views. The Soviets will find support for their positions on advertising, commercialization, and private enterprise (though they will be displeased with the recommendations on access and censorship). In general, Third World countries will find comfort in the recognition of their concerns and of the need to reduce and eventually eliminate existing communication gaps--though they will not find the Report as fully responsive to their interests as they had hoped. The United States, despite the presence of what it considers to be a lack of balance in treating the activities of private enterprise, holds the opinion that, in view of its minority voice on the Commission, values of importance to United States communications professionals were well preserved.

The MacBride Report, however, should be viewed much more positively than as an exhibit of successful "damage limitation." Despite its manifest weaknesses, it can be summed up *on balance* as largely an affirmation of freedom and diversity in the flow and exchange of information and an encouragement of actions toward increasing the ability of all peoples to participate in and benefit from the world's communication process.

Final judgement of the Report must wait upon the number of actions that stem from it that are of practical value in terms of developing effective international cooperation. That will be the test.[4]

A FINAL WORD--ALMOST

If asked to give my personal, absolutely and positively, unbiased opinion of the MacBride Report, I would probably resort to a ploy that a BBC friend advised me to use on my first visit to England.

"Look," he said, "your hosts will drag you around to look at all kinds of sculpture and paintings, some of which you will think are bloody awful. So to avoid offending your hosts, here's what you do. Back off a bit, narrow your eyes, sight along your thumb, and then say, 'Yes, hmmmmmmmmm, but it's a bit uneven, don't you think'."

Uneven? Yes, but on balance (despite manifest weaknesses), I believe the Report still stands as a testament to freedom and diversity and other important libertarian values.

---

[4]This critique and analysis was written by the author of this book in October 1980, shortly before the MacBride Report was submitted to the UNESCO General Conference at Belgrade. A less personal version was designed as an unofficial briefing paper for the U.S. delegation.

Chapter 17

CONCLUSION

Looking back from the perspective of a decade and more, how well did the MacBride Report meet the test, mentioned at the end of the 1980 critique?

While aware that many concomitant factors must have transpired in this interval, I believe the long range implications of the Commission's work on international relations and policy development have been rather substantial. Though the actual incorporation of its recommendations of "practical value" into the international system by the world community may have been moderate, its guidance and path-pointing have been obviously influential.

To begin, the Report focused world attention and aroused a higher level of interest in international communication matters and in the legitimate concerns of developing countries for redressing the recognized imbalance in world information flow. Additionally, it emphasized that communications must be viewed from a global perspective and, consequently, its improvement must be a cooperative and simultaneous undertaking.

One healthy result of the Commission's work was to bring to bear on UNESCO more views than ever before of all interested nongovernmental communities. It generated an enormous outpouring of papers, comments, criticisms, and suggestions by individuals, institutions, and organizations and, what is more, brought together in one place a useful collection of communication data that had previously been scattered.

The Report, I believe, could also be claimed to have played a significant role in the adoption of the International Program for Development of Communications (IPDC) at the Belgrade Conference--both substantively and atmospherically (that is, the general mood of the meeting) (see Appendix II).

Because the Commission had exhaustively analyzed and discussed all of the issues that had been argued during the past ten years, there was a general recognition that the time for talk was over; it was time to act. And here, too, the Report was helpful. Not only had it defused (or at least shunted aside) many divisive arguments (such as protection and licensing of journalists, right of reply and others), but its clarification of the issues and emphasis on pragmatic steps put the delegates in a mood for positive and cooperative action.

The Commission had clearly indicated that the crux of the controversy was imbalance in global news flows and recommended that redress lay not in restrictions but in a common effort to modify the state of dependency of the developing nations by strengthening their communication self reliance. And such an effort, the Report emphasized, should be to encourage the evolution of indigenous communication policies that would encompass adequate infrastructures and supply professional personnel for their operation. And this, of course, is precisely what the IPDC was designed to help accomplish.

In fact, much of the development of IPDC's list of priorities for making grants followed along lines suggested by the Report, as did the majority of the initial requests for grants. Another encouragement, not so immediately related, was the move toward greater openness in the many controlled societies in Eastern Europe. It is quite likely that the Commission's strong rejection of censorship in all its forms and insistence on access to all sources of information must have encouraged media workers in these societies and helped pave the way toward the establishment of *glasnost* in the Soviet sphere. This remarkable turnabout in Soviet policy proclaimed by President Gorbachev in 1984, which greatly relaxed the former rigid state control over freedom of expression and the media, could well have had its roots in the MacBride Report. Suddenly criticism was not only tolerated, but encouraged--via press, books, films, theater, radio, and television. And in 1990, legislation was passed lifting censorship and granting individuals the right to own newspapers.

Surely all this free-flow fervor in the USSR did not all stem from the MacBride Report, but--who knows?--it may well have been something of a seminal force.

Whether it influenced Gorbachev or not, the Report certainly influenced Federico Mayor, who took office on November 16, 1987 as the new Director-General, to institute far-reaching reforms in UNESCO. Many of its recommendations had already been incorporated in successive UNESCO work plans, but he carried them further. In particular, following the

Report's emphasis on the need for practical approaches (as opposed to normative actions), he steered UNESCO away from ideologically oriented programs (like journalistic licensing and international ethical codes) and focused it toward achieving the goal of wider and better dissemination of information by assisting developing countries in developing infrastructures, training personnel, and acquiring appropriate technology.   And these reforms hold the possibility of gaining the confidence and participation of the professional media personnel.   This does not mean that Western journalists will not continue to be skeptical and suspicious about activities in UNESCO in this field, but it does mean that, along with their wariness, they will no longer tend to regard UNESCO as the embodiment of threats to fundamental issues of freedom of the press and free flow.

Third World communicators, too, have altered their attitude, recognizing the meager awards of unrelenting confrontation and adopting the Report's guidance toward a less rhetorical and more pragmatic approach in achieving their goals.

And all parties have come to recognize that the relationship between the free flow of information and a better balanced flow of information requires that the developing world acquire the skills and equipment it needs to produce such a balance. All parties, too, seem to accept the Report's conclusion that the improvement of the world's communication system lies not in international interference but in international cooperation--in a common effort to adapt communication techniques and technology to the needs of the developing countries, who, in turn, must contribute their own efforts to improve their capabilities through national communication policies of their own. The emphasis on this latter point by the Commission resulted in a noticeable increase in requests to the IPDC for grants to establish national communication systems.

But the MacBride Commission could never have had such influence on these developments but for one decisive bit of behavior: the refusal, despite intense pressure from the nonaligned countries backed by the Soviets and from M'Bow himself, to endorse the establishment of a New International Information and Communication Order. Though the Commission indicated a framework in which such an order might be studied, it made clear that improvement in the world's communication system must be through a *process*, not by a radical ripping up of the present system in order to impose a single schematic.

Refusal to endorse establishing the NWICO had profound repercussions.   This phrase had become the mantra for the Third World and "fighting words" for the West, and over the years it became a "semantic omnibus." That is, it was so freighted with emotional labels and ideological attachments, that its mere mention in debate destroyed any chance that rationality could prevail. The Commission's action cut the ground out under the nonaligned nation's push for radical change. The campaign for a NWICO henceforth lost momentum and gradually faded away in UNESCO and the United Nations.

Thus, the Commission's "damning with faint praise" finally brought about the removal of the NWICO bugaboo and cleared out this emotional underbrush so that all participants could enter the discussions on a new, less-encumbered playing field. This has had a salutary effect on ensuing international communications meetings.

True the MacBride Report "neither clarified nor resolved the issues," but on the other hand, it revealed the complexity of modern communication problems and the difficulty of their solution and proved that some of the issues involved, despite mutual good intentions, are now (and probably forever will be) irreconcilable.

The lesson, then, is that instead of wasting energies in confrontational debate to resolve consensus-proof issues, efforts should be directed toward an inevitable long-range undertaking requiring a cooperative endeavor to understand the enormous potential for good of modern communication systems and toward being sensitive to the necessity for their application to basic needs of the entire human family.

The MacBride Report pointed the way.

Chapter 18

EPILOGUE

A PERSONAL PERSPECTIVE

With the exception of some modest but practical work in the period from about 1950 to 1970, UNESCO's record to date in communication matters has not been impressive.

The organization began life in 1945, built on the Western model of disinterested debate and cooperation, and with a constitutional commitment to freedom and the free flow of information. After the balance of power shifted to the developing countries and with the leadership of Amadou M'Bow as Director-General, there was a steady erosion of that structure and commitment. In part, this was attributable to the vigor with which the Third World majority, backed by the Soviets and with ready support by the Secretariat, heaped criticism upon the Western media and attempted to combat Western dominance through restrictions and restraints. It was also due in part to the rampant politicization of the organization's activities in this area.

Some politicization is, of course, inevitable in any organization, especially one made up of governments, but UNESCO's Secretariat never seemed able to separate politics and ideology from reality, nor to look hard enough at the social and cultural dimensions of the media rather than the political and technological factors--dimensions more persistent than they seemed to realize. Examples of this opacity are legion.

The Secretariat, sympathetic with Third World demands, pushed year after year for the formulation of an international code of journalistic ethics, ignoring the reality of the diversity of cultures and complexity of communication systems in today's pluralistic world. It relentlessly persisted in pursuing the establishment of a New World Information Order despite the unrealistic notion that there could ever be one grandiose "order" or global schematic that would be suitable for all countries. As Elie Abel once pointed out, "UNESCO does not have the function or need to give its blessing to any particular single planetary standard of conduct for the media. I think that this is insanity...each country has a right and need to make its own decision, consistent with its own cultural and political beliefs. In other words, let us try to deal with the world as it is, rather than as some enthusiasts would like it to be."[1]

As Sussman reminds us in his foreword to Gifford's *The New International Information Order*, "Not until 1983 did the organization officially begin to define the so-called order as a 'continuous and evolving process'... But by then the mind-set had been established and UNESCO was perceived as having a hidden agenda...and all the official denials by the Director-General could not undo the seven years of bitter controversy."

Despite the failure of repeated efforts to secure adoption of formal resolutions, that was not the course the Secretariat and the Third World power bloc chose to follow; the result was a systematic alienation of UNESCO's Western constituency. The constant clamor for an NWICO, the unrelenting repetition of charges against Western media, together with a growing perception that this behavior pattern was the result of calculated manipulation of the organization by the Secretariat and the Third World majority, helped to precipitate a drastic act of reciprocity. The untenable deadlock in the communications area, although by no means the only cause, finally brought the exasperated United States and United Kingdom to the end of their patience. They resigned.

The West was not without fault. The United States stubbornly clung to its conviction that its privately owned free press was the model suited for export to all the world. We and our allies were slow to admit that, indeed, there was an enormous imbalance in global news and information flow and that we should join in cooperative measures to modify that unhealthy situation. And the West was very late in developing a strategy of focusing on concrete and practical measures that, without impinging on press freedom, still moved in the direction of cooperative relationships. Furthermore, the Western countries, along with all other parties in the debate, exhibited a perverse reluctance to try to understand and come to grips with the arguments of others.

I once expressed the view that the delegates seemed to be shooting arrows at one another from within water-tight compartments. Others described UNESCO debating as a "dialogue of the deaf." Four scholars described the debate as "a remarkably vivid instance of communication involving high stakes by articulate agents advocating incommensurate positions."[2]

---

[1]Remarks in a seminar on communications, Edward R. Murrow Symposium, Washington State University, Pullman, Washington, 1979.
[2]"Many Voices, Many Worlds: Four Readings of the NIIO Debate in UNESCO," p. 4.

I would be less than fair if I were to leave the impression that all of the spokespersons for the Third World who were involved in the communications debate were fools and knaves or ideological idiots. Many were most sincere and reflected in their interventions deeply-held convictions about the necessity for redressing what they believed were grave injustices and inequalities in this field. A few, like Jean Ping (while ambassador to UNESCO from Gabon and leader of the African group), realized that continued vilification of the West was counterproductive to their interests and tried hard to cooperate with Western delegates to promote practical measures for strengthening Third World communication capacities. Other Third World leaders, though, invariably took the hard line, which I often thought was done for home consumption or recognition among their peers rather than from a firm sense of personal commitment. Socialist spokesmen were acting under strict orders and rarely ever strayed from the party line;[3] the result, understandably, was to perpetuate the rigidity in East-West relationships.

Despite the repeated rejection of resolutions concerning ethical codes, licensing of journalists, standards setting, and other normative actions, the Secretariat kept reintroducing them year after year into UNESCO's plans and conferences, though well aware that these ideas were anathema to the West. The predictable consequence of this spiteful practice was fruitless continued advocacy of incommensurate positions.

The reality, of course, was that there are some issues in this field that are (and always will be) irreconcilable; hence, a realistic approach would have been to put these aside and to concentrate on those areas in which some level of commonality could be found and, consequently, some possibility of consensus.

I am pleased that close observers of UNESCO are noting signs that the organization under new Director-General Federico Mayor is now accepting that reality and is moving toward trying to meet free-press concerns, or is at least dropping elements in its plan that the West has so long pinpointed as objectionable. The 1989 draft of the Third Medium Term Plan not only reaffirms Article 19 of the Universal Declaration of Human Rights, but in several instances rejects the old ideological approach in favor of practical activities to such an extent that the entire Communication Program has been shifted from controversy to pragmatism.

---

[3]This writer once took part in a discussion in Moscow between members of a U.S. National Commission for UNESCO and their Soviet counterparts in which no meaningful dialogue could take place because the Soviets were confined to reading word for word what had been prepared for them in their notebooks.

One paragraph sets the new tone:

Now that UNESCO, following the consensus reached at the 24th session...and without turning its back on the past, is setting out on a path of innovation, it is perhaps time to take the lessons of the past experience to heart and to explore the possibilities of a new strategy whereby the organization's global objective may be obtained in such a manner as to dispel the misunderstandings.[4]

In a speech that Director-General Mayor gave to a group of U.S. press executives in Washington in 1989, he said the NWICO was out, because "our constitution says we should work to guarantee the free flow of information."

These moves, although welcome, do not necessarily mean that the United States and the United Kingdom will be rejoining UNESCO in the near future. They will both have to be convinced that not only have substantial reforms been made, but also that there is a track record of adherence to these gains and continued movement in these positive directions.

Neither country will soon forget how, in return for their substantial contributions (United States 25 percent, United Kingdom 5 percent) they received a disproportionate share of aggravation and abuse. It can be said with certainty that without the change that took place in the Director-Generalship and the reform movement now underway, there would be no possibility of these countries resuming their membership in UNESCO. The possibility is probably being further enhanced by the democratic changes that have occurred in Eastern Europe.

If the United States does return to UNESCO, one hopes that it will have abandoned the reactive mentality that so long characterized much of its behavior in the organization, and that it will assume the positive leadership worthy of a great power.

AFTERWORD

Since the Commission completed its work, much has transpired in the world--in fact, it is not the same world.

Neither the commissioners or anyone else could have anticipated the seismic changes that have taken place in the old order, particularly the rise of the democratic spirit and urge for reform that transformed the Soviet Union and toppled the communist regimes of Eastern Europe (Poland, Hungary, East Germany, Czechoslovakia, and Romania) and swept aside

---

[4]Paragraph 25(c) of the Annex to 129 EX/Decision 4.1.

the Berlin Wall and the Cold War. As Elie Abel once said in summing up the situation: "The astonishing wave of revolutions that swept across Central and Eastern Europe in 1989 pronounced the doom of Joseph Stalin's external empire, raising hopes for a rebirth of democracy and the rule of law. As the Cold War passed into history, Communism was in retreat throughout the region."[5]

When Gorbachev came to power in 1985, he began cracking open the wall Stalin had imposed between the rulers and the ruled; he called this campaign *perestroika*. It was a strategy, reporter Hedrick Smith explains, which he manipulated for modernizing and adapting Soviet Socialism and offering promises of democracy and private enterprise, while still protecting the establishment.[6]

The Baltic states and many other nations started testing the waters of dissent. Citizens of the Central African nation of Zaire, for example, began pushing for rights of free speech and free press denied them by a repressive government. In many other nations of sub-Sahara Africa, from the Ivory Coast to Zambia, the quest for freedom and political reform is spreading. And the long fight in South Africa for ending the apartheid system is proceeding with renewed intensity.

Ohio University Professor John L. Gaddis believes that this remarkable transformation could not have occurred except for "the communications revolution which made it impossible for any nation to deny its citizens knowledge of what was going on elsewhere...A new kind of domino theory has emerged in which the achievement of liberty in one country causes repressive regimes to topple, or at least wobble, in others. Integration through communications has largely brought this about."[7]

Unquestionably what Hedrick Smith calls "a major bend in the path of history" has occurred, and communications across national borders has played an important role. Video and audio tapes and printed materials that once had to be smuggled into nations with rigid censorship have now become widely available. Never again will a government monopoly on information be possible. Now with the spreading ubiquity of photocopy and fax machines, short-wave pocket receivers, one-meter satellite dishes, and an array of other consumer products, Lenin's methods of media control can no longer be imposed.[8]

---

[5]Elie Abel. *The Shattered Bloc*, Houghton Mifflin, Boston, 1991, p. 1.
[6]Hedrick Smith. *The New Russians*, Random House, New York, 1990, p. XVII.
[7]John Lewis Gaddis. "Toward the Post-Cold War World," *Foreign Affairs*, Spring 1991, p. 104.
[8]For an extended treatment of this topic see *Power, the Press & the Technology of Freedom* by Leonard Sussman, Freedom House, 1989.

One of the most dramatic changes has been the sudden rebirth of newspapers. In the Soviet Union, under *glasnost*, journalism is undergoing a remarkable transformation. *Ogonyok*, a small weekly paper has gone from a circulation of 230,000 to more than three million; the *Moscow News*, formerly a propaganda weekly for tourists, is now a full-fledged newspaper in great demand. *Pravda* and *Izvetsia*, the official Soviet newspapers that had bored intellectuals, began reporting strikes, trials, and public protests (i.e. real news) and their readership shot up dramatically. The Moscow City Council, determined to be free of the Party organs, started its own paper and weekly magazine and, what's more, contracted with publishers in France and England to set up two new printing plants.

Independent newspapers began springing up or taking on new life in surprising places. In Zaire alone, 21 newspapers have appeared. In Zimbabwe, an independent paper sells out its press run in Harare, and similar examples could be cited in countries like Poland and Hungary.

To communications scholar Robert Stevenson of the University of North Carolina, this metamorphosis represents the triumph of independent journalism and the failure of "development journalism" based on mobilizing news media in support of nation-building, which often meant supporting the regime in power. "Development journalism--closely linked for ten years to the New World Information Order debate in UNESCO--now has a record, and it is one of failure." As evidence, he cites the Non-Aligned News Agencies pool (NANA), transmitting stories contributed by member news agencies, that has operated for 15 years "without any evidence of visibility or acceptance." Inter Press, which was also intended to serve the real information needs of the Third World, has lost its long-standing underwriting from the Friedich Ebert Foundation in Germany, and the Pan African News Agency, modeled on NANA, "limps along as an unloved and unused stepchild of its parent Organization of African Unity."[9]

The World Press Freedom Committee (WPFC), as well as other free-press organizations (including IFNE, IPI, IFPP, IAPA, and NANBA)[10] are participating in a broad program to help emerging news media in Central and Eastern Europe. The WPFC has published and distributed a special handbook for journalists, conducts training courses, and is providing manuals and other materials in a six-country region.

---

[9]Robert L. Stevenson. "International Communications: Four Things for the 1990s." Pacific Islands News Association/Islands Broadcast Association conference, Solomon Islands, October, 1989.

[10]International Federation of Newspaper Editors, International Press Institute, International Federation of the Periodical Press, Inter American Press Association, and the North American National Broadcasters Association.

The WPFC conducted a survey of needs in East Germany, Poland, Hungary, and Czechoslovakia and has prepared a list of possible "twinning projects." Similar to the "sister city" model, this approach would link up newspapers in the United States with newspapers in the area to share expertise. Other plans being considered include a training center for journalists in Warsaw, creation of a pool of consultants and trouble-shooters, donations of computers, printers, scanners, photo transmitters and other equipment, making available "journalists in residence," and providing a basic kit for establishing low-power local radio stations.

Clearly the Western media organizations are moving to react in a positive way to the new dimensions and opportunities that have opened up to foster the operation of a free press in a region where it has not existed for a long time or ever.

Manifestly, the world order has been transformed and the global agenda reshaped. The old East-West confrontation, which had so long dominated international relations, has become obsolete and the "communication ball game" in international forums has also changed, with new alliances being formed and old loyalties disappearing. Ideological unity has disappeared and no longer can the Third World nations, as they once did, count on automatic support from the Soviet Union, which even before its dissolution had shown a tendency toward moderation and cooperation with the West. Gone is much of the rigidity and aggressiveness that for so long has hobbled efforts to seek rational solutions and concerted action. And the fresh winds of democracy and capitalism also sweep into the places where delegates of nations gather to confront pressing issues of the day.

An earlier shift in the international structure occurred when the United States and the United Kingdom withdrew from UNESCO (1984 and 1985). Both nations withdrew in part because of the constant controversy over communications, although this was not by any means the only sore point. The then Assistant Secretary of State Gregory Newell, the principal architect of the U.S. withdrawal, perceived a persistent pattern of three problems:

1. excessive politicization.

2. endemic hostility toward basic institutions of a free society, especially a free market and a free press.

3. uncontrollable budgetary expansion coupled with serious management faults.

The United Kingdom's reasons were similar but with greater emphasis on UNESCO's inattentions to individual human rights and the need for program concentration, decentralization, and efficiency.

At this writing (summer of 1991), it appears likely that the United Kingdom may well return to UNESCO within a year or so. A parliamentary committee is leaning that way, recognizing that "by its absence from UNESCO, the United Kingdom is failing to participate as fully as it might in important international initiatives."

The United States may ultimately rejoin too, though currently its State Department remains opposed. However, there are some signs that the climate is improving; foremost among these, of course, is the fact that UNESCO has by now instituted many of the reforms that were considered mandatory, including dropping espousal of the NWICO. In addition, there is pressure from many nongovernmental organizations, especially in the sciences, because they are losing out on the opportunity to take part in UNESCO's work in combatting illiteracy, preserving historical monuments, protecting the environment, and researching food production and alternate sources of energy.

More significant, because the media played such a central role in criticizing UNESCO, the American Society of Newspaper Editors recently passed a resolution recommending that the United States resume its membership in UNESCO. This seems to reflect a growing feeling in the U.S. media that their interests are not being represented with sufficient vigor and vigilance by the sitting Western members.

Another phenomenon that must be noted is the extraordinary explosion of new communications technology, particularly in networking, bringing the opportunity for people and institutions geographically separated to work together in common tasks and economics of scale that reduce unit costs as the number of participants grows. Trends in telecommunications include using the computer as an interactive teaching machine and administrative tool; moves toward digitization of networks to integrate voice, data, and image; the widespread growth of cable systems; the increased use of direct satellite systems; and the surge toward deployment of fiber-optic facilities, with the dramatic increase in capacity that they offer for telecommunications infrastructures. Fiber-optic cables have already been laid across the Atlantic and the Pacific, thereby vastly increasing the carriage of transoceanic communication. National fiber-optic networks are being built in France, Japan, and Canada, and long-distance providers in the United States are rapidly introducing fiber-optics in their intercity networks. Ultimately, advocates foresee a two-way fiber-optic cable system capable of transmitting high-resolution video, digital-quality voice communications, and high-speed data to every American home, office, school, and institution.

The application of such technology to educational, economic, and civic needs of nations, both developed and developing, holds great promise. For the first time in human history, all peoples of the world could have unrestricted access to learning opportunities, remedial education, job training and retraining, and vocational advancement.

Although the dominance of the Western news services that motivated the NWICO debate still persists, it is becoming less so as new video, audio, and print global networks are springing up. The most successful new player has been the Cable News Network (CNN), now in 104 countries, which came into its own with its dramatic coverage of the war in the Persian Gulf, with even Saddam Hussein tuning it in to follow the progress of the war.

And Anglo-American media are not only global enterprises; the *China Daily* is distributed in locations around the world and the Egyptian daily, *Al Ahram*, is printed in London and New York. Other examples could also be cited.

The aforementioned Robert Stevenson believes that the search for national identity and the simultaneous resurgence of cultural conflicts in newly liberated countries suggest that the outline of a truly global culture is developing. This is also (in part, he thinks) a product of multinational corporate enterprise. He cites, for example, the cultural influence of Rudolph Murdock before his death, whose multimedia empire of films, television stations, magazines, newspapers, direct broadcast satellites (DBS), and program packaging firms stretched from the South Pacific across Britain to Europe and North America.

Other moguls are taking advantage of new technologies to extend their operations and influence beyond national and regional boundaries and foreign buyers--especially the Japanese--are buying up control of American communication conglomerates and the tapes, records, compact discs, and movies to go with them. And, as Stevenson predicts, the "exponential growth of international broadcasting promises to double--and perhaps to double again--the numbers of receivers, channels, and program hours by the end of the century." Although efforts will be made by countries in Western Europe and Canada to stave off this Hollywood flood, Stevenson believes the next century truly promises a global culture.

Whether, as Stevenson suggests, the continued dominance of Anglo-American communication, the resurgence of national identity, the cultural impact of multinational media organizations and the triumph of independent journalism, will indeed produce a global culture remains to be seen. (I am skeptical, since the resurgence of national identity and realization of sovereignty might also revitalize national cultures.)

If a global culture does indeed develop, it will tend to reduce much of the confrontational debate that characterized the communications discussions in UNESCO and the United Nations, and will bury once and for all the scheme that was a constant preoccupation of the MacBride Commission--the New World Information and Communication Order.

In a world that is fast changing to an information-based economy, one places a higher premium than ever before on communication and on the means and media that facilitate its services to humanity. One would hope that pluralistic communications would not only help to foster the welcome spirit of democracy that has blazed up from the Baltic to the Black Sea, but would also apply its wondrous mechanisms in such a way as to provide widespread access to new ideas and information, so that all groups in today's society can participate in and benefit from the implementation of new discoveries.

Trouble spots still remain in many places in the world today, especially places of religious and ethnic tension. Given the failure of communism,[11] the new credibility of the United Nations in repelling aggression and helping to restore peace and security, the end of the East-West confrontation, and moves toward disarmament of the super powers, together with the amazing assertion of independence and democratic aspirations of nations that had been 40 years under suppression, there is basis, I believe, for cautious optimism, and communications will have an important role to play in its fulfillment.

It was the assumption of the founders of UNESCO that if one could maximize the flow of ideas across international boundaries, then the causes of war would decrease. One could argue that the communication of the idea of liberal democracy built on systems that encourage free enterprise has won out in the competition for the hearts and minds of men. If indeed the next century realizes the establishment of liberal democracies now struggling to emerge, then we may have a new birth of freedom and peace. As Gaddis points out, history proves that liberal democracies do not go to war with one another. "From that perspective," Gaddis concedes (though with warnings that many forces of fragmentation are still at work), "the old 19th century liberal vision of a peaceful, integrated, interdependent capital-

---

[11]However, communist regimes continue in Cuba, Viet Nam, North Korea, and China; in the latter, a prodemocratic movement was brutally beaten down in June of 1989.

ist world may at last become true."[12] If this were to happen, the MacBride Commission could be considered as one factor, among many others, in steering history in that direction.

In the march of events away from political controls of communications and toward a greater sharing and access to information and ideas, and the enterprise that those concepts promote, the MacBride Commission played a positive role. In particular, it avoided supporting the central controllers of news and information, and in that way signaled the ultimate movement toward a freer flow of world communication.

POSTSCRIPT

There is an old Arab saying to the effect that at some point, one must take his foot out of the river. And so it is with the rapid flow of events in what was once the Soviet empire. I must arbitrarily sign off in my reporting and send this manuscript to the publisher.

Since the last chapter was written, there has been a bewildering see-saw of positive and negative events in the drive toward democracy. In August 1991, hard-liners attempted a coup against President Gorbachev, and early targets of their conspiracy were the independent Soviet press and television that had emerged during *glasnost*. When the hard-liners seized power, Hedrick Smith reported, "they moved swiftly to shut down liberal newspapers, clamp a tight lid on central Soviet television, and ban its rival Russian channel. Their obvious goal was to deprive opposition leaders, such as Boris Yeltsin (newly elected president of the Russian Republic), of the channels of mass communication."[13]

Before the failed coup, Gorbachev himself retreated from his *glasnost* and joined the hard-liners in a media crackdown; he thought the liberated Soviet media had gone too far in reporting and showing graphic pictures of the brutality of Soviet soldiers and tanks on innocent civilians as they were suppressed in Latvia, Lithuania, and other areas of unrest. Nevertheless, Russian journalists and broadcasters continued with great ingenuity to publish and transmit independently. Lithuanian radio, operating out of the office of the Lithuanian Society for the Blind, and the Russian Republic set up their own television station as a rival to Soviet Television-Moscow.

"Similar trends," reported Smith, "were at work on the print media, where the diversity of the press had been protected by various republic

---

[12]op. cit., *Toward the Post War World*, p. 104.
[13]Hedrick Smith. "The Perilous Struggle for a Free Press," *Parade*, October 20, 1991, p. 4.

leaders like Yeltsin and by democratic regimes who won control of city councils in places like Moscow, Leningrad, Sverdlovsk, and Volvograd."[14] On the political front, the drive toward democracy produced moves toward independence in many parts of the now Soviet "disunion." The Baltic nations of Lithuania, Estonia, and Latvia declared their independence. So did the Ukraine as a consequence of the powerful centrifugal forces loosed by the crumbling of the Communist regime.

The City Council of Moscow helped set up independent newspapers and journals. *Pravda*, the communist flagship paper, had its circulation fall in two years from 10 million to 2.3 million, while the *Moscow News*, a reformist paper, jumped from 500,000 to 2.3 million.

After the failed coup, Gorbachev and Yeltsin restored the liberal papers, but *Pravda* and *Izvetsia* still controlled the printing plants and the state still had a stranglehold on paper stock and distribution.

Freed from communist tyranny, the peoples of the Soviet Union and Eastern Europe resumed their historic quarrels and ethnic disputes, and nationalist fever, already a potent force, will lead to more drives for full independence, especially if the economic recession worsens. One step toward cohesion, after months of disintegration and drifting, was the signing in October 1991 of a treaty of economic union in which eight of the original fifteen republics pledged themselves to radical reform and to the creation of a voluntary economic community to replace the collapsed dictatorship.

Whether this loose association of independent states will work is questionable, because the treaty is vague in many respects and because it is spurned by the economically vital Ukraine. However, the treaty does clarify the murky question of central control in Moscow and thus opens the door to possible Western aid.

Many issues remain in determining what sort of structure will eventually emerge to replace the centuries-old central control exercised by the czars and the Bolsheviks. And while the Soviet press and television are not yet totally free, it is clear that they will be on the front lines in the battle for democracy and in widening the perimeters of freedom.[15]

---

[14]Ibid., p. 6.

[15]By press time, the Soviet Union had been dissolved and a loose federation of eleven republics was formed into the Commonwealth of Independent States. Boris Yeltsin, President of the Russian Republic, who led the defeat of an earlier attempted coup to overthrow Gorbachev, emerged as the new leader and is now attempting to install a democratic free-market system to replace the former communist controlled political and economic order.

APPENDICES

APPENDIX I

I. THE MAUVE SERIES
List of Pertinent Background Papers Prepared for the Commission

(The numbering system below embodies the numbers assigned by UNESCO.)

31. The new world information order (M. Masmoudi, Tunisia, member of CIC).

32. Aims and approaches to a new international communication order (B. Osolnik, Yugoslavia, member of CIC)

33. Communication for an interdependent, pluralistic world (E. Abel, United States, member of CIC)

33. Call for a New International Information Order:
bis Preliminary remarks (G. El-Oteifi, Egypt, member of CIC)

33. Shaping a new world information order
ter (Speech of the president of the International Commission at the "Forum 1979")

34. The New International Economic Order and the New International Information Order (C. Hamelink, Netherlands)

35. Some remarks on the relation between the New International Information Order and the New International Economic Order (J. Pronk, Netherlands, member of CIC)

36. The right to communicate (J. d'Arcy, France)

37. The right to communicate
    1. Concept (L. S. Harms, United States)
    2. Towards a definition (D. Fisher, Ireland)

38. The right to communicate
    3. Legal foundation (A. A. Cocca, Argentina)
    4. Relationship with mass media (J. Richstad, United States)

39. The right to communicate
    5. A socialist approach (J. Pastecka, Poland)

39.
bis Relation between the right to communicate and planning of communication
    (G. El-Oteifi, Egypt, member of CIC)

40. Communication: a plea for a new approach (F. Balle, France)

41. Communication and international development: some theoretical considerations (M. Tehranian, Iran)

42. Mass media and national development - 1979 (W. Schramm, United States)

43. Towards a national policy on communication in support of development (G. N. S. Raghawan and V. S. Gopalakrishnan, India)

44. A philosophy for development communications: the view from India (B. G. Verghese, India, member of CIC)

46. Mass media ownership (R. Cruise O'Brien, United States)

47. Communication accompanies capital flows (H. Schiller, United States)

48. Farewell to Aristotle: "Horizontal Communication" (L. Ramiro Beltran, Colombia)

49. Rural development and the flow of communication (H. Cassirer, United States)

50. Advertising and public relations in the arms industries: their role in the mass media (P. Lock, Federal Republic of Germany)

51.   Typology of restrictions upon freedom of information: from evident, recognized violations to hidden impediments (J. Louy, France)

52.   Obstructions to the free flow of information (F. Giles, United Kingdom)

53.   Responsibility and obstacles in journalism (prepared by the International Organization of Journalists)

54.   Imbalance in the field of communication (I) Asia

55.   Imbalance in the field of communication (II) Latin America and the Caribbean

56.   Export-import flows of news:
      1. Foreign news on foreign terms: Finland (U. Kivikuru, Finland)
      2. Flows of culture and information: Hungary (T. Szecsko, Hungary)

57.   The image reflected by mass media: Distortions
      a)   The image of Southern Africa in certain Western countries (R. Lefort, France)
      b)   Study of five reports on Ethiopia (R. Lefort, France)

58.   The image reflected by mass media: Manipulations--The nuclear axis: a case study in the field of investigative reporting (B. Rogers, United Kingdom)

59.   The image reflected by mass media: Stereotypes a) Race relations (C. Jones, United Kingdom)

59. bis   The image reflected by mass media: Stereotypes
      b)   Images of women (M. Gallagher, Ireland)

60.   International broadcasting (B. Bumpus, United Kingdom)

61.   Communication planning

62. Communications and communities: a North-American perspective (J. Halina, Canada)

63. A national policy for purposeful use of information: mass media in USSR (Y. A. Poliakov, USSR)

64. A national policy for socialization and self-management of information (V. Micovic, Yugoslavia)

65. Access and participation in communication (F. Berrigan, Australia)

67. Alternatives experiences (I)
     Local radio and television stations in Italy (G. Richeri, Italy)

68. Alternative experiences (II)
     Communication practices in Latin American (F. Reyes Matta, Chile)

69. Democratization of communication (J. Somavia, Chile, member of CIC)

70. The true problem; democratizing information (J. Schwoebel, France)

71. Education and learning innovations: use of communication technologies and facilities

72. Mass media education or education for communication (J. Dessaucy, France)

73. Strengthening the press in the Third World (prepared by the International Press Institute)

74. Communication and training: an indicative international review of facilities and resources

75. Culture and communication (V. Flores Olea, Mexico)

76. Interaction between culture and communication (M. Lubis, Indonesia, member of CIC)

77.   Cultural industry (H. Gutierrez, Mexico)

78.   The context of mass communication research (J. Halloran, United Kingdom)

79.   A critical look at communication (J. Vidal Beneyto, Spain)

81.   Communication technologies of the 1980s (I)

    1. The implications (K. Schaefer and A. Rutkowski, United States)

    2. The future of computer communications (D. Parkhill, Canada)

82.   Communication technologies of the 1980s (II)

    3. Development of television broadcasting technology (M. Krivosheev, USSR)

    4. Recent progress and its impact upon communication policy and development (R. Gazin, Yugoslavia)

83.   Communication technologies of the 1980s (III)

    5. The social implications (S. Komatsuzaki, Japan)

    6. Future trends (Yash Pal, India)

84.   Technology and change in modern communication (I. de Sola Pool, United States)

85.   Contribution of scientific and technological progress to the development of communication (V. S. Korobeynikov, USSR)

86.   New technological developments in the print media (A. Smith, United Kingdom)

87.   International allocation of frequencies to national broadcasting services (M. Chaffai, Tunisia)

88. Institutional configuration for large space communications structures: A basis for the development of international space communications norms. (D. Smith, United States)

89. The protection of the individual, his freedom and privacy, in particular in the computer field (J. Freese, Sweden)

90. The Protection of Journalists (S. MacBride, Ireland, president of CIC)

90. Professional Ethics in Mass Communication
bis (B. Osolnik, Yugoslavia, member of CIC)

APPENDIX II

THE INTERNATIONAL PROGRAM FOR DEVELOPMENT OF COMMUNICATIONS (IPDC)

Another major communication step at the Belgrade conference--and one influenced by the MacBride Report--was the adoption by UNESCO of what was primarily a U.S. initiative, the proposal for establishing an International Program for Development of Communications (IPDC). It was conceived as a central clearinghouse for information about communication developments around the world, whose purpose was to match contributed funds to the priority needs of developing countries, and it represents a sympathetic response by the developed countries to recognized needs of less-developed countries to help them help themselves to expand and strengthen their communication capacities via development of infrastructures and training.

The idea for the IPDC was first suggested at the 1978 UNESCO General Conference in a U.S. resolution in which it proposed hosting a meeting to plan a program for practical assistance in international communications. At the same time, Mustapha Masmoudi (then Tunisian minister of information) introduced a resolution calling for a meeting to define a New World Information Order (NWIO) and the creation of an international fund for promoting mass media in developing countries. The Washington planning meeting in November 1979 resulted in a nondecision between the two proposals. A follow-up meeting in Paris in April 1980 produced a proposal for establishing the IPDC.

If the truth be known, this idea was, in part, born of the determination of the United States to fend off Masmoudi's proposal to define the NWIO, although its major purpose was to find a way to achieve a better balanced dissemination of news while yet protecting the concept of free flow. It was a concrete manifestation of a principle long articulated by the United States and its allies: namely, the way to address imbalance is not by restricting communication activities of countries with advanced communication capacity, but by raising the communication capabilities of the developing countries so they can participate more fully in the world's communication system. The IPDC was designed as a mechanism to implement this philosophy.

Dr. Clifford Block of the U.S. Agency for International Development states that the adoption was the result of an implicit agreement growing out of the 1978 General Conference, whereby "the Third World would moderate its rhetoric on issues such as the licensing of journalists and worldwide journalistic codes [and in return] the industrialized world would assist the poorer nations more rapidly in developing communication capabilities.[1]

Those of us who were involved in fashioning the design of the IPDC (Roland Homet, then with the U.S. Information Agency, was the principal architect) considered it not only as a means of modifying the global news imbalance but as a means of turning away from the obsessive preoccupation with divisive and destructive politicizing in favor of positive and constructive action. The IPDC provided a new focus for UNESCO communication activities and a practical means for cooperatively narrowing the gap in this field between the developed and developing countries.

Governance of the IPDC is by the 35-member Intergovernmental Council, of which this writer was an original member. The council met for the first time on June 15, 1981 with representation of eight delegates from the West, three from the Soviet bloc, and twenty-four from the developing world. The Council is responsible for implementing the program, recommending priorities, and allocating funds for grants.

The original notion of the United States was that the IPDC was to serve as a clearing house for information about funding from other sources and as a broker between the developing countries and donors. At the insistence of the Third World delegates, however, it soon evolved into a funding mechanism itself, with a special account established to accept contributions directly. In this way, the Third World majority could control the funding mechanism that would make the awards, and it wanted all contributions to flow into this special account. Western members, on the other hand (including the United States), insisted on the option of support for IPDC-approved projects through no-strings, bilateral means, via UNESCO's Funds in Trust, which provides the opportunity to fund specific projects rather than have the money applied to a whole range of approved projects.

This issue of bilateral vs multilateral funding was a major argument within the IPDC from the start, and continues to be a source of controversy, because some Western countries are unwilling to provide funds that could conceivably support ideologically distasteful projects. Whatever contri-

---

[1]Clifford Block. "Instituting the Development Program for International Communications," article in *World Communications*, p. 475.

butions they make to the IPDC go into UNESCO's Funds in Trust and are earmarked for specific projects.

During the four years of membership on the Council, I was conspicuously unsuccessful in establishing two reforms: making the private sector eligible for grants and limiting the number of awards so that larger amounts of money could be given to fewer grantees. Because the IPDC, like UNESCO where it is housed, is an organization of governments, it is not surprising that there was little hospitality for the notion of sharing some of the limited funds with interlopers from outside the fraternity. Of the hundreds of grants that were made to governments, only three went to private sector applicants, and they were all tiny.[2]

My other concern was with a predictable situation in which money is being distributed: everybody wants a piece of the action. Since the Council members vote on who is to get the grants and there are always far more requests than there is money available, there is a great deal of the you-vote-for-me and I'll-vote-for-you business and a tendency for delegates to avoid bad feeling that might result from voting to reject a colleague's pet proposal. In consequence, efforts are made to stretch funds available as far as possible by making many small awards. This may be diplomatically sound but it is realistically foolish. The term "dibble-dabbling" meant that many countries received grants, all right, but most of them were of such tiny dimensions that they were next to useless in providing practical assistance.

Today, I am pleased to note that after ten years, the IPDC is undertaking reforms along two lines. At the 1989 General Conference, it was decided to grant eligibility to private sector applicants for UNESCO grants, and at the 1989 IPDC Council meeting (which I attended as an observer) it was clear that the Council had earlier begun tightening the prescreening procedure of projects, vastly reducing the number of projects accepted for consideration so that the resources could be allocated in sufficient dimensions to be worthwhile, and was now applying a drastic quota system in making awards. (In previous years, some $2 million might be spread out over 120 grants; this year only twenty grants were funded from the Special Account and ten referred to Funds in Trust.)

The IPDC's fiscal undernourishment was evident from the very start and continues to be its biggest problem. Its Special Account has never been

---

[2]At its 13th session (February 17-24, 1992), the IPDC amended project submission procedures to make a project's contribution to freedom of the press and principles of pluralism and independence a priority concern for selection for funding. It opened its procedures for direct submission of working relationship with UNESCO, and called on the Director-General to establish working relations with professional media organizations.

more than \$2.5 million in any year, and the same is true for Funds in Trust, whereas the total of project requests have averaged four times those amounts. It is understandable that Third World expectations would exceed reality, but this gap has caused bitterness and disappointment.

There are several reasons why the IPDC is chronically under-financed. Several industrialized countries that were expected to contribute never did or did so modestly. The United Kingdom never gave a shilling (it prefers to contribute through established multilateral agencies). Japan, Italy, and Denmark did not contribute until much later. The United States contributed only \$4.2 million over a period of four years (while still in UNESCO) and then only via Funds in Trust so it could determine where the money went and for what purpose. Only France and the Scandinavian countries (especially Norway) made substantial contributions from the start.

I had the conviction that the ultimate solution to the financial well-being of the IPDC is through involvement of the private sector in the United States and other industrialized countries. I visited executives of several communication-related corporations in 1982 and 1983 to sell them on the idea of protecting against the closing down (which I foresaw) of a major source of information as reprisal for lack of sympathetic attention to helping Third World countries improve their communications. No sale. Although they acknowledged that there might be long-range negative consequences from neglecting this situation, they could not see justifying such altruism to their stockholders. They always asked me why our government was not doing more to aid these countries and why it wasn't helping corporations in this country to combat the "unfair" competition they were experiencing as the result of Japanese government collaboration with its industries.

Despite meager funds, IPDC project support has made it possible to establish a number of national (read government) news agencies, training centers, and regional networks where none existed before, thus helping developing countries help themselves to strengthen and improve their communication capabilities.

There is some risk in this from a Western standpoint. Helping to establish national and regional news agencies may encourage an expanded drift toward government control of the media. On the other hand, there is a likelihood that introduction of new technologies can create an abundance of channels for diversified messages and encourage a richer exchange of opinion and flow of information. In any case, the IPDC's coordinated approach to international communications is far better than restricting or ripping up the present system as a means of achieving parity. And the

IPDC is helping bring about a needed restructuring, but in the way the MacBride Report emphasized it must be undertaken: as a slow, step-by-step, cooperative process.

If the IPDC could develop private sector involvement and continue to improve the procedures and working methods now underway, I believe the IPDC has a good possibility of fulfilling the substantial role among the family of nations that those of us who were its founding fathers envisioned.

If the United States were to return to UNESCO, the IPDC is one area where the U.S. presence would make a highly visible and beneficial difference.

APPENDIX III

EVENTS AND DOCUMENTS CONCERNING WORLD COMMUNICATIONS

1944   Following World War II, the United States, Great Britain, China, and the U.S.S.R. draft proposals for a United Nations charter at the Dumbarton Oaks Conference.

1945   Founding meeting of the organization with 51 member nations. Charter accepted.

1946   UNESCO established, with goal to further world peace by removing social, religious, and racial tensions, encouraging interchange of ideas, and improving and expanding education. Article 1.2 supports the free flow of information within and between countries.

1947   The United Nations adopts the International Telecommunications Union (established in 1934) effective in 1949, giving it responsibility for allocating frequencies, furthering low rates, and perfecting communications in rescue work.

1948   UN General Assembly adopted the Universal Declaration of Human Rights, stating that everyone has the right to freedom of opinion and expression. Article 19 guarantees freedom to hold opinions without interference and to seek, receive, and impart information and ideas through any media and regardless of frontiers.

1955   Nonaligned Countries movement is established at the Bandung Conference of Asian-African Countries.

1959   UN Economic and Social Council (ECOSOC) requests UNESCO to conduct world survey on mass media.

1961   ECOSOC passes Resolution on Mass Media in Developing Countries recommending that developed countries cooperate with less developed countries in meeting the needs of these for development of independent national information media. Also recommends that governments of underdeveloped countries review tariff and fiscal policies to facilitate development of information and media and the free flow of information within and between countries.

1962 UN General Assembly passes Resolution 1802 on Communication by Satellite, stating that satellites offer great benefits to mankind in permitting expansion of radio, television, and telephone transmission thus facilitating contact among peoples.

1963 Organization of Asian News Agencies is created.

1964 UNESCO General Conference authorizes Director-General to convene a meeting of experts on space communication.

1965 At that meeting, UNESCO is urged to undertake study of the problems for free flow of information, the spread of education, and cultural exchange posed by space communication.

1967 UN Outer Space Committee provides that all nations shall have equal access to outer space.

1968 UNESCO Broadcast Organizations on Outer Space meet in Paris.

1969 UNESCO Intergovernmental Meeting on Space Communication attended by representative of 61 countries.

1970 UNESCO General Conference passes Resolution 4.21 authorizing the Director-General to assist member states in formulating policies with respect to mass communication media.

    UN General Assembly formulates development strategy for the Second United Nations Development Decade.

    Nonaligned Nations hold summit conference in Lusaka to discuss the role of information in developing countries.

1971 World Administrative Radio Conference (WARC) for Space Communication passes Amendment of Radio Regulations, stating nations will do all in their power to reduce their broadcasting across borders via satellites unless they have reached prior agreement with those countries.

1972 UNESCO General Conference passes resolution 4.113 requesting the Director-General to prepare and submit a draft of a Declaration on the Use of Mass Media.

Adopts the Declaration of Guiding Principles on the Use of Space Broadcasting, stating that in using space broadcasting for the free flow on information, all nations should respect the sovereignty and equality of others, and affirming the need for a balanced flow of information between countries.

The UN General Assembly approves UNESCO Declaration on Space Broadcasting.

1973 Nonaligned countries' Fourth Conference of Heads of State and Government of Nonaligned Countries formulates a Program for Action for Economic Development, stressing need for greater interchange if ideas among developing countries and for reorganizing existing communication channels.

1974 UNESCO General Conference considers Draft Declaration on Role of the Mass Media. After agreeing the Draft and Amendments require further study, Conference authorizes intergovernmental meeting to prepare new Draft to submit to 19th session.

UN General Assembly passes resolutions 3201 and 3202 calling for establishment of a New International Economic Order.

1975 Conference on Security and Cooperation in Europe is held in Helsinki; Final Act aims to facilitate freer and wider dissemination of information and cooperation in its exchange.

UNESCO Intergovernmental Meeting on Use of Mass Media discusses Mass Media Draft 10 C/9. In dispute over amendment equating Zionism with racism, delegates of 12 Western nations leave the meeting.

Nonaligned Countries meet in Lima with Foreign Ministers of Information.

1976 UNESCO Intergovernmental Conference on Communication Policies in Latin America held in Costa Rica. Final Report stresses need to replace criterion of "free flow of information" with that of "balanced circulation."

UNESCO General Conference authorizes Director-General to hold further consultations on 19 C/9 to prepare final draft and also to appoint an international commission to study communication problems (the MacBride Commission). Adopts Medium-Term Plan 1977-1982 urging strategies likely to achieve a more equitable two-way flow of information.

Nonaligned Countries hold meeting of Information Ministers in New Delhi that notes existing global information flows were marked by serious imbalances and endorses constitution for Nonaligned Press Agencies Pool.

Nonaligned Countries hold Summit at Colombo, discuss concern with growing gap in communications capabilities of developing countries and stress new world order of information is just as important as a new international economic order.

Organization for African Unity (OAU) adopts Cultural Charter for Africa, stating African governments should ensure total decolonization of the mass media and cooperate to break monopolization of non-African states.

1977   WARC passes Final Acts for planning Broadcast Satellite Service.

United States Senate Subcommittee on International Operations of the Committee on Foreign Relations releases a report on WARC 1977 that reaffirms principles of free flow of information.

First Session of African Information Ministers in Kampala supports efforts of nonaligned countries to establish a new international information order in consonance with interests of Third World countries.

First Conference on Nonaligned Broadcasting Organizations is held in Sarajevo.

1978   UNESCO General Conference adopts Draft Declaration on Fundamental Principles governing Contributions of the Mass Media to Strengthening Peace and International Understanding and to Combating War Propaganda, Racialism, and Apartheid.

UNESCO Draft Program and Budget 1979-1980 gives priority to measures intended to improve communication between developed and developing countries.

International Commission for the Study of Communication Problems is established. Sean MacBride is chosen to head the 16-member Commission.

1979   MacBride Commission Report is submitted to Director General.
First meeting of the International Program for Development of Communications (IPDC) is held in Paris.
ITU. General WARC in Geneva is held; Third World countries press claims for equal access to spectrum and orbital spots.

1980   UNESCO General Conference at Belgrade does not formally consider MacBride Commission Report (because Director-General claims it was prepared for him personally), so the Report is merely "noted"; however, in the enabling resolution the Conference set forth eleven considerations that could be the basis for a New World Information and Communication Order.

The above was adapted from *World Communications: A Handbook.* George Gerbner and Marsha Siefert, Editors. Longman, 1984.

INDEX

Reactions from UNESCO member
  states, 188-190
  See also *Many Voices, One World:
  Communication and Society for
  Today and Tomorrow*
Finch, Tom, 65
First Amendment, 19
Food and Agriculture Organization, 63
France, 18
Free flow of news, 10
Freedom of information, 96-97
Freedom of the press, 121
Fuller, Keith, 65

Galliner, George, 25
Garcia Marquez, Gabriel, 36, 71, 109, 124,
  126, 131, 133, 168-169
Gardner, Mary, 53
Ghana, 161
Global issues, 22
Great Britain, 18
  See also United Kingdom
Group of 77 (G77), 12, 22, 29, 32, 173,
  190-191
Gunter, Jonathan, 38

Halloran, James, 78
Harikawa, Toskio, 120
Havana, 59, 72
Helsinki Conference on Cultural Policies,
  17
Holland, Mary, 115
Human rights: see Universal Declaration
  of Hungary, 162

Imbalance of news, 97-98, 207
Immunity for journalists, 56
  See also Protection of journalists
Indian Space Application Center, 118
INTELSAT satellite system, 24
Inter American Press Association, 38, 93,
  173, 177
Intergovernmental Coordinating Council
  for Information of the Non Aligned
  Countries, 72
Intergovernmental Council of Non Aligned
  Countries, 57
Interim Report, 1, 58-60, 63, 72, 78-79, 87,
  89-102
Intermedia, 180
International Center for Study and

Planning of Information and
  Communication, 139-140,
International code of ethics, 11, 55-56,
  104-106, 117
  See also Code of ethics
International Council of Jurists, 33, 116
International Herald Tribune, 170
International Network of Documentation
  Centers on Communication Research
  and Policies, 152
International Organization of Journalists,
  58
International Press Institute, 54-55, 58, 182
International Program for Development of
  Communication, 29, 160
International Telecommunications Union,
  11
Iran, 160
Iraq, 163
Israel, 22

Jakarta, 59
Jana News Agency, 55
Japan, 31, 50-51, 62, 65, 104, 162, 171-
  172
Johannesburg Post, 181
Jones, Byron, 34
Jones, Mervyn, 115, 121-122
Journalistic:
  accreditation, 55
  code of ethics, 143, 211
  freedom, 146
  responsibility, 146
  training and professional ethics, 99
    100, 214
  See also Code of ethics, International
    code of ethics

Kandil, Handy, 16
Keoloff, George, 38
Kirkpatrick, Clayton, 23, 38
Kissinger, Henry, 28
Koven, Ron, 31
Krasikov, Anatoly, 57
Krivocheev, M.I., 118

Lamb, David
Latin America, 53, 108
Latin American Views, 194
Learning To Be, 28
Lee, John, 78

ABOUT THE AUTHOR

William Harley has had three careers: in education, broadcasting, and diplomacy. He received his B.A. from the University of Wisconsin in 1935, his master's degree in speech in 1940, and an honorary Doctor of Laws degree in 1972.

He was a professor at the University of Wisconsin and Program Director of the Wisconsin State Radio Network. In 1954, he put the nation's fourth public television station on the air, in Madison, and was in charge of its operation until going to Washington in 1960 as president of the National Association of Educational Broadcasters. Under his leadership, the NAEB played a major role in securing FM and TV channels for education, established an instructional TV system in American Samoa, and organized a campaign that led to the Educational Broadcasting Facilities act (that provided funds to states to build educational stations) and the legislation that established the Corporation for Public Broadcasting and its offshoots, PBS and NPR. Harley also traveled widely in fostering educational applications of radio and television in developing countries (and served on various boards, including the U.S. National Commission for UNESCO and the Peabody Awards).

In his third career, Mr. Harley served as a consultant to the State Department on international communication issues. In that capacity, he represented the United States at many international conferences and was the U.S. representative on the UNESCO International Program for Development of Communications. In 1978, he was assigned as the Department's liaison with Elie Abel, the American delegate on the MacBride Commission. This role took him around the world for two years, reporting on the Commission's work.

Among honors awarded him are: Distinguished Citizen Citation, Creighton University, 1962; Distinguished Alumni Award, University of Wisconsin Alumni Club, 1967; Chancellor's Award for Distinguished Achievement in Journalism, University of Wisconsin, 1973; NAEB Distinguished Service Award, 1975; World Freedom of Information Award, Texas Tech University, 1983; and the George Foster Peabody Distinguished Service Award, University of Georgia, 1986. He belongs to the Cosmos and International Clubs and is a member of Beta Theta Pi, Phi Eta Sigma, and Phi Kappa Phi.

Mr. Harley lives with his wife Jewell on Lake Barcroft in Falls Church, Virginia, where he edits a newsletter for alumni of the NAEB and takes people out on his "martini boat."